50 Fast Digital Video Techniques

**BONNIE BLAKE AND
DOUG SAHLIN**

50 FAST DIGITAL
VIDEO TECHNIQUES

Wiley Publishing, Inc.

50 Fast Digital Video Techniques

Published by
Wiley Publishing, Inc.
111 River St.
Hoboken, N.J. 07030
www.wiley.com

Copyright © 2003 by Wiley Publishing, Inc., Indianapolis, Indiana

Library of Congress Control Number: 2003105634

ISBN: 0-7645-4180-3

Manufactured in the United States of America

10 9 8 7 6 5 4 3 2 1

1V/RX/QZ/QT/IN

Published by Wiley Publishing, Inc., Indianapolis, Indiana
Published simultaneously in Canada

For general information on our other products and services or to obtain technical support, please contact our Customer Care Department within the U.S. at 800-762-2974, outside the U.S. at 317-572-3993 or fax 317-572-4002.

Wiley also publishes its books in a variety of electronic formats. Some content that appears in print may not be available·in electronic books.

To our families, friends, mentors and fellow digital video enthusiasts.

PREFACE

This book presents 50 fast digital video techniques that are essential skills for any digital videographer who wants to take his or her productions to the next level by editing them in iMovie, or Windows Movie Maker. Each technique should take you no more than 15 minutes to perform. Some techniques are simple, and others combine multiple effects. Each technique is divided into two sections: one for iMovie users, the other for Windows Movie Maker users.

  This book is written for the digital video enthusiast who wants to create professional looking home movies, but doesn't have the time for an in-depth study of all the features of iMovie and Windows Movie Maker 2.

WHY THIS BOOK WAS WRITTEN

We have written several books on graphic software used to edit digital images for print and for the Web, as well as books on Web animation software, and nonlinear video-editing software. The books we have previously written were designed for professionals who use software on a daily basis to earn a living. While writing these books, we noticed a lack of books that show consumers how to use software in conjunction with their digital photography and digital video equipment. The 50 Fast series seemed like the ideal series for a book that shows video enthusiasts how to use iMovie and Windows Movie Maker to create eye-catching professional home movies to share with their friends and relatives. Fortunately the publishers of the series agreed with our vision. Not surprisingly, the book exceeds our expectations as authors, designers, and video editors. It also provides the perfect solution for aspiring independent filmmakers on a tight budget, as well as professionals looking to add pizzazz to their business presentations. After mastering the iMovie and Windows Movie Maker techniques we cover in this book, you will have a firm grasp of basic digital video editing and production techniques. From here, you can easily advance to higher-end post-production video-editing applications and modify these techniques to suit your future goals.

THIS BOOK IS DIFFERENT THAN OTHER DIGITAL VIDEO BOOKS

This book is results oriented. It's not intended to be a standalone reference that covers every feature iMovie or Windows Movie Maker has to offer. Our goal is to provide you with 50 cookbook recipes that you can use to take your home movies or independent productions to the next level. Each technique is task oriented and focuses on a given aspect of the movie-editing process. Each task features detailed step-by-step instructions that show you how to quickly achieve a given task. In addition, we have sprinkled all sorts of essential tips, notes, and creative suggestions throughout. These tips are gems you would never find in a reference manual or traditional how-to book.

In addition to the 50 Fast techniques, this book offers you several extras including the following:

- Detailed illustrations that augment the written steps.
- Thirty-two full-color pages, illustrating the most color-intensive effects.
- Over 50 royalty-free sample clips for each platform are included on the companion CD-ROM in a folder called Clips. We have provided clips in the QuickTime MOV format for iMovie users, and the Windows Media Player WMV format for Windows Movie Maker users. Each clip is 640 x 480 at 30 frames per second to ensure good results while performing each technique. These are the same clips used in each chapter and as such, you can use them to easily follow along with the steps in each technique. Optionally, you can substitute footage that you have captured to follow along with techniques. The book was written in such a way that it works with our clips or yours. When applicable, we tell you what type of footage works best with the technique being presented.
- All of the completed techniques are included as Flash SWF video files on the CD-ROM.
- We've also include trial versions of software and plug-ins for the Macintosh and PC.

WHO SHOULD READ THIS BOOK?

This book is for digital video enthusiasts who want to use the nonlinear video-editing software that ships with Macintosh OS X (iMovie) or Windows XP (Windows Movie Maker) to create professional looking movies for home or business. While not a necessity, it is helpful if you have a basic understanding of iMovie (Macintosh OS-X users) or Windows Movie Maker (Windows XP users) before proceeding. If you have not previously explored the powerful features of these applications, you can refer to the application help menu to learn the basics while working through the techniques in this book.

Armed with a basic knowledge of the application, you can use these techniques to add a level of professionalism to your productions that is guaranteed to make you the envy of co-workers, friends, and relatives who view your movies. This book will appeal to you if you need a cookbook of digital video recipes that you can mix and match to create eye-popping home movies to entertain yourself, friends, and relatives. If you've ever watched a movie or television show and wondered how you could add some of the same razzle-dazzle to your home movies, this is the book for you. In addition, this book is also essential for the professional who wants to incorporate digital video into their business. iMovie and Windows Movie Maker can help you produce stunning video for the Web, and for presentations. Video is fast becoming one of the most popular forms of visual communication in the new millennium. Using iMovie or Windows Movie Maker in concert with our book can get you up and running with this new technology in no time.

WHAT COMPUTER HARDWARE AND SOFTWARE WILL YOU NEED?

The minimum requirements to create home movies in iMovie or Windows Movie Maker are not especially demanding. In fact, if you're already using Macintosh OS X or Windows XP (Home or Professional), your system probably already meets the minimum requirements. However, you'll be happier, and as a result more productive, if your computer features a faster processor and more memory than the minimum requirements for each platform.

Here are the minimum requirements for each platform:

For Windows XP:

- PC with 300 megahertz (MHz) or higher processor clock speed recommended; 233 MHz minimum required (single or dual processor system); Intel Pentium/Celeron family, or AMD K6/Athlon/Duron family, or compatible processor recommended
- 128 megabytes (MB) of RAM or higher recommended (64 MB minimum supported; may limit performance and some features)
- 1.5 gigabytes (GB) of available hard disk space
- Super VGA (800 x 600) or higher-resolution video adapter and monitor
- CD-ROM or DVD drive
- Keyboard and Microsoft Mouse or compatible pointing device
- A digital (FireWire IEEE 1394) or analog video capture device

For Macintosh:

- Mac OS X v10.1.5 or later
- 400 MHz PowerPC G3 or faster required (700 MHz recommended)

> **NOTE**
>
> You'll get much better performance from your computer while editing digital video with Windows Movie Maker if you add additional memory to your system and upgrade to a faster processor. Your system will be better equipped to handle the demands of digital video editing if you have a 1.0 GHz or faster processor and 512MB RAM. We also recommend that you invest in a large hard drive with a capacity of at least 80GB, as you'll need a lot of available hard disk to capture video. You can augment your internal hard drive with a USB or FireWire hard drive. Both are excellent choices for storing overflow video, however they are too slow to use for capturing video.

■256MB RAM recommended 2GB of free hard disk space Macintosh with built-in FireWire ports ■ 1,024 x 768 screen resolution or higher QuickTime 6.1 required (download via Software Update)

CONVENTIONS USED IN THIS BOOK

In order to make this book as user-friendly as possible, we omitted technical jargon whenever possible. Each technique features information about the videos you'll be using to recreate the technique, as well as "before-and-after" figures to demonstrate the results you can expect when performing this technique. The text is broken down into easy-to-understand steps for each platform. Each example is illustrated with images of the steps you'll be performing with your computer to replicate the technique.

> **NOTE**
>
> You'll get much better performance from your Macintosh while editing digital video with iMovie if you add additional memory to your system and upgrade to a faster processor. If you plan on making movies that are longer than a minute, we recommend at least 512MB of RAM, if not more. In addition, you should consider investing in a large hard drive with a capacity of at least 80GB, as you'll need a lot of available hard disk to capture video. Make sure the drive is an ATA, UltraATA, or Ultra Wide SCSI, with a minimum spin rate of 7,2000 RPM. USB drives are fine for storage but too slow for capturing. In general, FireWire drives are not recommended for capturing, although they serve as excellent storage devices.

In the first and second chapters, you find techniques that show you how to shoot better home video, as well as techniques for capturing footage to your computer and editing the footage. The last chapter of the book contains information you can use to export your digital video to VHS tape, CD, DVD, and for the Internet. Sandwiched in between are techniques that add polish and panache to your home movies.

We break up each technique into major steps and explain what each step accomplishes. By following the steps and referring to the illustrations, you can reproduce the technique on your computer with the sample clips provided in the Clips folder on the book's accompanying CD-ROM.

In each technique, you are instructed to import the video clips we have provided from the Clips folder of the book's accompanying CD-ROM. Depending on the speed of your CD-ROM drive and computer, this task may take a while. If you have the available hard drive space, we recommend that you copy the sample clips into a folder and import them into the application from there. By doing this, you ensure that the clips import into the application more quickly, plus you'll still have the clips available if you remove the CD-ROM from its drive.

The "About the Video" section of each technique contains information about the equipment used to create the sample clips, as well as information about the settings using to record the video. Throughout the book we present tips, notes, and words of caution based on the experience we have gained editing our own videos.

BONNIE BLAKE'S ACKNOWLEDGMENTS

It has been a pleasure working with the Wiley team on such a fun book. Many thanks to Mike Roney who helped our vision for a great book on digital video become a reality. I would also like to thank Tim Borek for his creative insight and direction. Thanks to Beth Taylor and Maureen Spears for your hard work under tight deadlines, and careful scrutiny of our manuscript. Thanks to Laura Moss for keeping on top of the mountain of permissions required for this book. I would also like to express my appreciation and thanks to our friend Margot Maley Hutchinson for all her hard work up front and support from beginning to end.

Warm thanks to my models, Kelly Blake, Matt Cicitta, and Dale Kroll, who put up with endless hours of posing while I experimented to get each shot just right.

Special thanks to Mary Cicitta for her contribution to the iMovie Appendix resource section. Her research and input are much appreciated.

Lastly, thanks to Doug Sahlin for being such a wise, honest, ambitious, talented, and creative person. As always, working with you has been a delightful experience. Although there were some tense moments and late nights, you helped me survive with a dose of good old-fashioned humor, lots of laughs, Sixties rock trivia, and a positive outlook. As a result, I think we produced a great book. I know you are as proud of it as I am.

DOUG SAHLIN'S ACKNOWLEDGMENTS

This book was a great deal of fun to write, but would not have been possible without a vast support team. Special thanks to Mike Roney for making this book possible. Thanks to project editor Tim Borek for keeping my inbox full and providing direction and needed comic relief. Thanks to the production team at Wiley, with special thanks to copy editor Beth Taylor, pinch-hit project editor Maureen Spears, permissions editor Laura Moss, and media development specialist Angie Denny.

Special thanks to Bonnie Blake for your friendship, creative energy, and boundless enthusiasm. It's been a wonderful experience working with you on this project. When the going got tough and the hour became late, you responded with warmth, wit, and creative solutions and also proved the age-old adage, "Two heads are better than one." As Ricky might say, "We done good, Lucy."

Special thanks to the actors who assisted in the sample videos for this book: my good friends Barry Murphy — who in addition to playing a wonderful mystery man in a trench coat is also a talented songwriter and musician; and Larry Decker, a superb triathlete and a world-class human being. A boatload of thanks to my dear friend Cheryl Decker, the quintessence of effervescence and optimism, for getting me a VIP All-access pass to the Great Clermont Triathlon.

Kudos to Margot Maley Hutchinson, literary agent extraordinaire, for ironing out the fine points with the publisher. As always, special thanks to my friends and family, with fond regards to my lovely sister Karen, and my ebullient cousin Ted who sometimes goes by the alias of Tedster.

CONTENTS AT A GLANCE

CONTENTS

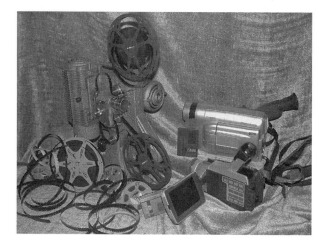

CHAPTER 5: CREATING VINTAGE MOVIE EFFECTS 119

CHAPTER 8: CREATING COMPELLING TITLES AND CREDITS 223

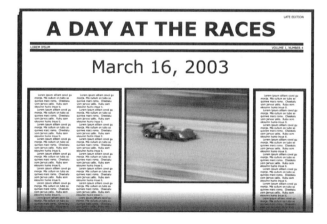

CHAPTER 9: EXPORTING YOUR MOVIE   269

CHAPTER 1

SHOOTING VIDEO LIKE A PRO

Armed with a digital camcorder, an interesting subject, and beautiful scenery, you have all the necessary elements to create some wonderful footage. By default, most digital camcorders do a credible job of capturing what you point them at. However, any piece of equipment has limitations. Your digital movies will be less than what they can be if you don't master a few skills to overcome the limitations of your equipment. In this chapter, we present techniques that help you get the most from yourself, your subjects, and your equipment.

Technique 1 shows you how to cope with adverse lighting conditions. You learn to film subjects with their backs to the rising or setting sun and still capture detail. Technique 2 shows you how to set up an indoor studio with *three-point lighting*. Three-point lighting makes your footage more dramatic by bathing the subject with a key light, erasing deep shadows with a fill light, and revealing subtle details with a back light. In Technique 3, we show you how to create a makeshift dolly to smoothly track a person in motion. Finally, Technique 4 shows you how to

capture a sporting event like a pro and overcome the mundane nature of most home movies of sporting events.

COPING WITH ADVERSE LIGHTING

1.1

1.2

Windows Movie Maker and iMovie have video effects that are similar to the filters you find in more sophisticated applications, such as Adobe Premiere and Sonic Foundry Vegas Video. You can use these effects to compensate for footage that is too dark or too light, but when you try to compensate for footage that is very dark or very bright, you end up washing out the detail of the clip. When faced with adverse lighting conditions, you end up with better results if you manually adjust your camcorder's exposure. As you can see in Figure 1.1, the camcorder's default setting compensated for the bright ambient light behind the subject, which washes out the subtle details in the subject's face as well as the violin he is playing. Figure 1.2 shows this technique applied, which brings back some detail in the subject's face.

SHOOT A BACKLIT SUBJECT

When your subject is between the camcorder and a strong light source, such as the rising or setting sun, your subject is backlit. If you don't compensate for this situation, your camcorder will meter the average brightness of the scene and expose the scene accordingly. The scenery surrounding your subject will be properly exposed, but your subject will be in the dark with details obscured in shadow.

- Aim your camcorder at the subject.
- View the scene with the camcorder's LCD viewer.
- Press your camcorder's Backlight button. The background will be overexposed, but you'll be able to make out the details of your subject matter (see **Figure 1.3**).
- Record your subject. If your camcorder is fairly economical with battery usage, you can frame the scene with your LCD viewer. As you're shooting the scene, pay careful attention to your subject, making sure that you're picking up the subtle details. When you override a camcorder's auto-exposure with a backlight setting, the scene background will be overexposed, but the subtle details of your subject will be faithfully recorded.

1.3

There are other factors involved while shooting in bright sunlight. The UV rays from sunlight can alter the color of your video. Consider investing in a skylight filter for your digital camcorder. Most camcorders have threads in the front of the lens that you use to attach accessory filters. Not only does the UV filter give you better-looking video, it's also cheap insurance that protects the expensive camcorder lens from scratches. Another accessory to consider is a polarizing filter, which is used to reduce or eliminate glare from reflective surfaces such as windows and water. After attaching a polarizing filter to your digital camcorder, you rotate the outer ring of the filter to "dial out" glare and reflections. For example, if you're filming goldfish in a pond, the polarizing filter will cut through any glare on the surface and enable you to faithfully record the fish swimming underwater.

SHOOT A SUBJECT IN HEAVY SHADE

You're bound to encounter the problem situation where your subject is in heavy shade. Sometimes you'll find the perfect subject for some footage sitting on a park bench under tall towering oak trees. The oak trees do a wonderful job of framing your subject on the park bench, but your camcorder exposes the scene for the average lighting, and the bright background wins out every time.

TIP

If your camcorder doesn't have a Backlight button, zoom in on your subject and manually adjust the exposure until you can make out the details of your subject. After setting the exposure, zoom out to frame the scene.

■ Zoom in on your subject. Zoom in as tight as you can. If your subject is a person, zoom in on the person's face.

■ View your subject through your camcorder's LCD viewer.

■ Switch to manual exposure mode.

■ Adjust the exposure until you have achieved the desired level of lighting (see **Figure 1.4**).

■ Zoom out and frame the scene using either the LCD viewer or the camcorder eyepiece.

Camcorders have different methods for manually adjusting exposure. On some camcorders you press an exposure button after which you move a dial while viewing the scene through the camcorder viewfinder or LCD. After dialing in the proper exposure, you shoot the scene. On many camcorders, pushing the focus button again returns the camcorder to automatic metering. Refer to your camcorder owner's manual for the exact procedure for manually adjusting the exposure of your model.

You should also consider manually adjusting the focus of your camcorder when you're shooting a scene in which you will be panning the subject. In a situation like this, if you let the camcorder automatically expose the scene, certain frames of your video may flicker when the camcorder quickly readjusts the exposure for brighter or darker objects in the scene. Manually adjust the exposure so that your subject is properly exposed and then record the scene.

SHOOT A NIGHT SCENE

Another tricky lighting situation is a night scene. Most camcorders do a fair job of exposing a night scene, but the camcorder's auto focus feature causes the focus to go out of whack when brightly lit objects move through the scene. For example, if you're shooting a night scene of a busy street corner and your center of interest is a street performer and his audience, you want that part of the scene to be in sharp focus at all times. However, the first time a car passes near the corner, the camcorder focuses on its bright lights, throwing your subject out of focus. To prevent this occurrence, you must manually focus on your center of interest.

■ Zoom in on your subject.

■ View the scene through your camcorder's LCD viewer.

■ Switch your camcorder to manual focus and then adjust your camcorder until your center of interest is in sharp focus.

■ Zoom out to frame your scene.

■ Film your subject. Note that when you film a stationary scene, you'll have better success if you use a tripod.

1.4

TIP

If your camcorder is equipped with a Smart Flash, you can use it to fill in shadows.

After you've set up your night scene, do not zoom in or out. If you manually adjust the focus as outlined in this technique, your focus goes out the window as soon as you start zooming. Take advantage of any bright ambient lighting, such as streetlights or a spotlight in front of a business. When you set up your scene, position your subject in bright ambient lighting to bring out the fine details in your subject. Otherwise, your subject will be a muddy indistinguishable blob of color.

1.5

TIP

When you compose a scene, imagine a grid of two vertical lines and two horizontal lines in your viewfinder, which effectively splits the scene into nine squares. Aim your camcorder so as to align your center of interest as close as possible to where the grid lines intersect (see **Figure 1.5**).

CREATING A THREE-POINT LIGHTING SETUP

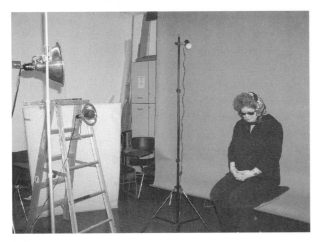

2.1

2.2

Light is one of the most important ingredients in a successful video production, particularly for indoor sessions. Indoor video lighting can be very tricky, especially if natural light sources are combined with the artificial light from lamps and overhead fluorescent fixtures.

In this technique, you learn a foolproof and inexpensive way to create near-perfect indoor lighting by using clamp-on utility lamps from a hardware store. This technique is based on the classic three-point lighting technique that photographers and videographers use as a springboard for their lighting setup. **Figure 2.1** demonstrates a makeshift lighting setup positioned around a subject. The light source comes from three inexpensive clamp-on light fixtures with incandescent light bulbs. **Figure 2.2** shows you the results of this three point lighting exercise from the camcorder's perspective. The three lights balance each other out resulting in a warm glow on the subject. As you will learn in this chapter, identifying the proper position for the back and side (fill) lights will result in near-perfect indoor illumination on a subject, as good as if you were using a professional lighting system.

7

To prepare for this technique, grab some photoflood lights (from photo supply stores) or any incandescent lights from a hardware store (**Figure 2.3**). Experiment with different lights and a variety of different watts to see if they cast a color on your subject that's suitable for the shoot. Find a room totally devoid of natural light, because for this technique you will rely only on the artificial light emitted from light bulbs. If blocking out natural light is too difficult, shoot your video at night.

STEP 1: SET UP THE KEY LIGHT

In a nutshell, three-point lighting involves a *key light,* a *backlight,* and a *fill light.* The key light is going to be your primary light source, so positioning it in just the right place is very important. In this step, you will identify the proper position of the lights in relation to a subject.

2.3

- Find a dark room. Have a friend, child, or a significant other act as your model and seat them in a chair in a dark room. Placing the subject in front of a solid-color background which always works well. A solid-color sheet of construction paper behind the subject does the trick. Stick with neutral colors, like mid-tone blues, greens, or grays, so the background won't detract from your subject.
- Position your camcorder in front of the subject on a tripod.
- Position one of your clamp-on lamps in front of the subject, but up higher than the subject and slightly on an angle. If you position the light above the subject, improvise by clamping it onto a hat stand, a tall lamp, a ladder, or a shelf. Experiment with the light by positioning it at different heights and angles, so that the light appears slightly off-center on the subject. In **Figure 2.4**, the key light is positioned so the key light source is dominant on the left side of the subject's face. It often takes a lot of experimenting to get the lighting to your liking. In fact, it's a good idea to use an inanimate object in place of the model to set up the lighting, and then call your model in when the lighting seems perfect. Otherwise, your model will get hot and tired of waiting under the lights.

STEP 2: SET UP THE BACKLIGHT

A backlight sits behind the subject so that the subject can be distinguished from the background. The backlight also eliminates the sense of flatness that limited lighting can create by balancing out the intensity of the key light.

■ Position a lamp behind the subject. You don't want the light or the stand to which the light is clamped to appear in the shot, so make sure that the light is positioned higher than the field in your viewfinder. Alternatively, you can position the light below, left, or right of the camcorder's field of vision. You may need some extension cords to reach the wall outlet to give you the freedom to move the lights around the space. In **Figure 2.4**, although the light is clamped onto a stand, the backlight is not visible in the camcorder viewfinder. Alternatively, you can position the backlight below a subject. Experiment with positioning the light closer and farther away from the subject until the light balances perfectly with the key light.

2.4

STEP 3: SET UP THE FILL LIGHT

A fill light, angled to the side of the subject, casts a subtle illumination on the subject. This soft light creates a balance between the key light and the back light. Otherwise the key light and backlights will cast harsh highlights on the subject.

BULB WATTAGE

Although you can use regular household light bulbs for this technique, film lights provide the best results. House lights tend to cast shadows that are too warm in saturation because the wattage tends to be too low to produce a strong color spectrum. You can buy photoflood lamps in any photography/video supply store for about $3.00 each. They typically come in 250 to 650 watts and last from two to four hours before burning out. Make sure that your electrical outlets can handle the high-wattage bulbs. If you think that you may blow a fuse, start out with the lower wattage bulbs to be safe.

WARNING

Incandescent bulbs are very hot, so wear utility gloves when handling them. Also, never touch a bulb with your bare hands, even if the bulb has cooled to room temperature. The oil on your hands can cause a bulb to explode when it heats up.

■ Position a lamp to the side of the subject. Experiment with bulbs that emit a softer light for the fill light position. If your light is too harsh, you can also experiment with holding up a white board (foam core or illustration board) to allow the fill light to bounce off the board (also known as a "bounce card"), diffusing the light even more. Because all scenes are different depending on the light intensity, wattage of the bulbs, and the nature of your environment, you need to experiment to find the right light balance.

■ Now, adjust all the lights until the scene looks visually balanced. The placement of the three lights, subject, and camcorder should resemble the positioning of these elements in **Figure 2.5**. To perfect the scene, try moving the lights farther away from and closer to the subject and also try different angles. You notice that moving the lights even slightly casts a mélange of hard shadows, soft shadows, and light on the subject.

Now for the fun part you've been waiting for. You are ready to shoot your video.

ADJUSTING WHITE BALANCE

White balancing is calibrating your camcorder so it displays color accurately. Many camcorders have an automatic white balance setting. Because automatic white balance presets are often inaccurate, your composition will look better if the white balance is adjusted manually. Check your users manual to find out if your camcorder has this feature.

To perform a manual white balance, set up your lighting, position your camcorder for the shoot, and point your lens toward the subject. Set your camcorder's white balance to manual and fill your viewfinder frame with a white object like foam core, white posterboard, or paper. If you're shooting a subject, put the white board in front of the subject. Finally, press the white balance button on your camcorder, and voilá! You now have the perfect balance of light and color in your composition.

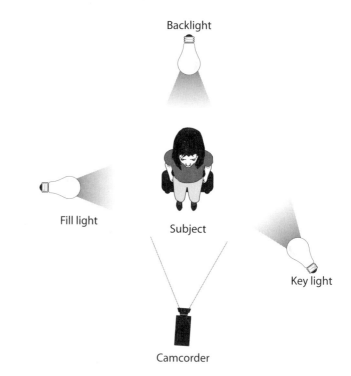

2.5

CREATING A MAKESHIFT DOLLY

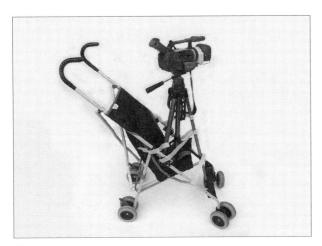

3.1

3.2

Following a moving subject can be a difficult task using a hand-held camcorder. As you follow the person, the camcorder moves in synch with you and does not remain level. Professional moviemakers use expensive *dollies* to film people in motion. You can create a makeshift dolly by improvising with items you may have hanging around in your garage or attic. Financially challenged independent filmmakers are renowned for coming up with makeshift devices to use as dollies. In **Figure 3.1**, we've mounted a tripod with a camcorder on top of a baby carriage. Tape was used to secure the tripod to the carriage as well as the straps on the carriage used to secure the child. **Figure 3.2** shows a camcorder person following the motion of a subject with a tripod with a camcorder, mounted on a baby carriage. Independent film makers and students often invent variations of this "dolly" by using wheelchairs, skateboards, rolling tables, shopping carts, virtually anything with wheels that can turn smoothly to create fluid motion. Sure, you might look a little silly to the outside world wheeling around a camcorder, but by strapping a camcorder onto a makeshift dolly, you can achieve some very smooth motion shots.

11

STEP 1: LOCATE AN OBJECT WITH WHEELS

In our example for this technique, we use a baby carriage. Baby carriages make excellent makeshift dollies because they fold up easily for transport and are relatively easy to obtain.

- Place a tripod inside the baby carriage. You want to make certain that it's secured, so if the carriage has straps for the child, attach them to the base of the tripod.
- Mount your camcorder on the tripod and then adjust the tripod to the correct height for your moving subject.
- View the scene through the camcorder viewfinder to make sure that your camcorder is level. If not, adjust the legs of the tripod until the camcorder is level.
- Use any kind of secure tape that won't cause a sticky residue, like electrical, masking, or gaffers tape to further secure the camcorder in position. If taping the tripod to the carriage (or alternate object with wheels) does not feel secure enough, you can use common household items like string, rope, or bungee cords to further secure the tripod in place.

STEP 2: REHEARSE THE SCENE

If you've used the makeshift dolly before, all you need to do is aim the camcorder at your subject and begin filming. However, if you are improvising with material you've obtained on the scene, such as a borrowed shopping cart, you can save yourself a bit of grief by making sure that the makeshift dolly performs without a hitch.

- Instruct your actor(s) to begin moving.
- Follow your subject with the makeshift dolly.

As you move your makeshift dolly, make sure that the motion is smooth and none of the wheels are out of round. If your scene involves following your subject around a corner, make sure that the wheels turn smoothly. Also pay attention to any squeaky wheels that might ruin the audio for your clip. If the makeshift dolly performs suitably, you're ready to begin shooting. If not, find another item to use as a makeshift dolly or grease the squeaky wheels.

> **TIP**
>
> Make sure that the tires on your makeshift dolly are devoid of gashes and dents, and when you turn the dolly, make sure the wheels turn in a fluid movement. Otherwise, when you shoot your video, the movement will be choppy.

STEP 3: BEGIN SHOOTING

After rehearsing the scene and testing your makeshift dolly, it's time for the fun part. Lights . . . Camera . . . Action!

- Switch your camcorder to Pause. In the viewfinder, make certain that your lens clears the makeshift dolly. You don't want part of the dolly to appear in your video.
- Open your camcorder's LCD viewer so that you can preview the motion.
- Now, get in front of or in back of the subject.
- Instruct the person to begin walking, roll the tape, and stroll along with the carriage while they walk.
- Watch the LCD viewfinder to make certain that your motion is fluid alongside the subject.
- Depending upon the effect you want to achieve, you can track your subject in one of three ways. You can follow them from behind as shown in **Figure 3.3**, walk backwards in front of the subject, or track the person from the side as shown in **Figure 3.4**.

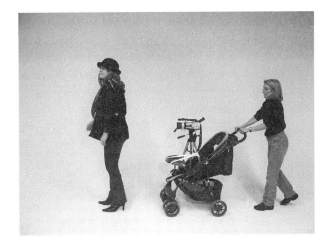

3.3

3.4

STEP 4: USING YOUR CAR AS A MAKESHIFT DOLLY

You can take this technique one step further and use your car as a makeshift dolly. You'll find this version of the technique especially useful if you travel through scenic country roads, or through a historic neighborhood. All you need for this version of the technique is a tripod that fits on the passenger's seat of your car, some bungee cords (which can be purchased from your local building supply or hardware store), and your camcorder's remote control.

- Position the tripod in the passenger's seat of your vehicle with two legs of the tripod parallel to the front of the seat.
- Fasten the seatbelt around the tripod.
- Clip enough bungee cords together to encompass the tripod and wrap snuggly around the seatback. Thread the bungee cords through the center post of the tripod and around the seatback. Clip the open ends of the bungee cords to create a loop around your passenger seat, thus securing the tripod.
- Clip two bungee cords together, thread them through the legs of the tripod that are parallel to the front of the seat and secure them to the under-

side of the seat. Each car is different. Look under your seat for springs or mounting hardware to which you can clip the bungee cords. Note that you may need more bungee cords if your vehicle is a large car, SUV, or pickup truck. On the other hand, if you drive a compact sports car, you may need only one bungee cord.

- Mount your camcorder on the tripod and turn the LCD viewer so that it is visible from the driver's seat (see **Figure 3.5**).

- Using the LCD viewer, adjust the tripod to aim the camcorder between the windshield supports. You may have to zoom in to avoid including the windshield wipers or roof in your video. It's also beneficial to position the camcorder angled to the left as if a passenger were looking to the left.

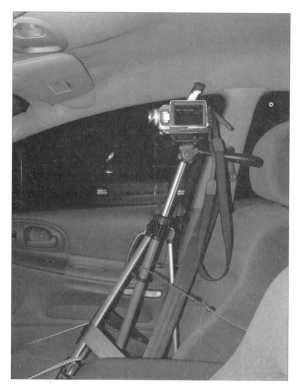

3.5

TIP

When you use this version of the technique to record video from inside your car, you may encounter glare from the windshield. You can eliminate glare with the use of a polarizing filter, an accessory that attaches to your camcorder lens. You twist the outer ring of a polarizing filter while viewing the scene through your camcorder's LCD viewer to dial out the glare. Polarizing filters are also great for eliminating reflections from water and windows.

After the camcorder is securely fastened, you're ready to begin recording video. To record video, park your car by the side of the road, turn your camcorder on and use your camcorder remote to begin recording. Merge onto the road and you'll faithfully record the scenery as you drive. Note that this technique works best on smooth roads. If you try this technique on a bumpy road, or on one with potholes, the camcorder may bounce slightly as the upward force of your vehicle and the weight of the camcorder cause the bungee cords to expand when you encounter a bump.

CAUTION

When using this technique, be cautious when changing lanes. When you look to your right, you'll see the images from your camcorder LCD viewer, as well as the traffic in the right lane. This can be a bit disconcerting, as you're not expecting the extra visual input. In this regard, it's advisable to perfect this technique in a quiet neighborhood before venturing out onto unfamiliar or crowded roads.

4

SHOOTING SPORTING EVENTS LIKE A PRO

4.1

4.2

ABOUT THE VIDEO

The sample video for this technique was compiled from footage shot at the Great Clermont Triathlon, where athletes test their physical stamina by swimming 1.5 miles, biking 25 miles, and then running 6.2 miles. Watching the event unfold as the athletes in their colorful garb compete and then transition from one stage of the event to the next makes a triathlon an interesting event to watch and capture on video.

A sporting event can provide the basis for a compelling home video. However, most people film sporting events from a single vantage point, causing all the footage to look the same. To truly catch the excitement of athletes in competition, you've got to be mobile. You should also be prepared to tell a story. A sporting event is about more than the actual competition. Strive to get some behind-the-scenes footage (see **Figure 4.1**) before the event starts, then capture the beauty and excitement of the athletes in competition (see **Figure 4.2**), and then for your denouement, shoot some footage as the event winds to a conclusion.

STEP 1: SHOOT ATHLETES PREPARING FOR THE EVENT

Athletes are like modern day gladiators; they suit up prior to the event and get ready to compete. If you can get behind the scenes and shoot the athletes as they're suiting up, you've got an excellent beginning for your video. Football players don shoulder pads, baseball players wear cleats, and racecar drivers wear fireproof suits and colorful helmets.

■ Contact the event promoters ahead of time. Tell them what you're doing and try to obtain a VIP pass.

■ Arrive at the event ahead of time and scope out the best positions for recording the event. If possible, attend pre-event practice to familiarize yourself with the athletes and shoot some preliminary footage from different vantage points. This will familiarize you with the participants and will help you anticipate their actions when you record the event. If you're covering an event like a triathlon, arriving early will give you the opportunity to watch athletes limber up with some easy swimming or a slow jog.

■ Get behind the scenes and shoot the athletes as they suit up with protective gear and warm up for the event (see **Figure 4.3**).

■ Shoot any other pre-event formalities, such as introduction of the athletes, a coin toss, runners stretching, and so on.

4·3

When you're shooting behind the scenes, pay attention to any rituals the athletes may go through while preparing. Some athletes go through elaborate stretching routines, while other athletes prepare for the event by focusing their thoughts. Shoot any dramatic expressions on the athletes' faces while they prepare to compete, to add an element of drama to your production.

STEP 2: SHOOT THE START OF THE EVENT

Every athletic event has some sort of formal beginning. A football game begins with an opening kickoff; in auto racing there's a parade lap, and so on. If you're familiar with the sporting venue, you probably have a pretty good idea of the best vantage point for filming the beginning.

■ Claim your position well ahead of time. If you're attending a crowded event that will be recorded by many people, you don't want the back of other people's heads in your video.

■ Turn on your camcorder and switch to Pause a half minute before the event starts. Note that some camcorders will power down after a given period of time to conserve battery life. With some camcorders, you can use the camcorder menu to reset the default time to a setting of your choosing. Alternatively, you can start your camcorder within your device's default power down window and press the Pause button.

■ Press the record button several seconds prior to the start. Shooting a few seconds of lead-in footage is a good idea. Having extra footage gives you some leeway when you use iMovie or Windows Movie Maker to edit the footage, add titles, transitions, and so on.

■ Record at least 30 seconds of the beginning. Many beginning moviemakers make the mistake of only recording a few seconds per clip, which makes transitioning from one scene to the next difficult.

STEP 3: CAPTURE ATHLETES IN MOTION

Every sporting event involves athletes in motion, whether you're filming a baseball game, a figure skating event, or a triathlon. In the case of a triathlon, the athletes compete in three stages. At the start of the event a horn sounds or a gun fires and the athletes race into the water and when deep enough, begin swimming. At the end of the swim, the athletes exit the water and race towards their bikes. During this transition, the athletes don their biking shoes and protective helmets before mounting their bikes and racing off into the distance. The final stage of the event involves locomotion of the biped variety as running shoes meet tarmac.

■ Shoot your footage from different vantage points. If you're filming a football or basketball game, film from the sidelines if possible and shoot from the end zones. The different viewpoints will pique viewer interest when you screen your finished production.

■ Shoot from different elevations. Film the event from ground level and high in the grandstands. If you're shooting an event like a triathlon, you can even position your camcorder on the ground to catch the athletes from a unique vantage point as they run or bike past.

■ Follow the athletes. Instead of filming the event from a distance, zoom in on individual athletes in motion and pan your camcorder as the athlete moves (see **Figure 4.4**). Doing this takes some practice, which is why arriving ahead of time is important. You need to become familiar with the athletes and their motion. You can use a tripod to stabilize the camcorder while you pan. However, if you're covering an event like a triathlon, a tripod can be a hindrance. You want to have the flexibility to capture the athletes in each stage of the event and a heavy tripod can slow you down as you move from stage to stage. With a bit of practice, you can pan smoothly without a tripod.

TIP

When shopping for a tripod, consider purchasing a model with a level and a fluid head. These options ensure that your scenes will be level, and you'll be able to pan smoothly when capturing motion on film.

4.4

STEP 4: CAPTURE THE HEAT OF BATTLE

If you do nothing but film the athletes as they move from one end of the field to the other, you're missing a good bit of the action. Film the athletes as they interact with each other on field — the defense tackling the running back, the goalie taking a defensive stance against the onslaught of a soccer running back, triathletes riding their bikes in close quarters, battling for position as they race towards a corner.

- Keep your camcorder at the ready. Follow the flow of the event through the camcorder viewfinder.
- Anticipate exciting events. Keep your finger poised on the record button.
- Press the Record button when it looks like things are beginning to heat up. As the event unfolds before you, watch for signs of impending action. For example, you'll want to be ready to shoot when you see basketball players rushing towards a basket, or a gaggle of bikers queuing up for a corner (see **Figure 4.5**).

When filming athletic events, practice makes perfect. Before capturing a big event on film, consider recording similar events as practice. For example, if you're going to fly to New York to film friends and

> **TIP**
>
> If possible, record the awards ceremony as the final scene for your movie. If the event doesn't have an awards ceremony, or you're unable to attend it, create ending credits (see Chapter 8) that list the winners or score of the event.

family running the New York Marathon, record a few local running events first. By practicing, you can fine-tune the technique presented here and then capture some eye-popping video when you do record the big event.

> **TIP**
>
> To pan smoothly without a tripod, spread your feet apart and move your arms close to the sides of your chest while cradling the camcorder with both hands. Take a normal breath, press the record button, and then exhale slowly as you move the camcorder in synch with the motion of the athlete. Follow through after you release the record button, otherwise the motion may not be smooth at the end of the sequence.

4.5

CHAPTER 2

FROM CAMERA TO CUTTING ROOM FLOOR

After capturing several minutes of video or filling up a 60-minute cassette, you can view your videos through your camcorder's LCD. Of course, doing so is rather limiting because the screen is small. You can also connect your camcorder to your television set and play your videos. Whichever way you use to view your recordings, you'll find some flaws that detract from the overall quality of your video. For example, you may not have panned steadily, or perhaps you forgot to switch off the record button and captured several minutes of your feet as you walked to your next scene.

Therein lies the beauty of working with programs such as iMovie and Windows Movie Maker. You capture your raw footage into your computer and edit your videos to produce a professional-looking production. In this chapter, you learn the basics of editing. First and foremost, you learn to capture the footage to your computer as clips. Next, you learn to trim unwanted footage from your video clips. You also

learn to add still images to your productions. The final technique in this chapter shows you how to assemble your clips on the timeline to create a professional-quality presentation.

5

CAPTURING FOOTAGE AS CLIPS

5.1

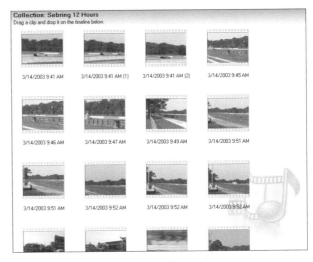

5.2

Capturing digital video footage is always an event filled with anticipation. The idea of capturing moments in time and being able to rearrange them in any order you see fit takes you from the realm of being a camcorder jockey to a digital producer. When DV footage is moved from the camcorder to the desktop, it is already in a digital state. So when you capture clips into an application, such as iMovie or Windows Movie Maker, you are actually *importing* the digital footage into your video editing application.

Figure 5.1 depicts the Clip pane in iMovie after several scenes have been captured. **Figure 5.2** represents the clip gallery in Windows Movie Maker. As you can see, both applications organize, name, and store the clips in a neat little window, ready for you to assemble in the order you want your movie to take shape.

This technique reviews the basic steps involved in the capturing process in both iMovie and Windows Movie Maker and some additional tips to help streamline the task. Although both applications offer "plug and play," capturing is one of the most important steps in the movie-making process.

Capturing the clips the way you want them to look the first time around can save you the trouble of having to go back and capture moments in scenes you may have missed.

iMOVIE

STEP 1: SET UP THE DV CAMCORDER

We want to record children playing with wild berries and leaves on a lazy summer day in Cape Cod. But before capturing the footage into individual scenes, the camcorder and the Mac have to be set up properly.

- Connect the camcorder to the FireWire port on your Mac. Plug the camcorder into a wall outlet. Using a battery while capturing may cause frames to drop in addition to wearing out your battery.
- Turn on your camcorder and put it in VCR or VTR mode.
- Launch the iMovie application and in the Save As dialog box, give the movie a name and click the Save button. The location you save the file to also determines the location of the scenes you are about to capture. These clips, or scenes, will be saved in a folder named Media that resides within the new movie folder you have just created.

The Camera mode icon should be selected, because iMovie will sense that your camcorder is all set up and ready to roll (see **Figure 5.3**). The words Camera Connected appear in the Monitor window. iMovie can now take over your camcorder's control functions. Note you can also control your camcorder at this time using the control features in VCR/VTR mode.

STEP 2: CAPTURE SCENES
FROM YOUR FOOTAGE

You can capture a clip in iMovie in one of two ways: You can enable iMovie to automatically decide what constitutes a scene, or you can manually create your own scene. Note that the word *clip* in iMovie is synonymous with what iMovie refers to as a *scene*. This step requires you to click the control buttons at the bottom of the Monitor window to rewind, stop, play, pause, and fast forward, respectively, to specify the beginning of a

NOTE

The capture process in iMovie was designed for DV camcorders, so you can't utilize the capture feature if you want to capture from an analog camcorder. You can, however, buy a device to convert your analog footage to digital and then import this footage into iMovie. Dazzle Multimedia manufactures one such device for Mac users, the Dazzle Hollywood DV Bridge. As of this writing, the street price for this converter is about $200.00. If you are using clips from a USB device such as a digital camera, you can copy the clips from the camera to your hard drive. Generally they are converted to QuickTime format for Macs.

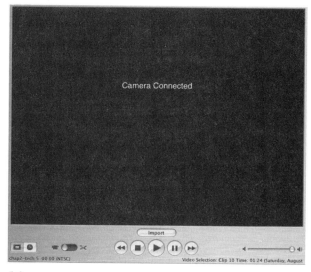

5.3

scene you want to capture (see **Figure 5.4**). Either way, make certain you play your video from beginning to end before you capture any scenes. This way, you will have a clearer idea of where activity begins and ends in your video. In addition, you can formulate an idea of how you are going to assemble the clips after you capture them.

■ By default, iMovie automatically detects where a scene begins and ends by examining breaks in timecode on the original footage. This method works fine if you have meticulously shot your footage so that a scene begins and ends approximately where you want it. Many times, however, you don't have time to think about the postproduction process when you're behind the lens. Fortunately, you can change the way a movie is captured in the Preferences dialog box. In the Import section of the box, shown in **Figure 5.5**, the default setting for importing a clip is Automatically start new clip at scene break.

5.4

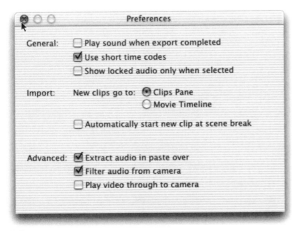

5.5

Choosing this setting decides when a scene begins and ends. To manually select the end of a scene, deselect this box and close the Preferences dialog box by clicking on the red button with an *X* in the upper-left of this window.

■ To manually end a scene after disabling automatic scene detection, click the **Play** button to roll the footage to where you want the scene to begin. Click the **Import** button once to specify where you want the scene to begin and click it again when you want the scene to end. When you're ready to shoot the next scene, click the **Import** button again until you have gathered all your scenes together in the Clip Shelf. Don't worry about the extra footage you may have grabbed. You can trim this later in the editing process.

■ If you accidentally click the **Import** button to capture a scene and then change your mind, just click the **Stop** button on the controls under the Monitor window. Doing this stops the scene from being stored on the Clip Shelf.

■ When you are done, turn off your camcorder. When you do this, the Mode icon below the iMovie monitor switches to the Edit Mode, which is represented with a Scissors icon (see **Figure 5.6**).

STEP 3: ORGANIZING SCENES IN THE SHELF

After you've captured a bunch of scenes, you'll need to examine them again and decide which clips will be useful in your assembled movie.

■ To preview a clip stored on the Shelf, double-click its thumbnail image. A preview of the clip plays in the Monitor window.

5.6

■ To delete a scene from the Shelf, first select the thumbnail of the scene in the Shelf. (The selected scene takes on a blue tint.) Drag the clip to the Trashcan to the bottom right of the window. The Trash window indicates the size of the clip you just deleted. However, the clip is not deleted from the movie until the Trashcan is emptied. Empty it by clicking it. The Empty Trash dialog box warns you that the clip will be removed from the Shelf if you click OK (see **Figure 5.7**).

■ To restore a deleted scene, press **Command-Z** to undo your last move. Note that because of iMovie's non-destructive nature, the clip still exists in the Media folder where you stored the movie from which you are capturing. Clips must be manually trashed from this folder if you want to permanently get rid of them. In fact, you should trash clips you don't plan on using as clips take up a lot of room on your hard drive.

Now your movie is ready to be assembled on the timeline.

5.7

WINDOWS MOVIE MAKER

After shooting some exciting footage, the next step is to put the crowning touch on the creation by editing your work in Windows Movie Maker 2. Before you can edit your footage, however, you first have to capture it. If you've shot several minutes of footage, finding exactly what you want can be a cumbersome task. Fortunately, Windows Movie Maker can automatically break down

> **CLIP SIZE CONSIDERATIONS**
>
> Video clips take up a tremendous amount of hard drive space. As you watch the timecode on the scene thumbnail in the Clip pane tick away while you capture a clip, keep in mind that full-screen video eats up about 3.5MB of hard disk space per second. This means that a minute-long clip consumes about 210MB of disk space. Make certain that you're aware of remaining hard disk space on the disk you use for capture. If it's an unlimited amount of remaining space (additional hard drives), you don't have anything to worry about. Otherwise, make sure that you are prudent when capturing scenes. Keep them short—less than a minute. You also don't want your scenes to be too short if you're planning on adding transitions and overlay titles. Transitions need at least several seconds clip overlap on the tail of one clip and the head of another to successfully transition one clip into another. See Chapter 3 for techniques for applying transitions.

footage into scenes, enabling you to preview scenes and choose the right clips for your digital masterpiece.

STEP 1: CONFIGURING YOUR CAMCORDER FOR CAPTURE

Before you launch Windows Movie Maker, you have to attach your camcorder to the PC. The actual steps for doing so vary depending on whether you capture video through a USB interface, an IEEE 1394 FireWire card, or an analog video card. If you use the latter device and plan to capture audio as well, you need to make the connection from the camcorder's audio out port to your sound card.

■ Connect your camcorder to your PC capture device.

■ Turn on your camcorder and select VCR or VTR mode. If you connected your camcorder to a FireWire or USB port, Windows will make a sound alerting you that the device is connected properly.

■ Launch **Windows Movie Maker 2** and then choose **File ➤ Capture Video.** The Video Capture Device section of the Video Capture Wizard appears. The dialog box lists all the available capture devices that are connected to your PC.

■ Select the device from which you want to capture the video and then click **Next.**

■ Type a name for the footage you are capturing, select the folder in which you want to store the captured video clips, and then click **Next.** The Video Setting section of the Video Capture Wizard, which you use to configure compression settings for the footage that you'll capture, appears.

STEP 2: CAPTURING THE FOOTAGE

After configuring your camcorder, you are ready to begin capturing footage. The options you have available depend on the type of device you are using to capture your footage. In this section, you find out how to capture footage from a digital camcorder hooked to a FireWire card installed in your computer.

■ Choose the desired video setting (see **Figure 5.8**). The actual setting you choose depends on what you'll use to play back your rendered movies. If you intend to play the videos on your computer, choose the default setting to compress the file for Windows Media Player's native WMV format. If you're going to burn your finished movies to a DVD disc, choose Digital Device Format. Note that this setting takes up quite a bit of room on your hard drive, with one minute of video

> **TIP**
>
> Choose a compression setting that produces a better quality clip than you actually need. You can always choose a higher compression setting and then choose a lower quality compression setting when exporting the movie.

requiring 178 MB. If you're creating a movie for delivery over the Internet, click the **Other Settings** radio button and choose one of the presets. After choosing a video setting, click **Next.**

■ If you've connected a digital camcorder to a FireWire card or USB port, the Capture Method section of the Video Capture Wizard becomes available (see **Figure 5.9**). Here you can choose to

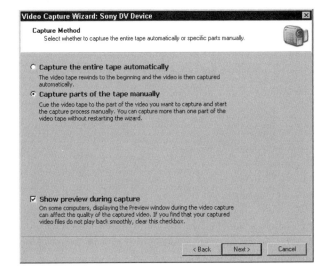

5.8

5.9

capture parts of the tape or the entire digital tape.
If you've got a powerful computer, you can enable
the Show preview during capture option and preview the footage as you capture it. You have better
control over the process if you decide to capture
parts of the video manually. After choosing a capture method, click **Next**.

■ In the Capture Video section of the Video
Capture Wizard, you capture the actual footage.
If you decided to manually capture parts of the
video, the Start Capture and Stop Capture buttons
become available and VCR-style controls appear at
the bottom of the preview window. You use these
controls to preview the footage on your camcorder.
When you see what you want to capture, click **Start
Capture.** Click **Stop Capture** to stop capturing.
You can then capture other parts of the tape as
needed. If you select the **Create clips when wizard
finishes** option, Windows Movie Maker breaks the
capture into individual clips. This option is the
desired capture method, especially when you're
capturing many minutes of footage. As you capture the footage, Windows Movie Maker displays
the length of the selection you've captured, as well
as the size of the resulting clips (see **Figure 5.10**).

■ Click **Finish** when you've captured the desired
footage from your camcorder.

STEP 3: SORTING YOUR FOOTAGE

After you capture your video, Windows Movie Maker
creates a collection. You assemble your movie by dragging clips from the collection to the timeline at the
bottom of the Windows Movie Maker window. If you
opted to divide your capture into clips, Windows
Movie Maker creates a thumbnail for the first frame of
each clip and assembles the captures clips as a collection, like the KeyWest collection shown in **Figure 5.11.**

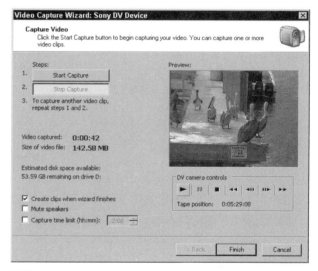

5.10

You can take care of most of your collection house-keeping by right-clicking a clip and then choosing one of the following options from the shortcut menu:

- **Add the clip to the timeline.**
- **Play the clip in the Preview Pane.**
- **Cut the clip.** After you cut the clip, you can select another collection and paste the cut clip into that collection.
- **Copy the clip.** After copying the clip, you can paste it into another collection.
- **Paste the clip into another collection.**

- **Rename the clip.** Renaming a clip will make it easier to identify.
- **Create clips.** You can use this option to break lengthy footage you capture or import into clips.
- **Combine clips.** This option is available when you have more than one clip selected and will combine the selected clips into a single clip.
- **Browse for missing file.** This option becomes available if you move a clip from the folder in which it was captured to a different folder. Missing files are designated by a movie clip symbol with a large red *X*.

5.11

6

TRIMMING UNWANTED FOOTAGE

6.1

6.2

If you take advantage of iMovie and Windows Movie Maker's ability to capture video footage and convert the footage into clips or scenes, you've jumped over the first hurdle in creating your digital masterpiece. However, even though both programs do an excellent job of converting long footage into scenes, you may still find instances where you need to eliminate some frames in your clip. For example, if a scene shows a few frames of your significant other in an unflattering pose, diplomacy dictates that you remove the offensive frames. Another time you would want to trim a clip is if you manually captured it and did not properly set the out point. Fortunately iMovie and Windows Movie Maker provide easy methods you can use to remove any undesirable footage. **Figure 6.1** shows a clip in the Monitor window in iMovie ready to be edited. **Figure 6.2** shows the in and out points at the bottom of the Monitor window reset to reflect the newly trimmed (or "cropped" as it is called in iMovie) clip. The interface in Windows Movie Maker offers a similar trimming feature as you will read about in the Windows Movie Maker section of this technique.

iMOVIE

iMovie offers a couple of different ways to trim clips. You can trim clips after you arrange them in the Timeline, enabling you to go back and tweak a movie to perfection even after it's all assembled. You can also trim a clip right off the Shelf, before you even begin thinking about the order in which the scenes are going to appear. Here, we demonstrate how to trim a clip by selecting one on the Shelf.

STEP 1: OPEN A PROJECT

Open a project with some clips that have just been captured. As an alternative, capture a group of clips and then jump to Step 2. (See Technique 5 to learn about effective scene capture.) In this technique's example, we cut out two children playing make-believe cooking to leave only the latter half of the clip, which shows a little boy walking.

STEP 2: PREVIEW A CLIP

Before each clip is trimmed, you need to navigate through the clip to decide if it needs to be trimmed, and if so, at what point. Remember, iMovie is a non-destructive editing application; the original clip you captured always stays intact on your scratch disk, no matter how much you cut, crop, or trim it. Let's consider the easiest way to navigate through a clip.

■ Select a clip on the Shelf to view it in the Monitor window. Using the control buttons under the Monitor window (Rewind, Stop, Play, Pause, and Fast Forward), navigate through the clip to decide where it needs trimming, as shown in

Figure 6.3. To expedite the navigation process, you can use shortcut keys. Press the **spacebar** to play and stop a clip respectively. Press the **Home** key to return to the beginning of the clip you're currently viewing. Press the **End** key to bring you to the end of the clip.

■ The Scrubber bar is the blue bar directly under the Monitor window. Click and drag in this bar to pinpoint an exact place in time on the clips. Clicking the Scrubber bar gives you control of the *Playhead*, the inverted triangle on the Scrubber bar that indicates the timecode for the clip.

■ To precisely navigate through each frame, press the left and right arrow keys. When you're familiar with the sequence of the clip, you can crop it.

STEP 3: SET THE IN AND OUT POINTS

Before trimming, you need to identify the *in* and *out points* of the clip. The in point represents where you want the clip to begin playing, and the out point represents where you want it to end. In the clip shown in **Figure 6.4**, the in and out points are set so the two children playing in the clip are trimmed out.

Scrubber bar

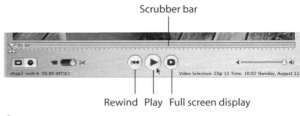

Rewind Play Full screen display

6.3

* Use one of the navigation methods to identify where you want a clip to begin. We used the manual scrub method to identify a point in time.

* Use one of the navigation methods to identify where you want a clip to begin. We used the manual scrub method to identify a point in time.

* Click and hold the pointer under the blue Scrubber bar. The right and left triangle markers that appear to the left will now be under your pointer. The triangle pointed left indicates the in point, and the triangle pointing right indicates the out point. In this clip, we placed the in point right when the boy appears in the scene and the out point almost at the very end of the clip.

* Drag the in point to the place in time where you want the clip to begin. Note the yellow bar that appears in between the in and out points designates the new area. Repeat the process by dragging the out point to determine where you want the clip to end (see **Figure 6.4**). After you've identified the area you want to trim, you can crop the clip or cut the clip.

STEP 4: CROP A CLIP

After you've set a clip's in and out points, you've determined which area of the clip you want to use in your movie. When you *crop* a clip, you are trimming the part of the clip you want to keep.

* Keep the in and out points set as they were set in the last step and choose **Edit ➤ Crop** from the

menu (or **Command-K**), as shown in **Figure 6.5**. Notice that the thumbnail in the Shelf now changes to reflect the new crop. The timecode on the thumbnail indicates a shorter length of time for the clip. To undo your cropping, choose **Edit ➤ Undo Crop** from the menu (**Command-Z**).

CUTTING A CLIP

In addition to cropping a clip, you can also *cut* a clip. Cutting a clip takes out the area you want to discard from a clip. When you cropped a clip in Step 4, you selected the part of the clip we were going to use. When you cut a clip, you select the in and/or out points of an area you want to eliminate in the clip. To cut a clip, you identify the area to be discarded with the in and out points. Then you choose **Edit ➤ Cut** from the menu, and the unwanted portion disappears.

In point   Out point

6.4

6.5

After you've trimmed your clips, the next step is assembling them in the Movie Track. Keep in mind that many iMovie users opt to assemble the clips on the Movie Track prior to trimming them. Trimming clips in the Movie Track involves the same process as trimming from the Clip pane. The only difference is the clip location in the iMovie window.

WINDOWS MOVIE MAKER

After you capture video and store it as a collection, you can then begin picking and choosing clips for your movie. When you choose a clip from the Collection pane, the first frame of the movie appears in the Preview pane. After selecting the clip, you can preview the clip and visually select the point where the trimmed clip begins and ends.

STEP 1: PREVIEWING THE CLIP

When you preview a clip, you can use the VCR-type controls to play the clip, pause the clip, stop the clip, fast forward the clip, rewind the clip, or advance forward or backward one frame at a time. Using these controls or their keyboard shortcuts, you can navigate to a desired frame. If you've just captured some footage from your camcorder, the clips are neatly arranged in a collection.

- Click a movie clip to select it. The first frame of the selected clip appears in the Preview pane (see **Figure 6.6**).
- Click the **Play** button to begin playing the movie, or, if you prefer, press the **spacebar**. After doing either, the Play button becomes the Pause button.
- Click the **Pause** button or press the spacebar to pause the movie.

- Click the **Fast Forward** button to advance to the end of the clip.
- Click the **Rewind** button to rewind the clip to the first frame.

STEP 2: SETTING THE START TRIM POINT

After previewing the clip, you probably have a pretty good idea of which parts you want to trim. The first step in trimming your clip is determining where you want the new clip to begin playing. This is often referred to as the start trim point.

- Click the **Play** button or press the **spacebar** to begin playing the clip.
- Click the **Pause** button or press the **spacebar** when you see the spot where you want the trimmed clip to begin. If you don't pause the movie at the precise point, you can advance forward or backward a frame at a time.
- Click the **Next Frame** button to advance to the next frame in the movie. Alternately, you can press **Alt** and the **Right Arrow** key.

6.6

■ Click the **Previous Frame** button to step back to the previous frame. Alternately, you can press **Alt** and the **Left Arrow** key.

■ Click the **Split** button (second button from the end in the Preview pane) to split the clip at the selected frame (see **Figure 6.7**).

STEP 3: SETTING THE END TRIM POINT

After you split the clip, Windows Movie Maker places the trimmed clip in the collection. The clip with your start trim point remains in the Preview pane. The trimmed clip has the same name as the original appended by *(1)*. Preview the clip again to make sure

that it's acceptable. After previewing the clip, you may decide that you need to trim some footage from the end by setting the end trim point.

■ Begin playing the clip.

■ Pause the clip when you reach the desired end trim point.

■ If necessary, move forward or backward a frame at a time to select a desired frame.

■ Click the **Split** button to set the end trim point (see **Figure 6.8**).

After setting the end trim point, the unwanted frames from the clip are in the Collection pane appended by the next available number, which will be *2*, unless you've trimmed a clip several times. You can delete the clip with the unwanted footage by selecting the clip, right-clicking, and then choosing **Delete** from the shortcut menu. Before trimming additional clips, you may want to consider renaming your trimmed clip to avoid confusion. You can rename a selected clip by pressing **F2**, typing a new name for the clip, and then pressing **Enter**. After trimming your clips, you're ready to begin adding clips to the timeline.

6.7

6.8

ADDING STILLS TO YOUR MOVIE

7.1

7.2

ABOUT THE IMAGES

Figure 7.1 is From the Photodisc collection, "Volume 28, People, Lifestyles, and Vacations." Figure 7.2 is an image of Half Dome in Yosemite National Park. The picture was taken with a Minolta 35MM SLR and captured to PC using a Hewlett Packard 5370 scanner with default resolution of 200 dpi.

U sing an application called iMovie or Windows Movie Maker to create movies doesn't mean that every single clip in your production has to be a movie. Adding still shots to your movie is an effective way to create viewer interest. You can use a still shot as a basis for a movie's title or ending credits. Another effective use of a still image is to suspend animation and allow the viewer a close-up look at a specific item in your movie, for example, a painting in a museum or a piece of antique furniture. If you have a series of pictures of a person or a scene at different points in time, you can add these to your production. An effective use of several images (also known as an *image sequence*) would be to examine the choreography of a pit stop in an auto race, or a triathlete's transition from swimming to biking, and then from biking to running, where each image is held onscreen for a few seconds to give viewers a better idea of what is happening.

When you use a digital camcorder to capture images for your movies, use a resolution setting of 1600 x 1200 or higher if your camcorder supports it. The image will have smaller dimensions when you add it to iMovie or Windows Movie Maker, but it will look better. If you're scanning an image for use in a video project, use a resolution of 200 DPI or higher.

iMOVIE

Whatever the origin of your picture (scanned in, digital camera, stock photography that you purchased), chances are you need to change the size of the picture in a photo-editing application before importing the picture into iMovie. In iMovie, pictures must be sized to 640 x 480 (NTSC) to display correctly. Otherwise a black border will appear around the image. If you own an application such as Photoshop or Photoshop Elements, you can use the crop tool to crop the photo

> **NOTE**
>
> You may wonder why you should import still pictures that are sized as 640 x 480 instead of the DV NTSC standard frame size of 720 x 480. iMovie logically expects you to size still pictures to suit the final output, which is 640 x 480, the QuickTime (and non-widescreen TV) standard.

> **TIP**
>
> If you take GraphicConverter out for a spin and decide to keep it, you are obligated to pay for this application. The latest version of GraphicConverter (Version 4.5) can be downloaded from the CD `www.lemkesoft.de/gcdownload_us.html`. The current price for this application as of this printing is $30.

to 640 x 480. If you don't own a photo-editing application, there's an inexpensive shareware application you can use, named GraphicConverter. GraphicConverter is great for quickly resizing images and changing their resolution. A tryout copy of this application is on the CD-ROM. Load the application onto your hard drive before you proceed.

In addition, keep in mind that if you are using someone else's pictures in your production and you plan on going public with it, you should get permission to use their pictures. This could avoid legal problems you may have if you use pictures without authorization.

STEP 1: TRIM THE STILL PICTURE

Figure 7.3 demonstrates that when a picture is not in the proper proportion to the iMovie frame, a black bar appears both above and beneath the picture to compensate for the incorrect ratio. We'll trim the picture so that the size fits perfectly in iMovie.

■ Copy the GraphicConverter folder to your hard drive. Open the **GraphicConverter** application in this folder and choose **File ➣ Open** from the menu. Navigate to the Clips folder on your CD-ROM and open the file named **Photodisc_ball1.jpg**. The dimensions of this file

7.3

are currently 772 x 510, which means the image will have black bands on the bottom and top in the iMovie frame. First, save the image in GraphicConverter.

■ From the GraphicConverter menu, choose **Picture** ➢ **Show Position** and then click the **Selection tool** in the toolbar (rectangular marquee icon).

■ Click and drag on the picture to select the area you want to crop. Watch the W and H position numbers in the title bar to determine when your selection is exactly 640 x 480 pixels, as shown in **Figure 7.4**. Click and drag on any of the nine handles surrounding the selection to resize it after you've made your initial selection.

■ When you're done making the selection, choose **Edit** ➢ **Trim Selection** from the GraphicConverter menu. Next, choose **File** ➢ **Save As** from the menu. Save the file on your hard drive as photodisc_ball2. jpg. Now you're ready to import this picture into iMovie.

STEP 2: IMPORT THE STILL IMAGE INTO iMOVIE

■ Begin a new movie and save it. Choose **File** ➢ **Import** and in the Import dialog box, navigate

---

IMPORT FILE FORMATS FOR iMOVIE

In the previous technique, we imported a file into iMovie that was saved in a JPEG format. You can import many other image formats into iMovie inclusive of PICT, GIF, .Photoshop, .TIFF, and EPS. Keep in mind that the JPEG format offers *lossy* compression, meaning that each time you save a JPEG file, the quality is diminished. To avoid this problem, save it in another file format in your photo-editing application. When you're ready to save it again, do a Save As back to the JPEG format. This way, you'll have a working file and a JPEG copy of this file, thus retaining the high quality of the original.

---

to where you saved the file you just created (photodisc_ball2.jpg). Click **OK.**

■ The thumbnail preview in the Shelf indicates that the duration of the still image is 5 seconds (see **Figure 7.5**). Five seconds is the default duration for still images. You can change the duration so the picture will display for longer or shorter duration. You can learn about more adjusting still images in Technique 17.

7.5

7.4

WINDOWS MOVIE MAKER

After capturing your vacation footage, you view a family member's photos from the same trip and see several images you'd like to include in your finished movie. The artful placement of still images along the timeline augments your movie by filling in the blanks, so to speak. When you add still images to the Windows Movie Maker timeline, they are displayed for five seconds by default. You can increase the amount of time the images are displayed, a technique you can learn by reading Technique 8.

STEP 1: COPY THE PHOTOS TO YOUR HARD DRIVE

If the photos are from a digital camera, you can easily add them to your hard drive and use them in a Windows Movie Maker production:

> **NOTE**
>
> When you scan images, always use a fairly high resolution of 200 dpi to 300 dpi. Even though your finished movie will have a much lower resolution (72 dpi or 96 dpi), choosing the higher resolution rate assures you of the best possible quality image in your finished production.

> **NOTE**
>
> You can select one of your recent projects by choosing File and then selecting a project name from the list at the bottom of the menu.

■ Connect the digital camera media to your system by following the instructions in your camera user manual.
■ Copy the desired photos to a folder.

If the photos are from a film camera, you can scan them into your system for use in your production:

■ Place the photo in your scanner.
■ Use the scanner software to scan the image to a folder. **Figure 7.6** shows an image being scanned using the HP PrecisionScan software.

STEP 2: ADD THE IMAGES TO A COLLECTION

After you copy the still shots to a folder in your system, you're ready to add them to a Windows Movie Maker project. After you finish the project for which the Collection was created, you will still have the Collection in your system and can use the stills (and movie clips) in a different project.

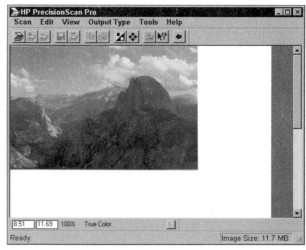

7.6

■ Choose **File ➤ Open Project** and select the project to which you want to add the still images.

■ Choose **View ➤ Collections** and then select a collection from the list.

■ Click the **Tasks** button.

■ In the Capture Video section, click **Import Pictures** to open the Import File dialog box.

■ Select the image you want to add to the collection. You can select multiple images by holding down the **Shift** key while clicking the last image you want to select to select a range of sequential images, or by pressing **Ctrl** while clicking additional images to select non-sequential images.

> **NOTE**
>
> If you add still shots to a movie that are not sized to the aspect ratio of the video (4:3 for normal video, 16:9 for widescreen), a black border appears on each side of the image when you add it to the timeline. If you own image-editing software, you can rectify this by creating a document that is the same aspect ratio as your video (720 x 480 for NTSC video, 640 x 480 for computer viewing) and paste your still shot into the document and save it into one of the popular image formats supported by Windows Movie Maker. When you import the image into a video, the background color of the document surrounds the image instead of black borders.

■ Click **Import** to add the image(s) to the current Collection.

■ Click the image to display it in the Preview pane, as shown in **Figure 7.7**.

After adding one or more images to a collection, you're ready to add them to a project timeline, a technique you can master by reading Technique 8.

7.7

ASSEMBLING YOUR TIMELINE

8.1

8.2

The timeline is the ultimate command post in your digital video editing suite. Here, decisions about clips are made and assembled, and your movie begins to come alive. After clips are assembled in the timeline, you can finesse the movie with effects, transitions, titles, and sound, which are all covered in subsequent chapters. Here, we start with the building blocks of a movie by assembling the simplest kind of movie, a rough cut.

iMOVIE

In iMovie, what would be considered a conventional timeline is called the Movie Track. You can display the Movie Track in two different ways. It can be viewed as a traditional timeline, called the Timeline Viewer, or in storyboard style, as the Clip Viewer. The Timeline Viewer gives you a more physical representation of the way a movie is assembled. You can tell which clips are longer and shorter just by looking at the timeline. The Clip Viewer displays clips just as they appear in the Clip Pane, only assembled in the order that they will play in the movie. Many users feel the Clip Viewer is easier to work with because it's more like assembling 35 mm slides on a slide shelf. In this technique, we assemble a simple movie in Clip Viewer.

STEP 1: START A NEW PROJECT

■ Begin a new project and save the project to your hard disk.

■ Choose **File** ➤ **Import** from the menu. In the Import dialog box, navigate to the Clips folder on the CD-ROM and select **MacClip001.mov**, **MacClip002.mov**, **MacClip003.mov**, and **MacClip004.mov**.

STEP 2: ASSEMBLE THE TIMELINE

In this example, we assemble a movie in the Clip Viewer. Then switch to the Timeline Viewer to see the difference between the two views.

NOTE

When you create a new document in iMovie, a Media folder is also created alongside your new document. This is where the movie clips, sound clips, and still images are stored in the movie. When you import files into an iMovie document, a copy of these files is placed in the Media file associated with the iMovie document. The clips appear in the Shelf.

■ Click the **Film** icon (to the bottom left of the monitor, right above the timeline) to see the timeline in Clip Viewer mode. Drag the clips from the Clip pane in sequential order to the Movie Track, as shown in **Figure 8.3**.

■ Play the Movie Track by rewinding the movie. Do this by clicking the **Go to the beginning of the movie** button, the first control button under the Monitor window. Next, press the **Play** button. (Alternately, you can return to the beginning of the movie by pressing the **Home** key and press the spacebar to play the movie.)

■ Drag the third clip, **MacClip003.mov**, from the Shelf to the beginning of the Movie Track and replay the movie in the Monitor window. Assembling clips on the Timeline in iMovie is easy.

■ Now, get rid of the last clip, **MacClip004.mov**, by selecting it and dragging it back onto the Shelf. If you delete the clip by clicking it and pressing the **Delete** key but then decide to use it again in the movie, you have to repeat the import process on

---

TRIMMING CLIPS IN THE TIMELINE VIEWER

Trimming is not limited to clips on the Shelf. Clips in the Timeline Viewer can be trimmed using the same methods as in the section "Adding Stills to Your Movie". In many cases, trimming clips directly in the Timeline Viewer may be easier. The reason for this is because when you crop or cut a clip, the excess footage from the clip gets deleted and the right adjoining clip scoots down so that it's still butted up against the tail of the clip you just trimmed. As a result, the movie assumes a shorter duration in time. In many editing applications, after a clip is trimmed, the subsequent clips need to be moved over to butt up against one another. When you trim in the Timeline, iMovie repositions all the clips for you.

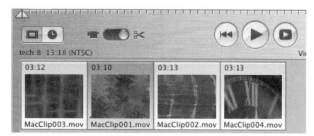

8.3

this clip. Now, if you decide to bring the clip back into the Movie Track again, just drag it back to the Track again.

■ To see the clips in the Timeline View, click the **Clock** icon in the bottom left of the Monitor window, next to the Movie Track icon. In the Movie Track view, you can see the sound track on a movie (if there is one) and change the speed of an individual clip from fast to slow.

WINDOWS MOVIE MAKER

After you capture footage from your camcorder into a collection, import still images into a collection and trim your clips. Assembling the clips and still images on the timeline is the real fun. In Windows Movie Maker, you can assemble your production using two modes: timeline or storyboard. As you become more familiar with editing in Windows Movie Maker, you'll find yourself switching between both modes as you create your movies. Each has its advantages. For this technique, you'll begin assembling a three-clip movie on the timeline and fine-tune the production with the storyboard.

STEP 1: START A NEW PROJECT

When you begin a new project, you capture video into a collection, open an existing collection, or import existing clips to create new collections. You can assemble your project by adding individual clips from one or more collections to the timeline.

■ Launch Windows Movie Maker and then choose **File** ➢ **New Project.**
■ Choose **File** ➢ **Import into Collections.** Navigate to the CD-ROM that accompanies this book and select the files **WinClip001.wmv, WinClip002.wmv,** and **WinClip003.wmv.**

Windows Movie Maker creates a new collection entitled with the name of each clip. A Windows Movie Maker collection doesn't store the actual media; it only stores the path to the directory where the media is stored on your computer. If you remove the CD-ROM and open the collection, the media is no longer available and each thumbnail only shows a red *X* indicating the media is offline.

STEP 2: ASSEMBLE THE TIMELINE

The Windows Movie Maker timeline is a visual reference of your movie as you create it. At the top of the timeline is a time ruler that gives you a visual representation of how long a clip is after you add it to the timeline and the current time of the movie as you preview it. Windows Movie Maker displays the first frame of each clip as well as the clip's name.

> **TIP**
>
> When you import media into collections, Windows Movie Maker creates a new collection for each clip you import. You can condense several clips into a new collection by choosing View ➢ Collections and then selecting the Collections icon at the top of the tree. Right-click the Collections icon at the top of the window, and from the shortcut menu, choose New Collection. Type a name for the new collection before you do anything else. You can now click different collections and drag media from each collection into your new collection folder. If you don't want to delete the media from the old collection, hold down the Ctrl key while dragging and dropping and Windows Movie Maker copies the media into the new folder.

■ Click the **Collections** button on the toolbar if the Collections pane is closed.

■ Click **WinClip001.wmv** and Windows Movie Maker displays a thumbnail of the movie clip in the Collections pane.

■ Drag and drop the movie clip on the timeline. When you release the mouse button, Windows Movie Maker snaps the clip to 00:00, the beginning of the timeline. Before adding the next clip to the timeline, hold your cursor over the movie clip. After a few seconds, a tool tip appears with information about the clip.

■ Click **WinClip002.wmv** to open the collection and then drag and drop the movie clip on the timeline. When you release the mouse button, the clip snaps to the last frame of the first clip.

■ Add **WinClip003.wmv** to the timeline following the previous steps.

■ Select the first clip and then click the **Play Timeline** button (which looks like the Play button on your VCR controller) to the left of the Show Storyboard icon to preview your handiwork, which should resemble **Figure 8.4**.

As you preview the movie, you may notice that the middle clip seems out of place and should logically be shown as the end of the movie. You can easily solve this dilemma by sorting the clips on your timeline.

STEP 3: SORTING THE CLIPS

You can click a clip on the timeline to select it and then drag it over another clip to reposition it. However, sorting clips is easier if you switch to Storyboard mode.

■ Click the **Show Storyboard** icon to switch to Storyboard mode. When you work in Storyboard mode, the timelines for each movie clip are condensed to a single thumbnail image of the clip's

8.4

NOTE

After you add clips to a timeline and preview the project, you may find you need to trim some footage. You can trim a clip on the timeline by selecting it and then dragging the handle at the beginning of the clip to the right to set the start trim point and dragging the handle at the end of the clip to the left to set the end trim point. As you drag one of these handles, the Preview pane updates in real time giving you a visual reference of the start trim or end trim Frame. Alternately, you can select a clip and in the Preview pane use the VCR controls to advance to the desired start trim point and then choose Clip ➤ Set Start Trim Point. Advance the clip to the desired end trim point and then choose Clip ➤ Set End Trim Point. Windows Movie Maker trims the clip on the timeline leaving the original unaffected.

first frame. In Storyboard mode, you can still get information about a clip by holding your cursor over a thumbnail.

■ Click the second clip and then drag it to the right of the third clip. After you release the mouse button, Windows Movie Maker repositions the clips (see **Figure 8.5**).

Before you explore a different technique, experiment with moving the clips to different positions in the storyboard. Drag and drop the first clip to the right of the second. Notice the vertical blue line that appears as soon as your cursor clears the second clip. That's your notification that the clip can be placed in this position.

WinClip001   Winclip003   WinClip002

8.5

BRIGHTENING DARK FOOTAGE

9.1

9.2

ABOUT THE VIDEOS

The video clips for this technique were filmed at the University of Tampa in Tampa, Florida. The university offices and many of the classrooms were originally part of the Tampa Hotel that was constructed in 1891. The video was filmed using a Sony DCR-TRV27 set in auto mode. The clips were captured to PC using an IEEE1394 FireWire card and trimmed in Windows Movie Maker.

Most camcorders on the market do a good job of choosing the correct settings to ensure that your video creations are properly exposed for existing lighting conditions. However, even the best camcorder can be fooled in difficult lighting conditions as seen in **Figure 9.1**. If you find you have some footage that is a bit dark, you can compensate for this by applying effects in iMovie and Windows Movie Maker. Granted, neither application has the sophisticated filters you find in an application, such as Adobe Premiere or Sonic Foundry Vegas Video, but you can still correct footage that needs a little boost in the brightness department and end up with a better looking video clip as shown in **Figure 9.2**. You can also use these effects as part of a special effect for illuminating your movies.

iMOVIE

STEP 1: START A NEW PROJECT

In this technique, we import clips into the project a little differently than we did in the previous techniques. Instead of importing them into the Clip pane, we change the location preference of imported files. This way we can control whether the clips end up in the Shelf or in the timeline.

■ Begin a new project and save the project to your hard disk. Display your Timeline in the Clip Viewer by clicking on the film icon above the Movie Track.

■ In the menu, choose **iMovie ➢ Preferences.** In the Preferences dialog box, for Import: Files go to, check the **Movie Timeline** radio button next to Import: New clips go to, as shown in **Figure 9.3.** Click the *X* in the upper-left corner of the dialog box to close it.

■ Choose **File ➢ Import** from the menu. In the Import dialog box, navigate to the Clips folder on the CD-ROM and select **MacClip005.mov** and **MacClip006.mov.** Instead of the clips importing to the Shelf, they now import sequentially into the Movie Track.

■ Preview these files in the Monitor window by pressing the **spacebar.** Note that when you preview these clips, the first clip, an image of an outside corridor, has quite a bit of extreme contrast because of the position of the sun when the footage was shot. The left portion of the clip (the building) appears very dark.

STEP 2: ADJUST THE LIGHTNESS

■ Click the first clip, **MacClip005.mov** and then click the **Effects** tab at the bottom of the pane window. In addition to storing thumbnail preview clips, the pane window also houses Effects, Transitions, Audio, and Titles, depending on which tab is selected.

■ In the middle of the Effects pane, navigate through the list of Effects and select the **Adjust Colors** effect. A real-time preview thumbnail in the top of the Shelf demonstrates the effect on the selected clip. Play the thumbnail again by clicking on the effect.

■ At the bottom of the Effects Pane, drag the **Lightness** slider a little bit to the right, toward the Bright setting as shown in **Figure 9.4.** The thumbnail displays the results of your adjustment.

■ Apply the effect by clicking the **Apply** button at the top of the Effect pane. Now the brightness on your clip is more evenly balanced. Press the **Home** key to return the Playhead back to the beginning and then press the **spacebar** to play the movie.

9.3

RENDERING EFFECTS

When you apply the Adjust Colors effect on a clip, a red progress line gradually travels across the top of the clip in the timeline, indicating that the effect is rendering on the clip. Rendering involves complex mathematical calculations that are performed on the clip, so the effect can be seen. iMovie handles rendered effects by duplicating the rendered clip so that the original clip is left intact. Transitions and titles are also rendered. This, of course, increases the size of the production as you end up with more clips than you bargained for. So if you're wondering why your iMovie project folder is growing in size, it may be because you are using a lot of effects, transitions, and titles.

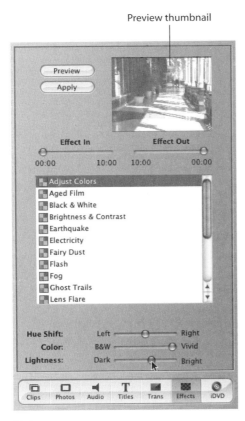

Preview thumbnail

9.4

WINDOWS MOVIE MAKER

Whether you're compiling vacation footage into a movie or you've imported video you've captured from a VHS tape, it's always disheartening to see that some of the clips are just a little too dark to show fine detail. When this happens to you — and it will if you shoot enough video — you can compensate for dark footage by applying the Brightness video effect.

STEP 1: START A NEW PROJECT

You generally discover that one or more clips you've captured need a bit of enhancing at the beginning of your project. After you capture video from your camcorder, or import video into a collection, you preview the video to see what you've got to work with. (You do preview your video clips, don't you?)

■ Launch Windows Movie Maker and choose **File ➢ New Project**.
■ Choose **File ➢ Import into Collections**. Navigate to the CD-ROM that accompanies this book, select the files **WinClip004.wmv** and **WinClip005.wmv** and click **Import**. Windows Movie Maker creates a new collection for each clip.
■ Select the media from each collection and arrange them on the timeline in numerical order.

9.5

- Click the **Play Timeline** button directly above the timeline.

As you watch the clips in the preview window, notice that the second clip is a bit too dark (see **Figure 9.5**). In Windows Movie Maker, you can modify the color characteristics of a movie clip or make it lighter or darker by applying a video effect. You can apply video effects while working in Storyboard or Timeline mode. For this technique, you'll be using Storyboard mode.

STEP 2: APPLY THE BRIGHTNESS EFFECT

After you ascertain that a video clip needs a bit of enlightenment, it's time to call out Windows Movie Maker's Video Effects pane. Within the collection of Video Effects, you'll find several effects you can use to modify a clip's color characteristics, and a whole lot more.

- Click the **Show Storyboard** icon to switch to Storyboard mode. Windows Movie Maker collapses the timelines into thumbnail images.
- Click the **Tasks** button on the toolbar. The list of available Windows Movie Maker tasks appears in the left side of the workspace.
- In the Edit Movie section, click **View Video Effects**. Windows Movie Maker displays its collection of video effects.
- Click the **Brightness, Increase** effect and then drag it on the star in the lower-left corner of the second clip's thumbnail image. Windows Movie

Maker highlights the star in blue, your indication that an effect has been applied to the clip.
- Click the first clip and then click the **Play Storyboard** button. As you preview the movie, notice that the second clip is a bit brighter but still needs more work (see **Figure 9.6**).
- Click the **Brightness, Increase** effect and drag it on the second clip again. In Windows Movie Maker, you can apply a video effect more than once to increase its intensity.

When you preview the movie again, you'll notice that the second application of the effect did the trick. Before wandering off to another technique in the book, try applying the filter again, or experiment with the Brightness, Decrease effect on the first clip to see what that effect does.

9.6

CHAPTER 3

ARTFULLY CHANGING SCENES WITH TRANSITIONS

When you use iMovie or Windows Movie Maker to assemble video clips to create a movie, you can assemble the clips and then export the movie for an intended destination as outlined in Chapter 9. Most of the time, your production will make perfect sense to your viewing audience. However, if one scene differs radically from the next, your viewers may not understand that one scene has ended and another has begun. For example, if you're showing a video compilation of projects you've done during the year and a summer scene ends in a dwelling, and then a winter scene begins in the same dwelling, your viewers won't notice the change of seasons until they pick up a visual clue such as frost on a window. You can provide a visual hint that something different is about to occur by bridging two scenes with a transition. And as the chapter title implies, you can also use transitions as an artful way to change scenes.

Each application has many transitions available to choose from. The actual transition that you use depends on the type of footage you're editing and what type of effect you're after. You can simply fade one scene into another, or visually grab your viewing audience by the throat with a more compelling transition such as a rotating wheel, a wipe, or a page curl. The techniques in this chapter introduce you to the fine art of scene transitions. We urge you to experiment on your own footage and modify our cookbook recipes to suit your artistic muse.

CREATING A CROSS-FADE

10.1   10.2

The cross-fade transition (next to fade-to-black) is probably the most common type of transition used in video editing. Cross-fades are like the color black; they are always in good taste and never go out of style. The classic cross-fade transition does just as its name implies: One clip fades out as another fades in, sharing a moment where the clip that's fading in changes from transparent to completely opaque. **Figure 10.1** represents the tail of a clip that cuts abruptly into another clip. Figure **10.2** represents the tail of the same clip transitioning into a clip of a blazing fire against a black background, using a Cross Fade technique. As you can see, the image from the first clip fades as the new image becomes stronger. Because there are so many transitions to choose from, if you can't decide which transition to use in a project, consider using cross-fades. They are always a good choice, especially when used at the beginning and end of a movie.

iMOVIE

STEP 1: START A NEW PROJECT

In iMovie, the equivalent to a Windows Movie Maker cross-fade is called a Cross Dissolve. A Cross Dissolve tastefully blends one clip into the other by briefly overlapping two clips.

In this technique, you apply a simple Cross Dissolve between three clips on the timeline.

■ Begin a new project and save the project on your hard drive.

■ Choose **iMovie ➢ Preferences** and in the Preferences dialog box, for Import: Files go to, click the **Movie Timeline** button. This way, the clips you are about to import will appear in the Movie Track instead of the Clip pane.

■ Choose **File ➢ Import** from the menu, navigate to the CD-ROM, and select **MacClip007.mov**, **MacClip008.mov**, and **MacClip009.mov**.

■ Display the timeline in Movie Track view. Now, you can apply a Cross Dissolve transition in between each clip.

STEP 2: PREVIEW AND ADJUST THE DURATION

Before applying the transitions to the clips in the Movie Track, you should preview the transition and tweak the speed setting. This setting allows you to set the duration of the Cross Dissolve transition as it gradually transforms one clip into another. You can make the transition occur slowly or quickly, depending on what speed setting you choose. Also, depending on the length of the clips you are transitioning to

and from, the speed may have to be accelerated and, in some cases, the clips might not be long enough to hold a transition at all.

■ Click the first clip in the timeline and note that the duration time of the clip as indicated in the thumbnail is 03:13. In the Shelf, click the **Trans** (transitions) tab. In the Transitions list, click the **Cross Dissolve** transition. A real-time preview of the transition appears in the thumbnail preview.

■ On the **Speed** slider, drag the button until the thumbnail preview displays 2:00, as shown in **Figure 10.3**. The Fade In will last for 2 seconds, which will overlap two seconds on the tail of the first clip (clock) and two seconds of the head of the second clip (fire).

■ If you click the **Preview** button to the left of the thumbnail preview in the Transition Shelf, you can see a larger preview in the Monitor window.

10.3

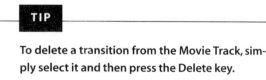

TIP

To delete a transition from the Movie Track, simply select it and then press the Delete key.

STEP 3: APPLY THE CROSS DISSOLVE

■ To apply the transition, drag the **Cross Dissolve** icon from the Transition pane and drop it in between the first two clips. The clip to the right scoots over to make room for the transition. Repeat the process for clips two and three, as shown in **Figure 10.4**.

■ Press the **Home** key to send the Playhead back to the beginning of the movie and then press the **spacebar** to see your transitions come alive in the Monitor window.

NOTE

If your clips have a duration of 10 frames or less (the lowest setting on the Speed slider), transitions are out of the question.

TIP

When a transition is rendering, you can continue working in iMovie. In fact, several transitions can render at the same time, and you can still keep on editing your movie. You cannot, however, add effects while transitions render or play the movie until the transitions are done rendering.

10.4

To become familiar with various types of transitions, take notice of them the next time you watch a movie or television. Developing an awareness of different types of transitions and the mood they create will help provide you with an education on how to use them effectively.

WINDOWS MOVIE MAKER

The transition from one scene to the next can make or break your movie. Choose a transition that enhances the content of your video clips. You can transition your viewers gently from one scene to the next with a slow, subtle transition, or yank them by the scruff of their necks into the next scene with a short-duration transition.

STEP 1: START A NEW PROJECT

When you assemble your clips on the timeline or storyboard, you have some important decisions to make. When one scene segues into another, you can simply butt one clip against the next if the clips are similar in content. If the clips are dissimilar, however, the sudden transition can be visually disconcerting to your viewers. If this is the case in your production, add a transition between clips. Windows Movie Maker has lots of intriguing transitions, but the Fade video effect gently blends one clip into the next. In other words, it's a classic cross-fade.

■ Launch Windows Movie Maker and then choose **File ➤ New Project**.

■ Choose **File ➤ Import into Collections**. Navigate to the CD-ROM that accompanies this book and select the files **WinClip006.wmv**, **WinClip007.wmv**, and **WinClip008.wmv**. Windows Movie Maker creates a new collection for each clip.

■ Click the **Show Storyboard** button if you're currently in Timeline mode.

■ Arrange each clip on the storyboard in numerical order (see **Figure 10.5**). Now you can add a little magic to the production, courtesy of the Windows Movie Maker Fade transition.

STEP 2: APPLY THE VIDEO TRANSITIONS

If you're new to digital video, the whole concept of video transitions may seem like magic. And it really is magic when you think about it. To turn your footage into something truly special, all you need to do is drag a transition from the Video Transitions pane and drop it into the little slot between each storyboard thumbnail. What could be simpler? But, of course, the true artistry is in selecting the right transition.

■ Click the **Tasks** button on the main toolbar and then click **View Video Transitions** from the Edit Movie section. Windows Movie Maker displays a bunch of gnarly icons that bear little resemblance to the effects you can achieve with these jewels.

■ Drag the **Fade** effect to the slot between the first and second thumbnail. You could repeat this step for the slot between the second and third clip, but Windows Movie Maker gives you more than one way to make a clean transition.

■ Click the slot between the first and second thumbnail to select the transition, right-click, and then choose **Copy** from the shortcut menu.

■ Click the empty slot between the second and third clip, right-click, and then choose **Paste** from the shortcut menu. Your storyboard should resemble the one shown in **Figure 10.6**.

■ Click the first clip and then click the **Play Storyboard** button to preview the movie. Alternatively, if you like to use menu commands, choose **Play ➤ Play Storyboard.** Presto — a perfect cross-fade!

STEP 3: ALTER THE FADE DURATION

The default time for a Windows Movie Maker transition is 3.5 seconds. This works well in most instances.

> **TIP**
>
> You can also use the keyboard shortcut Ctrl+C to copy a selected transition and Ctrl+V to paste a copied transition.

10.5

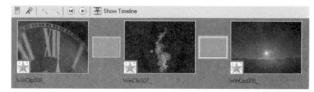

10.6

However, there are times when video footage is so perfect, you don't trim it quite as tight as you would normally. When you've got a killer clip that begs to stay on stage longer, you can lengthen the duration of the fade. Or maybe you want to express a sense of urgency. In that case, you can shorten the duration. If you're from the old school and you're used to working with 8mm or 16mm movies, manually splicing clips together, you'll be happy to know you can manually adjust the duration of the fade.

■ Click **Show Timeline** to switch to Timeline mode. Notice that there is a separate timeline for transitions, and each transition is designated by a small rectangle where two clips overlap (see **Figure 10.7**). If you hold your cursor over the rectangle, the name of the transition and the duration of the transition are displayed. (The clips supplied for this technique are short, and Windows Movie Maker adjusts the duration of the second transition to compensate for this.)

■ Click the first transition to select it, and then move your cursor towards the transition beginning until your cursor becomes a double-headed red arrow.

■ Clicking and dragging left increases the duration of the fade and dragging right decreases it.

■ Preview the movie. If you like the transition's new time duration, select the first transition, press **Ctrl+C**, select the second transition, and press **Ctrl+V**. Both transitions are now of equal duration (see **Figure 10.8**).

> **TIP**
>
> If you're working with short clips like the ones supplied for this technique, click the Zoom Timeline In button that looks like a magnifying glass, until you can easily see all of the transitions and video clips.

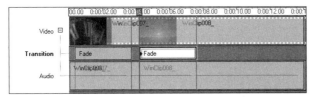

10.7

10.8

CREATING A PAGE CURL AND SCALE DOWN

11.1

11.2

ABOUT THE VIDEO

The video clips for this technique were shot in St. John, U.S. Virgin Islands. The footage was shot with a JVC GR10-DVF-U and captured to PC using a FireWire connection to a Sony HandyCam. The clips were trimmed in Windows Movie Maker 2.

Transitions are all about changing scenes, so the viewer will look forward with great anticipation to the next scene. Windows Movie Maker has a very cool transition effect that shouldn't go unmentioned — Page Curl. **Figure 11.1** shows a tropical island scene that transitions (see **Figure 11.2**) into a view from the beach. Page Curl transitions are a staple in many high-end video-editing applications and a welcome addition to Windows Movie Maker 2. Although iMovie does not offer a Page Curl transition, it offers a few exciting alternatives that will equally delight the viewer. For iMovie, you perform a technique using the Scale Down transition, which, as you will see, creates another attention-grabbing cut between two clips.

iMOVIE

The Scale Down transition creates a temporary picture in a picture during its transition into another clip. In these picturesque scenes, the first clip gradually shrinks away toward the upper-left corner of the screen. The longer you set the duration (assuming that your clips are long enough to handle the transition), the longer the clip hovers as a second scene. This transition is commonly used on travel and news channels to emphasize a place or an event.

STEP 1: START A NEW PROJECT

- Begin a new project and save the project on your hard drive.
- Choose **iMovie ➤ Preferences** and in the Preferences dialog box, for Import: New clips go to, click the **Movie Timeline** button. This way, the clips you import will appear in the Movie Track instead of the Clips pane.
- Choose **File ➤ Import**, navigate to the Clips folder on the CD-ROM, and select **MacClip010.mov** and **MacClip011.mov**.
- Display the timeline in Movie Track View. Now, let's preview the transition.

STEP 2: PREVIEW AND ADJUST THE CIRCLE

- Click the first clip in the Movie Track and click the **Trans** tab at the bottom of the Shelf panes. In the Transitions list, click the **Scale Down** transition.

> **TIP**
>
> If you had your heart set on a page curl in iMovie and were disappointed to find out there was none, there is a solution at `www.virtix.com`. Virtix offers an inexpensive bundle (approximately $30 US dollars) of plug-in effects for iMovie called the Echo package, which includes a Page Peel effect. The accompanying CD provides a few samples of other Virtix plug-in transitions and effects.

11.3

■ In the Transition Shelf, drag the **Speed** slider all the way to the right (04:00) to slow the transition down as much as possible (see **Figure 11.3**). Before you apply the transition, note that the current time on the clips in the timeline is 07:01 for the first clip and 09:04 for the second clip.

STEP 3: APPLY THE SCALE DOWN

■ Click the **Scale Down** transition in the Shelf and drag it in between the two clips in the timeline. Note that the addition of the new transition to the timeline has shaved off time from the first clip and the second clip. The first clip now reads as 03:01 and the second clip reads as 5:01. The Scale Down blends into 04:00 seconds of the tail on the first clip and 04:00 seconds on the head of the second clip to accommodate the transition.

■ To check out the transition, press the **Home** key followed by the **spacebar**. The first clip gradually shrinks into the sky above a distant sailboat, as shown in **Figure 11.4**.

11.4

WINDOWS MOVIE MAKER

When you have clips of beautiful scenery like the ones you're using in this technique, it's only fitting to choose a transition that will enhance the footage. When you create a movie, you're telling a story and the transition from one scene to the next begins a new chapter in your story, which you can signify as the turn of a page with the page curl transition.

STEP 1: BEGIN A NEW PROJECT

In Windows Movie Maker, you can arrange the order in which your movie plays by dragging and dropping clips on the timeline. However, in the beginning stage of a project, the timeline can work against you, especially if the clips you are combining are long. We recommend beginning a project using the Storyboard because you can arrange several minutes of clips into a few slots on the Storyboard.

■ Launch Windows Movie Maker and then choose **File ➤ New Project**.
■ Choose **File ➤ Import into Collections**. Navigate to the CD-ROM that accompanies this book and select the files **WinClip009.wmv** and **WinClip010.wmv**. Windows Movie Maker creates a collection for each clip.
■ Click the **Show Storyboard** button to display the Windows Movie Maker Storyboard.
■ Arrange the Storyboard by dragging and dropping the clips in numerical order to their respective slots in the Storyboard.
■ Select the first thumbnail and then click **Play Storyboard**. As you preview the movie, notice how abrupt the transition is from the first clip to the second. An abrupt change of scenes such as this doesn't give viewers a chance to catch their breath and can be greatly improved with the proper transition.

STEP 2: APPLY THE TRANSITION

After you initially preview the clips you've chosen, it's time to add the artistic touches. As a moviemaker, you're telling a story and scene transitions give viewers subtle hints as to what might happen next. You can choose transitions that create suspense or anticipation. This step shows you how to use a Page Curl transition to artfully segue to the next scene.

- Click the **Tasks** button and from the Edit Movie section choose **View video transitions**.
- Select the **Page Curl, Up Right** video transition.

11.5

- Click and drag it into the slot between the first and second clip.
- Select the first clip and click **Play Storyboard** to view the transition in the Preview pane. As the movie plays, notice that gentle transition from one scene to the next as the page curls. The bottom side of the page is like looking at the back of the scene (see **Figure 11.5**). The movie looks good, but could be improved if the page curl lingered on-screen a while longer.

STEP 3: PREVIEW AND FINE-TUNE YOUR PROJECT

After you add transitions to your movie, you're ready to preview and fine-tune the movie. When you preview your movie, pay attention to how each scene transitions into the next. The duration of the transition should be suited to the subject matter.

- Click **Show Timeline** to switch to Timeline mode.
- Click the **Zoom Timeline In** button; it looks like a magnifying glass with a plus (+) sign. When you magnify the timeline, you have better control when manually trimming clips or changing transition duration.
- Click the transition and move your cursor over the start of the transition clip. When your cursor becomes a double-headed red arrow, click and drag to the left. As you drag the transition, a tool tip displays the current duration.

> **TIP**
>
> As a rule, when you're creating transitions for landscape footage such as that used in this technique, the transition duration can be longer.

■ Release the mouse button when the duration is about 4 seconds.

■ Click the **Play Timeline** button. Notice how altering the duration of a transition can have a marked effect on a movie.

TIP

If you find that most of your movies require longer or shorter transitions, you can modify the Windows Movie Maker default transition duration by choosing Tools ➢ Options to open the Options dialog box. Click the Advanced tab and then in the Transition duration: field, click the up or down arrow to modify the default duration of video transitions (see **Figure 11.6**).

11.6

WIPING ONE CLIP INTO ANOTHER

12.1

12.2

ABOUT THE VIDEO

Subways are exciting and New York City has miles of underground railway. When you travel the subway, it's like being in another world. The sound of the wheels on the tracks combined with the gentle swaying from side to side, and then you're abruptly rousted from your rapture by the squeal of brakes. This subway footage was filmed with a Canon GL-2 DV camcorder using automatic exposure and captured in iMovie. The sample footage on the CD-ROM was exported in QuickTime format, 29.97 fps using Sorenson 3 compression.

Many of the transitions in iMovie and Windows Movie Maker are similar in effect on both platforms, but they go by different names. In this technique, you explore two transitions that produce a similar outcome. In iMovie this transition is called a *push*, and in Windows Movie Maker it's known as a *wipe*. These transitions change from one scene to another by wiping out, or pushing, the previous scene out of the way to reveal the new scene as if it's waiting in the wings. In this technique, you get to jazz up some scenes of the New York City subway system. **Figure 12.1** represents the first clip in the sample movie for Technique 12. **Figure 12.2** represents the transition between the first and the second clips. As you can see, the second clip pushes the first clip up to move it out of the frame. The Push transition can be adjusted to push a clip in four different directions, inclusive of up, down, left, and right.

iMOVIE

A ride on a New York City subway train makes a terrific backdrop for a Push transition. There is always movement in a subway and a push transition forcefully pushes one scene out of the way to make room for another. A push transition lends itself to the sentiment of a busy movie.

67

STEP 1: START A NEW PROJECT

- Begin a new project and save the project on your hard drive.
- Choose **iMovie ➢ Preferences** and in the Preferences dialog box, for Import: New clips go to, click the **Movie Timeline** button. This way, the clips you import appear in the timeline instead of the Shelf pane.
- Choose **File ➢ Import** from the menu, navigate to the Clips folder on the CD-ROM, and select **MacClip012.mov, MacClip013.mov, MacClip014.mov,** and **MacClip015.mov**.
- Display the timeline in Movie Track View. Now, you can apply a Push transition in between each clip to see what happens.

STEP 2: ADJUST THE DURATION

Before applying the Push transition to the clips in the Movie Track, you can preview the transition and adjust the speed settings. The speed settings enable you to adjust the speed at which one clip pushes the other out of a frame. A fast speed quickly shoves the clip out of the way, creating a sharp scene change. A slow speed gently nudges the previous scene away, creating a softer scene change.

- Click the first clip in the Movie Track and then click the **Trans** tab. In the Transitions list, click **Push**. A real-time preview of the transition appears in the thumbnail preview.
- On the **Speed** slider, drag the button until the thumbnail preview displays 00:25. Doing this causes the push to occur quickly, as shown in **Figure 12.3**.

STEP 3: ADJUST THE DIRECTION

When you select the Push transition, you can change two parameters, the duration (as you did in Step 2) and the direction of the push. Do this by clicking the

up, down, left, or right directional arrows to the left of the thumbnail preview.

- With the first clip in the timeline still selected and the Push transition selected in the Shelf, click the upward-pointing directional arrow. In the

TIP

You cannot apply a Push transition at the beginning of a movie or at the end. The push transition, like most other transitions, needs a clip to transition into. The only exception to this rule would be the Fade In and Fade Out and the Wash In and Wash Out transitions, which are generally used to begin and end movies.

12.3

thumbnail preview, you see that this direction allows the new scene to push the old scene upward (see **Figure 12.4**). You can achieve a different feeling depending upon which direction your frame is pushed.

STEP 4: APPLY THE PUSH TO CLIPS

■ After the Push transition is adjusted, drag the **Push** transition icon in between the first two clips.
■ Repeat the process by dragging another in between clips two and three, and another in between clips three and four. Note, as the red bar crawls slowly across the bottom of the scenes in the timeline, that the transitions render simultaneously.

NOTE

Depending on how fast your processor is and the duration of the transition, your transition may take awhile to render. While clips are rendering you won't be able to play the movie in the Monitor window until the rendering is complete.

12.4

■ Press the **Home** key and then the **spacebar** to admire the results of your new movie.

WINDOWS MOVIE MAKER

Need to add a sense of urgency to a movie? You know — out with the old, in with the new? Windows Movie Maker has an ideal transition when you need to achieve that type of transition. This gem of video transition is called the Wipe. If you've ever traveled on a packed subway car during the morning or evening rush, you may feel as though you're being pushed or wiped out of the train when you get to your stop.

STEP 1: START A NEW PROJECT

After you capture or import clips for a new movie, you generally have a pretty good idea of what type of footage you have when you preview the clips. When the creative juices start flowing, you begin thinking of ways to spice things up. After you've got the movie mapped out in your mind's eye, you can begin assembling your production.

■ Launch Windows Movie Maker and choose **File ➤ New Project**.
■ Choose **File ➤ Import into Collections**. Navigate to the CD-ROM that accompanies this book and then select **WinClip011.wmv**, **WinClip012.wmv**, **WinClip013.wmv**, and **WinClip014.wmv**. Click **Import**, and Windows Movie Maker creates a new collection for each clip.
■ Click **Show Storyboard** if you're currently working in Timeline mode.
■ Drag **WinClip011.wmv** to the first slot in the storyboard.
■ Finish assembling your storyboard by dropping the remaining clips in the next empty slots. Arrange the clips in numerical order. That is, of course, unless you used to draw outside the lines in school. In that case, you're permitted to arrange the clips as you see fit.

■ Select the first clip and click **Play Storyboard** (see **Figure 12.5**). As you preview the assembled storyboard, you see there's plenty of action, but a greater sense of urgency can be achieved with the right transition.

STEP 2: ADDING THE TRANSITIONS

Windows Movie Maker 2 includes six wipes. Choosing the right wipe is like choosing the right paper towel to sop up a spilled soft drink, but a whole lot more fun. To simulate the effect of being shoved out a subway door, the Wide Wipe Right transition is just the ticket.

■ Click the **Tasks** button and then click **View video transitions**. You'll find the wipe transitions doing yeoman's duty at the bottom of the Video Transitions pane.

■ Click the **Wipe, Wide Right** transition and drag it to the box between the first and second thumbnails.

12.5

■ Drag the **Wipe, Wide Right** transition into the slots between the remaining clips in your production.

■ Select the first thumbnail in the Storyboard and then click the **Play Storyboard** button. As you preview the scene, you see that there is definitely heightened excitement as one clip transitions into the next (see **Figure 12.6**). However, with a little tweaking, you can get an even better effect.

STEP 3: SPEEDING UP THE TRANSITION

If a crowd of people anxious to get home has ever propelled you out of a subway car, you know you're on the platform in a New York minute. To up the ante in our little production, you're going to speed up the transition between scenes.

■ Click **Show Timeline** to switch to Timeline mode.

■ On the Transition timeline, click the first transition and move your cursor towards the start of the transition. When your cursor becomes a double-headed red arrow, click and drag to the right. As you drag, notice that the information in the tool tip changes to reveal the current duration of the transition.

12.6

- Release the mouse button when the tool tip reads about 2.20 (see **Figure 12.7**).
- Right-click the first transition and choose **Copy** from the shortcut menu.
- Click the next transition, right-click, and choose **Paste**. Repeat for the last transition.
- Click the **Play Timeline** button. Notice how much faster each transition occurs. Kind of makes you feel like you're there, doesn't it? When you can convey that kind of emotion and feeling to your audience, you've taken the giant leap from home moviemaker to video maven.

While you still have all the clips assembled on the timeline, try some of the other wipe effects to see the difference they make on the finished movie. While working in timeline mode, you cancel a transition when you drop a different one in the same place. Alter the transition duration of the transitions to see the different effects you can achieve with this family of transitions.

12.7

TRANSITIONING WITH CIRCLES

13.1

13.2

ABOUT THE VIDEO

The lone kayaker was filmed from Cinnamon Bay, St. John, with a Sony DCR-TRV 27 digital camcorder during a balmy November afternoon. The footage was captured to PC with a FireWire connection and trimmed in Windows Movie Maker 2.

Circles can provide an interesting way to transition a clip into another. The lone man in the kayak in **Figure 13.1** proved to be an interesting subject, but he took his time getting beyond the surf line. The initial footage was boring, as it seemed to take him forever to finally start surfing the waves. The solution was to trim the footage and apply an interesting transition to signify the passing of time (see **Figure 13.2**).

When you use shapes to transition from one scene to another, choose a shape transition that suits the footage to which you are applying it. This technique shows you how to use a circular shape to transition from one scene to another. If a circular transition doesn't suit your footage, explore the other shape transitions to find something more suitable.

iMOVIE

The Circle Opening and Circle Closing transitions in iMovie are perfect for clips that may have a central object of some sort that you want to emphasize or highlight. As the circle transitions from one clip to another, it creates a circle around part of one clip and then gradually opens all the way or closes up, depending on which circle transition you selected. Circles are particularly useful for clips toward the beginning or end of a movie because they help add a sense of heightened drama to the story.

STEP 1: START A NEW PROJECT

In this technique, you apply a Circle Closing in between two clips so that the kayaker becomes the main focus in the scene.

- Begin a new project and save the project on your hard drive.
- Choose **iMovie** ➤ **Preferences** and in the Preferences dialog box, for Import: "New clips go to," check the **Movie Timeline** box. This way, the clips you import will appear in the timeline instead of the Shelf pane.
- Choose **File** ➤ **Import** from the menu, navigate to the CD-ROM, and select **MacClip16.mov** and **MacClip17.mov**.
- Display the timeline in Movie Track view. Now you can preview the transition.

STEP 2: PREVIEW AND ADJUST THE CIRCLE

The default speed of the circle was a little too fast, so you can adjust it.

- Click the first clip in the timeline, and in the Shelf, click the **Trans** tab. In the Transitions list, click the **Circle Closing** transition. In the thumbnail preview located in the Trans pane, you will see the default settings for this transition.

- If you drag the **Speed** slider to the left, the circle opens so quickly that it clashes with the soft rhythm of the kayak floating on the waves. Instead, drag the **Speed** slider to the right, to 03:15, which slows it down and gives you a nice balance between the transition and the clip movement (see **Figure 13.3**).

STEP 3: APPLY THE CIRCLE CLOSING

- Click the **Circle Closing** transition in the Shelf and drag it in between the two clips in the Movie Track.
- To preview the transition, press the **Home** key and then the **spacebar**. Notice on the first clip that the kayaker appears to have a spotlight effect as

13.3

the movie transitions into the next clip, which shows the kayaker far out in the ocean, riding a wave, as shown in **Figure 13.4**.

To fully understand the results of this technique, look at the sample movie provided on the book's CD-ROM. Using the circle transition to spotlight a moving object gives the appearance of tracking an object in time. Although the circle transition does not perfectly track a moving object, in many cases, you can come close to suggesting this type of effect.

WINDOWS MOVIE MAKER

After initially viewing the two clips used in this technique, it seemed logical to begin the transition from a central point, a task to which the Circle transition is well suited. Alternative transitions for unfolding a new scene from the center include Diagonal, Rectangle Out; Diagonal, Cross Out; Diamond; and Eye. When you select transitions for your own movies, choose one that matches an element in either scene to create an artistic segue between clips.

13.4

STEP 1: BEGIN A NEW PROJECT

Creating a new project is an exciting process. If you closely monitor the capture process, you end up with a collection of clips that need little or no trimming. After you cut the wheat from the chaff, you're ready to begin assembling your movie.

- Launch Windows Movie Maker and then choose **File ➤ New Project**.
- Choose **File ➤ Import into Collections**. Navigate to the CD-ROM that accompanies this book and select the files **WinClip015.wmv** and **WinClip016.wmv**. Click **Import** to create a collection for each clip.
- Drag each clip from its collection and place it on the timeline in numerical order.
- Select the first clip and then click the **Play Timeline** button. The footage of the kayaker's strong arms pushing the double-edged paddle against the waves, and then riding the surf, is good stuff, but the movie needs a transition to achieve the polish the footage deserves.

STEP 2: APPLY THE TRANSITION

The first scene unfolds and the camcorder zooms in on the kayaker. As the first scene ends, the subject is almost perfectly centered in the scene. The Circle transition seems like the perfect choice as it expands from the center of the scene like a ripple after a drop of rain hits a still pond.

- Click the **Tasks** button and then select **View video transitions**.
- Click the **Circle** transition and drag it between the two clips. If you're working in Storyboard mode, place it in the empty slot between the clips; otherwise, drag the transition to the Transition timeline and release the mouse button when the transition snaps between the two clips.

■ Select the first clip and click the **Play Timeline** button. The action unfolds as the kayaker paddles toward deep water and then the next scene appears from the center showing the kayaker riding a big wave to shore (see **Figure 13.5**).

STEP 3: MESSING WITH SUCCESS

The Circle transition certainly does a good job of attracting the viewer's attention to the center of the movie when the next scene begins and the default transition duration suits the footage well. Sometimes, however, you can get better effects by experimenting, or messing with success, so to speak.

■ Select the **Eye** transition from the Tasks pane.
■ Drag it and drop it on the existing transition. The Eye transition replaces the Circle transition.
■ Click the **Play Timeline** button and the movie plays in the Preview pane (see **Figure 13.6**). Notice that while the transition is similar, the Eye transition spreads out in an oval that almost perfectly matches the aspect ratio of the movie.

13.5

13.6

CHANGING SCENES WITH A RADIAL WHEEL TRANSITION

14.1

14.2

Sometimes less is more. When you take the journey, it's very Zen to be in the moment and experience each step. However, if you create movies that show every bit of footage you capture from an event, you'll quickly bore your viewer. The footage shown in this technique is a prime example. A 12-hour automobile race (see **Figure 14.1**) tests the endurance of man, machine, and spectators. To signify the passage of time in this technique, you apply a transition that looks like revolving spokes of a wheel, as shown in **Figure 14.2**), the perfect transition for an auto race.

iMOVIE

STEP 1: BEGIN A NEW PROJECT

In events like automobile races where there is a burst of excitement when the cars appear, then a long wait before it happens again, it's necessary to imply the passing of time. Otherwise, your movie would end up with a lot of long pauses. A radial transition tells the audience time has passed. Notice the transition almost resembles a stopwatch, which clearly symbolizes something is about to happen soon.

- Begin a new project and save the project on your hard drive.
- Choose **File ➤ Import** from the menu, navigate to the CD-ROM and select **MacClip018.mov**, **MacClip019.mov**, and **MacClip020.mov**.
- Drag these clips from the Clip pane to the Movie Track in sequence.

STEP 2: PREVIEW AND ADJUST THE RADIAL TRANSITION

Being able to preview a transition in the Transitions pane in real time is a wonderful feature. This feature makes playing with any adjustment settings associated with a particular transition easy. In the case of the Radial transition, you can adjust the speed of the transition with a slider, much like the Circle transition in Technique 13.

- Select the first clip in the Movie Track, and click the **Trans** tab to display the Transitions.
- In the Transitions list, click the **Radial** transition. In the thumbnail preview, as with other transitions, the duration of the transition is listed in the bottom left of the thumbnail (see **Figure 14.3**).
- Drag the **Speed** slider to the right until the duration of the transition reads 02:00 (the center of the slider). The slowing down of the transition alerts the viewer that things have happened and they're moving on to the next scene.

STEP 3: APPLY AND TWEAK THE TRANSITIONS

- To apply the transition to the first clip, drag the **Radial** icon in between the first and second clips.

14.3

14.4

Note how the clips to the right bounce horizontally to accommodate the new transition.

- Drag another **Radial** transition in between the second and third clips. The red render bar crawls slowly across the bottom of both transition clips, telling you that it's still cooking. When the red bar stops, the clip is rendered and subsequently, you can preview it in the Monitor window, as shown in **Figure 14.4**.
- To test your very cool movie, press the **Home** key to rewind the movie and then press the **spacebar** to play the movie in the timeline.
- You may feel the radial needs tweaking at this point. To edit a transition in the timeline, click the transition and make the proper adjustments in the Transitions pane. In the case of a radial transition, you can only adjust the duration of the transition. When you're done, click the **Update** button. The new transition updates the old in the Movie Track.

The Radial transition does a good job of delivering the message on these clips. This transition takes the audience forward in time. Keep in mind that you can also use a Radial transition to imply going back in time. For example, if someone is telling a story or reminiscing, a Radial could be used. Radial transitions can give visual clues to help the audience gauge the passing of time.

WINDOWS MOVIE MAKER

Trying to portray the drama of a long event in a short video can be a daunting task. You're faced with the age-old decision of what to leave in and what to leave out. Choosing three clips to portray a 12-hour auto race also proved to be a difficult task. We finally settled on three clips: a gaggle of cars racing to a corner at the beginning of the event, a fast parade of cars racing into a glorious Florida sunset, followed by a dazzling display of the cars' headlight patterns as they exit a sweeper (road racer-speak for a gentle radius curve taken at high speed) at over 160 miles per hour.

STEP 1: BEGIN A NEW PROJECT

- Launch Windows Movie Maker and then choose **File ➤ New Project**.
- Choose **File ➤ Import into Collections**. Navigate to the CD-ROM that accompanies this book and select the files **WinClip017.wmv**, **WinClip018.wmv**, and **WinClip019.wmv**. Click **Import,** and Windows Movie Maker creates a collection for each clip.
- Drag the clips from their collections and place them in numerical order on the timeline.
- Click the first clip and then click the **Play Timeline** button to preview the scene in the Preview pane (see **Figure 14. 5**). Even though these clips have no audio, you can almost hear the roar of the engines and squeal of the tires as the cars skitter through the curves and roar down the

14.5

straightaway, and then suddenly it's sunset, and then darkness. Exciting stuff for sure, but viewers are jerked too abruptly from one scene to the next. It's time to call in the video transitions.

STEP 2: WHEEL INTO THE NEXT SCENE

Choosing transitions is largely a matter of taste, while at the same time taking the content of the clips into account. Some video transitions seem to be ready-made for a particular type of clip, the **Wheel, 4 Spokes** transition being a prime example. This compelling transition is ideally suited for automotive transportation, or perhaps sailing activity. In previous techniques, you used the Storyboard to apply transitions between two scenes. For this technique, you'll use the timeline, which enables you to manually change the default transition time between scenes.

- Click the **Tasks** button and from the Edit Movie section click **View video transitions** to display the transitions in the Task pane.
- Select the **Wheel, 4 Spokes** transition and drag it towards the **Transitions timeline**. As you move your cursor between the first and second clips, a blue vertical line appears, indicating that the transition has been properly positioned between the two clips (see **Figure 14.6**).

- Release the mouse button to apply the transition.
- Position the **Wheel, 4 Spokes** transition between the last two clips as described previously.

STEP 3: PREVIEW AND TWEAK THE TRANSITIONS

Now that your timeline is in order, it's time to preview your handiwork. Many moviemakers make the mistake of applying exciting transitions and—thinking that their work is done—render the movie. Sometimes they get lucky and create a movie that doesn't need any tweaking, but this is the exception rather than the rule.

- Click the **Play Timeline** button to preview the movie. Now the movie conveys the excitement of motor racing without giving the viewer whiplash when scenes change. However, the

14.6

default transition duration makes the movie seem a little lethargic compared to the fleet-footed race-cars in the clips. A change is in order.

■ Click the **Zoom Timeline In** button until the rectangles on the Transition timeline start to separate. Whenever you have some short clips on the timeline, zooming in on the timeline enables you to examine each transition in detail. If you zoom in close enough, some of your video clips will not be visible in the workspace. You can navigate to hidden clips by clicking and dragging the scrollbar at the bottom of the timeline.

■ Click the second transition, move your cursor towards the beginning of the transition until it becomes a double-headed arrow, then click and drag to the right. As you drag, a tool tip displays the current duration of the transition.

■ Release the mouse button when the tool tip reads about 0:00:02.00 (see **Figure 14.7**).

■ Change the duration of the first transition to 2 seconds as described previously.

When you preview the movie now, you've still got all the excitement of racecars being skillfully piloted at high rates of speed and each new scene unfolds rapidly with just the right transition.

14.7

CHANGING SCENES IN SLOW MOTION

15.1

15.2

ABOUT THE VIDEO

The snowboarder video in this technique is from the Artbeats Digital Film Library, Recreation and Leisure Series. The clip itself is saved in a QuickTime format, NTSC frame size (720 x 480, 30 fps) and compressed as a Photo JPEG, high quality. The original source for this clip was 16mm film. The clip was imported into iMovie and Movie Maker, assembled, edited, and exported in their respective formats.

When you're shooting action footage, some scenes go past so quickly that viewers don't have time to appreciate the beauty of motion. A prime example is a pole vaulter. After the athlete plants the pole, the ensuing action occurs so rapidly that viewers can't make out the fine details of the pole bending, the athlete contorting his body to clear the bar, or the landing. When you have footage like this, you have three distinct events, the athlete's preparation, the actual event, and the aftermath. Neither iMovie nor Windows Movie Maker has an actual slow motion transition. However, by creatively using each program's toolset, we have created one for you.

Figure 15.1 shows a snowboarder launching off of a mogul in mid air. This segment of the clip is in slow motion, capturing every detail of the brief event. **Figure 15.2** shows the segment of the clip when the snowboarder lands and the motion returns to normal.

iMOVIE

iMovie makes slowing down the action on a clip very easy. The only ingredients you need to bring to the mix are some compelling images and a great idea on how to alter the motion on your clip so the technique works to your advantage.

We use a clip of a snowboarder taking a spectacular jump over a mogul. Just at the point when the snowboarder becomes airborne, the action slows down to emphasize the drama of the jump. This is a fun technique to use on action clips of friends and family who aspire to be weekend athletes.

STEP 1: START A NEW PROJECT

- Begin a new project and save the project on your hard drive.
- Choose **File ➤ Import**, navigate to the CD-ROM, and select **MacClip021.mov**. Drag this clip from the Clip pane to the Movie Track.

STEP 2: SPLIT THE CLIP

Because you are only using one clip, in order to slow the motion on part of the clip, you need to split it in a couple of places. Split the clip two times to produce three new clip segments.

- Drag the Playhead in the Monitor window to a point in the clip where the snowboarder starts to jump.
- Choose **Edit ➤ Split Clip at Playhead**. The clip on the timeline now splits in two.
- Drag the Playhead to the right in the timeline to the point in the clip where the snowboarder begins to land. Choose **Edit ➤ Split Clip at Playhead** to split the clip again. Now the clip has three segments as shown in **Figure 15.3**.

STEP 3: SLOW THE MOTION OF A CLIP

To slow the motion in a clip, you use the Fast/Slow slider. This slider is located at the bottom of the Movie Track, and you will only see it when your Movie Track is in Timeline view (see **Figure 15.4**). This slider is easy to spot because there is a hare (as in rabbit) icon to the left on this slider indicating that sliding toward this direction speeds up the motion.

> **TIP**
>
> For a very cool variation of this technique, try adding an Overlap transition in between the first and second clip segments. The Overlap transition will make the snowboarder appear as a ghost image, almost as if his spirit is jumping out of his own skin.

15.3

Concurrently, the tortoise icon to the right on this slider indicates that dragging in this direction slows down a clip. The duration of a clip that's speed has been adjusted changes accordingly as you will notice in the timecode readout. In this step, you slow the middle clip down to see what happens.

- Click the **Clock** icon at the bottom of the Monitor window to display the Movie Track in Timeline view.
- Click outside the Timeline view to deselect all clips. Then click the middle clip segment. Click and drag the **Faster/Slower** slider all the way to the right to slow the clip down, as shown in **Figure 15.4**. As you do so, note how it grows in length in the timeline.

TIP

If you have trouble viewing the options at the very bottom of the Movie Track when in the Timeline viewer, because the Dock from the OSX desktop is obscuring it, you can easily remedy this problem. From the Apple menu, choose **Dock ➢ Turn Hiding On.** Doing this temporarily hides the Dock so that you can work freely in the iMovie timeline. To turn the Dock back on, go back to the Apple menu and choose **Dock ➢ Turn Hiding Off.** To use the Dock while in iMovie, position your pointer at the bottom of the screen, and it will reappear.

15.4

- Press the **Home** key to rewind the movie back to the beginning and then press the **spacebar** to play it. The snowboarder now makes his leap in slow motion. Then, when he lands, the motion returns to normal.

If you preview the sample movie, you can get the feel of a frozen moment in time when a snowboarder makes the perfect jump. Splitting clips and adjusting the speed on the newly created segments is another trick you can use to bring attention to a particular point in time or an event in a clip sequence.

WINDOWS MOVIE MAKER

Necessity is the mother of invention as they say. Even though Windows Movie Maker doesn't have the toolset of a video editor, such as Adobe Premiere or Vegas Video, when you need to do something that seems otherwise impossible you can by creatively mixing and matching Windows Movie Maker's transitions, effects, and other tools to achieve the needed result. And that's exactly what you'll be doing to increase a snowboarder's hang time.

STEP 1: CREATE A NEW PROJECT

This technique uses one solitary clip that you'll manually divide into three scenes. Consider this your indoctrination into the creative moviemaker's guide, "How to Do More with Less."

- Launch Windows Movie Maker and then choose **File ➢ New Project.**
- Choose **File ➢ Import into Collections.** Navigate to the CD-ROM that accompanies this book, select **WinClip020.wmv,** and then click **Import.** Windows Movie Maker creates a collection for the file.

■ Select the video clip and press the **spacebar** to preview the clip in the Preview pane. The footage is good but doesn't do justice to the snowboarder's form and technique. You'll solve this by splitting the clip into three scenes.

STEP 2: SPLIT THE CLIP INTO SCENES

In previous techniques, you used Windows Movie Maker menu commands and buttons to edit clips. You can speed up your workflow if you get in the habit of using the keyboard shortcuts in this step.

■ Press **Alt+ Right Arrow key** to advance the clip to timecode 0:00:00:20, as displayed in the Preview pane (see **Figure 15.5**).

■ Press **Ctrl+L** to split the clip. Windows Movie Maker creates a new video clip called WinClip020(1). This clip begins with the snow-boarder about to jump.

■ Press the **spacebar** to resume playing.

■ Press the **spacebar** to pause the clip as close as possible to timecode 0:00:01:40, the point in the video where the snowboarder lands. Remember, if you don't pause the movie at the right spot, you can advance forward or back a frame at a time by using either the VCR-style controls or the previously discussed keyboard shortcuts.

■ Press **Ctrl+L** to split the clip. Windows Movie Maker creates a clip named WinClip020(2).

STEP 3: SLOWING THE MOTION OF A SCENE

After you split the clip into three distinct scenes, you're ready to assemble the clips on the Storyboard and slow down the middle scene, effectively increasing the snowboarder's hang time.

15.5

- Click the **Show Storyboard** button to switch to Storyboard mode.
- Drag each clip from the collection and place them in order on the Storyboard.
- Click the **Tasks** button and, from the Edit Movie section, choose **View video effects**. Windows Movie Maker displays the video effects you have at your beck and call.
- Click the **Slow Down, Half** effect and then drag it to the star in the clip's lower-left corner. Windows Movie Maker highlights the star in blue, indicating a video effect has been applied.
- Select the **Slow Down, Half** effect and apply it to the middle clip again. Windows Movie Maker's effects don't have any parameters you can adjust. However, you can apply an effect more than once to achieve a desired effect, in this case, very slow motion.

- Select the first clip on the storyboard and press the **spacebar**. When your finished movie plays, the snowboarder appears to float slowly in mid-air (see **Figure 15.6**), giving viewers a better chance to experience the subtle beauty of an athlete in motion.

TIP

For a variation on this technique, apply the Speed Up, Double effect to the last clip in an action sequence to finish off the scene with panache.

TIP

When you split your clips into scenes, give them unique names. You can name a clip by selecting it in the Collections pane, right-clicking, and choosing Rename from the shortcut menu. Type a new name for the clip and press Enter.

15.6

CHAPTER 4

CREATING COMPELLING SPECIAL EFFECTS

When you begin capturing and editing your digital video in iMovie or Windows Movie Maker, you begin to realize what a powerful tool a nonlinear video editor can be. With a few mouse movements and menu commands, you can create a finished product that looks almost professional. And best of all, you can cut out those less than perfect clips when you didn't pan steady or forgot to press the Record button after filming and captured several seconds of your shoes moving across the ground. After you create a production or two, you begin to look at video in a new way. Suddenly, when you're watching a movie and you see something really cool, you start asking yourself, "How'd they do that? How could I . . . ? What if . . . ?"

In this chapter, we provide the answer to some of these questions. If you have an artistic bent, you'll love the Posterizing technique. If you like your movies with a lot of razzle-dazzle, the Cinematic Effects technique is right up your alley. If you've got some clips that are too digitally perfect, you can make them look like they're a hundred

years old by applying the Antiquing a Movie technique to your clips. When you work through the techniques in this chapter, start to think of ways you can mix them or modify them to suit your movies.

POSTERIZING A MOVIE

16.1

16.2

ABOUT THE VIDEO

The video for this technique was filmed as the sun was setting on a Florida lake. The sky was cloudy from an approaching cold front; the setting sun tinting it shades of blue and pink. The video was filmed with a Sony DCR-TRV 27 digital camcorder. The resulting footage was captured to PC through an IEEE1394 FireWire card, and the clips were trimmed for your viewing and editing pleasure in Windows Movie Maker.

When you capture colorful footage such as sunsets, beach scenes, and fall foliage (see **Figure 16.1**), the clips can stand on their own. As an alternative, you can transform colorful clips into moving artwork by using the technique presented here (see **Figure 16.2**). With the right footage, you can use this technique to create posterized movies that would make even Andy Warhol jealous.

iMOVIE

Posterizing in a photo-editing application reduces an image's colors and/or value levels. In iMovie, however, posterizing is a good way to make a scene appear as if it were created from an animated illustration instead of photographic imagery. There are many different ways to achieve a posterized effect in iMovie. Manipulating the settings in the Adjust Colors effect is one way you can give your clips a posterized look. In this technique, you will learn how to apply this effect and then control the Adjust Colors settings to create some very cool looking footage.

91

16.3

16.4

STEP 1: START A NEW PROJECT

First you have to set up the timeline.

- Begin a new project and save the project on your hard drive.
- Choose **File ➢ Import** from the menu, navigate to the Clips folder on the CD-ROM, and select **MacClip022.mov**. Drag the clip from the Clip pane into the Movie Track. Now you're ready to preview the effect.

STEP 2: PREVIEW AND ADJUST THE COLORS

In this step you apply the wash transitions.

- Click the first clip in the Movie Track and then click the **Effects** tab.
- From the Effects list, click **Adjust Colors**. Note that you can ease in and ease out a color adjustment, enabling you to animate the color. But look at the bottom of the Effects pane to see what other additional options you have for adjusting a color.
- At the bottom of the Effects pane, iMovie provides three settings: Hue Shift, Color, and Lightness. Depending on the way the sliders are dragged, you can change the color of a clip dramatically. For **Hue Shift**, drag the slider all the way to the left. For **Color**, drag the slider almost all the way to the right, toward Vivid. For **Lightness**, drag the slider slightly left of center, toward the Dark setting (see **Figure 16.3**).

Now that the settings are just right, you're ready to apply the effect.

STEP 3: APPLY AN EFFECT

- In the Effect pane, click the **Apply** button. The effect renders on the selected clip.
- To see the results, press the **Home** key and then press the **spacebar**. The clip now appears to have a posterized effect, as shown in **Figure 16.4**, which makes it appear as if it is an illustration as opposed to a movie clip.

TIP

There is another way you can use the Adjust Color effect on a colorful clip and really wow your audience. This technique involves using the Effect In and Effect Out sliders in the Effects Pane (see sliders in **Figure 16.4**). You can make your clip appear in black and white and then gradually turn into full color as the clip plays. To do so, click on a clip in the Movie Track and click on the Effects tab. From the Effects list, choose adjust Colors. At the bottom of the pane, drag the Color slider all the way to the left to the B&W setting. Doing this desaturates the clip color so the clip appears in grayscale like an old black-and-white TV program. Adjust the Hue Shift and Lightness sliders to the middle of their slider bars. Now, drag the Effect In slider all the way to the left (0:00). Drag the Effect Out slider all the way to the left (10:00). When you play the clip (press Home and the spacebar), color is gradually added to the clip as it plays so it goes from black and white to full color through the duration of the clip. A sample of this effect can be found in the Chapter 16 Movie Samples folder.

WINDOWS MOVIE MAKER

When you use Windows Movie Maker video effects, you're not limited to using just one effect per clip. You can stack effects to get the look you're after. You can also arrange the order in which the effects are stacked. To achieve the posterized technique, you'll be stacking two effects on a clip.

STEP 1: START A NEW PROJECT

In previous techniques, you applied effects while working in storyboard mode. However, Windows Movie Maker is very flexible, giving you the alternative to apply effects while working in timeline mode.

- Launch Windows Movie Maker and choose **File ➤ New Project**.
- Choose **File ➤ Import Into Collections**. Navigate to the CD-ROM that accompanies this book, select **WinClip021.wmv,** and then click **Import**. Windows Movie Maker creates a new collection for the clip.
- Select the clip and then drag it to the timeline. Windows Movie Maker snaps the clip to timecode 0:00:00.00.
- Click the **Play Timeline** button to preview the clip. This particular clip shows a sunset through cloudy skies. Notice that there are some subtle blues and pinks that you can exaggerate to good effect with a little bit of effects magic.

STEP 2: APPLY THE EFFECTS

If one effect is good, then two are better, right? In certain instances, such as applying certain color effects to a clip, yes. However, you can go over the top and apply too many effects, which may cause the clip to appear muddy. Fortunately, if this occurs you can easily add, delete, and rearrange effects in Windows Movie Maker.

- Click the **Tasks** button and then click **View video effects** in the Edit Movie section.
- Select the **Hue, Cycles Entire Color Spectrum** effect and then drag it to the clip. Notice in the Preview pane that the blue colors are now purplish. If you preview the entire clip, you'll notice the colors change to reflect the color spectrum.
- Select the **Posterize** effect and then drag it onto the clip. Windows Movie Maker updates the clip, which you can view in the Preview pane. Notice that the video clip now looks like a pop art poster (see **Figure 16.5**).
- Click the **Play Timeline** button to preview the clip. The clip now resembles a light show from a '60s rock concert.

STEP 3: TAKING IT TO THE NEXT LEVEL

This is one of those techniques where stacking more than two effects will — if you choose an additional effect to alter the color — muddy the waters so-to-speak — but that doesn't mean that you can't mix and match different effects to achieve different results.

- Select the clip, right-click, and then choose **Video Effects** from the shortcut menu. Windows Movie Maker displays the Add or Remove Video Effects dialog box. This dialog box is split into two panes: Available effects and Displayed effects (see **Figure 16.6**).
- To remove an effect from a clip, select it in the Displayed effects: pane and then click the **Remove** button.
- To add an effect, select it in the Available effects: pane and then click the **Add** button.
- To change the order in which the effects are rendered, select an effect and click the **Move Down** button to move the effect down the order or click the **Move Up** button to move the effect up the order. Note that if the effect you select is at the top of the list, the Move Up button is dimmed; if you select an effect at the bottom of the list, the Move Down button is dimmed.

Before you clear the clips from the timeline and explore another technique, try creating your own concoction of color effects. We suggest replacing the Posterize effect with the Smudge Stick effect. Can you say, "Monet"?

16.5

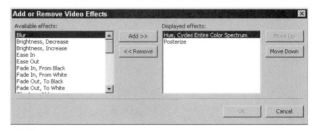

16.6

PANNING AND ZOOMING WITH STILL PICTURES

17.1

17.2

These pictures could be a montage from a typical vacation at the seashore — an old curious rowboat, a girl pensively examining the flora in the dunes; a woman doing a silly balancing act on the railing of a beach house. In this technique, you breathe life into still images by adding motion. They are from the Photodisc collection, Volume 28, *People, Lifestyles, and Vacations*.

M aking a slide show with still pictures is easy in iMovie and Windows Movie Maker. Even if you brought only your digital camcorder with you on vacation and left your camcorder at home, you can still make a movie out of your pictures. In Technique 7, you learned how easy it is to import still footage, but suppose that you want something a little more exciting than just your average "five seconds and on to the next one" slide show to e-mail to your friends. In this technique, you learn how to zoom and pan a still image. Applying this technique gives your still pictures the illusion of frame-by-frame movement when in reality it's just the still picture moving. **Figure 17.1** shows the still picture as it appears in the first frame. **Figure 17.2** shows the result of applying the pan and zoom effect in iMovie. It zooms up on the picture over time. The Windows version of the effect is slightly different because Windows Movie Maker does not have a zoom video effect, nor do you have the option to pan a still image. But with Windows Movie Maker, you can rotate an image, something iMovie cannot do for you.

iMOVIE

iMovie 3 sports a brand new pan-and-zoom effect for still pictures. This new effect is known as the Ken Burns effect. Ken Burns is well known for his PBS documentaries on historical subjects. Because most of his subjects are pre-film era (the Civil War, for example) Ken uses pan-and-zoom techniques to make still pictures come alive with movie-like movement. The iMovie effect isn't quite as sophisticated as some of Ken Burns' creations shown on PBS, but it is capable of jazzing up a series of still pictures by adding some movement to the pictures themselves. Here, we're going to apply a pan-and-zoom effect to a few still pictures in the timeline.

STEP 1: START A NEW PROJECT

- Begin a new project and save the project on your hard drive.
- Choose **File ➢ Import** from the menu, navigate to the Clips folder on the CD-ROM, and select **MacClip023.jpg**, **MacClip024.jpg**, and **MacClip025.jpg**. In the Shelf, click the **Photo** tab to view these, as shown in **Figure 17.3**.

STEP 2: ADJUST THE EFFECT

When you import pictures into iMovie, two default settings are applied. The first is the duration of the still picture, which we discuss in Technique 7. The second

> **TIP**
>
> Before importing pictures, don't forget to size them to 640 x 480 pixels to avoid having black bands appear in the picture. To learn about sizing pictures, turn to Technique 7.

17.3

17.4

default setting is a pan-and-zoom effect, which is automatically applied to each still picture. Press the **Home** key to rewind the Playhead and press the **spacebar** to play the movie, so you can see this pan-and-zoom effect in action. In this step, you learn how to change the direction and the amount of the default zoom.

- The images you imported as well as the adjustment parameters for the Ken Burns Effect appear in the Photos Pane.
- Click the first image in the shelf (image of boat). Click the **Reverse** button in the Photos pane to reverse the way the image zooms from start to finish. The default zoom makes the image go from small to large, so reversing it will make the boat go from large to small. Press the **Apply** button. When you do this, the clip appears in the Movie Track, and the effect renders.
- Click the second clip (woman sitting on stairs). Now click the **Finish** button. Drag the **Zoom** slider to approximately 4:50, so the picture will zoom up 4½ times its original size. Click the **Apply** button to apply this adjustment to the clip in the Movie Track, as shown in **Figure 17.4**.
- Click the third clip (woman balancing) and click the **Reverse** button to reverse the default zoom. Click the **Apply** button to apply the adjustments. Press the **Home** key and then the **spacebar** to play the movie. Notice that the action goes from large to small, then small to large, and then large to small again. The still pictures appear as if they are actually animated.

STEP 3: EDIT THE ADJUSTMENT

Like transitions, effects are never permanent. If you decide later on in the editing process that you don't like an effect, you can always go back and change it. In this step, you edit the pan and zoom that you applied to the second clip of the woman sitting on the stairs.

- Click the middle clip in the Movie Track.
- In the Photos pane, drag the **Duration** slider button to approximately 10:00 to lengthen the duration of the zoom, as shown in **Figure 17.5**.
- Click the **Apply** button and play the movie again. The tempo on the middle clip has been slowed down. The pause it creates appropriately places emphasis on the first and last pictures.

> **TIP**
>
> To get rid of a pan and zoom on a still picture, set the Start and Finish Zoom to 1:00.

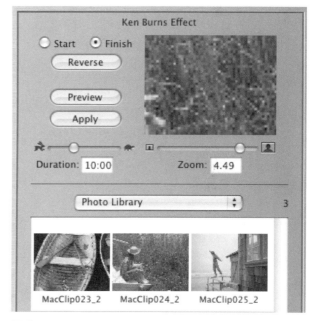

17.5

TRANSITIONS AND STILL PICTURES

You can add transitions to still pictures, too. Try adding a Cross-Dissolve between the second and the third clips to give your still pictures even more personality. Then, try adding a Wash In before the first clip and a Wash Out after the last clip. The Wash transition can be very effective for beginnings and endings because it creates an otherworldly entrance and exit.

WINDOWS MOVIE MAKER

When you look at Windows Movie Maker's video effects, it is obvious Microsoft hasn't paid homage to Ken Burns or anyone else from PBS for that matter. But that doesn't mean you can't do cool things with still pictures in Windows Movie Maker. In this technique, you turn a single image on its ear, flip it, and then return it to its upright position.

STEP 1: START A NEW PROJECT

■ Launch Windows Movie Maker and choose **File ➢ New Project**. Windows Movie Maker gives you a blank canvas with which to work.
■ Choose **File ➢ Import Into Collections**. Navigate to the CD-ROM that accompanies this book, select **WinClip022.jpg**, and then click **Import**. Windows Movie Maker imports the image into the current collection.

■ Drag the image from the collection and drop it on the timeline. If you're not working in timeline mode, click **Show Timeline**.

STEP 2: ALTER THE DURATION OF THE IMAGE

In Windows Movie Maker, still images display for 5 seconds by default. However, when you're applying special effects to the same image, you can spice things up by decreasing the amount of time the clip displays.

■ Select the clip and move your cursor towards the clip's handle until your cursor becomes a two-headed red arrow.
■ Click the handle and drag to the left. As you drag the handle, a tool tip tells you the current duration of the clip.

TIP

Although dragging and dropping from an existing collection to another is the only way you can add a video file to an existing collection, you have another option with still images. Click the **Tasks** button and choose **Import pictures** from the Video Capture section. Doing this opens the Import File dialog box from which you select multiple images to import into the currently selected collection.

- Release the mouse button when the tool tip reads approximately 0:00:02.00 seconds.
- Select the clip and choose **Edit ➢ Copy**. Alternately, you can press **Ctrl+C**.
- Choose **Edit ➢ Paste** or, if you prefer keyboard shortcuts, **Ctrl+V**. Windows Movie Maker pastes a copy of the clip on the timeline.
- Repeat the **Paste** command until you have five copies of the clip on the timeline (see **Figure 17.6**). Note that the timeline in this image has been zoomed to a higher magnification for clarity.

STEP 3: APPLY THE EFFECTS

You have three effects at your disposal to rotate a clip or image. Windows Movie Maker doesn't have an option for zooming in on an image, but you can simulate zooming in by using the Ease In effect and simulate zooming out by using the Ease Out effect.

- Click the **Tasks** button and then click **View video effects** in the Edit Movie section.
- Drag the **Ease Out** effect onto the first clip.
- Drag the **Ease In** effect onto the second clip and then drag the **Rotate 90** effect onto the clip. The clip rotates 90 degrees in the Preview pane.

- Drag the **Ease Out** effect onto the third clip and then drag the **Rotate 180** effect onto the clip. The clip rotates 180 degrees in the Preview pane.
- Drag the **Ease In** effect onto the fourth clip and then drag the **Rotate 270** effect on the clip. The clip rotates to 270 degrees in the Preview pane (see **Figure 17.7**).
- Drag the **Ease Out** effect onto the fifth clip.
- Select the first clip and then click the **Play Timeline** button. The movie zooms in and out on the image while rotating it in 90-degree increments.

17.6

17.7

CREATING CINEMATIC EFFECTS

18.1

18.2

ABOUT THE VIDEO

The clips used for this technique were shot in Yosemite National Park in California using a Sony DCR-TRV 27. The camcorder was set to infinite focus due to the vast panorama being recorded. Manual exposure was used for the third clip to safeguard against the camcorder adjusting the brightness as it was panned towards the shadow side of the valley. The clips were captured to PC using a FireWire card and trimmed in Windows Movie Maker.

*C*inematic implies motion picture, and unedited raw home video footage is a far cry from the lush beauty of a film narrative. Shooting and editing a movie so that it deliberately looks as if it were shot on film requires some planning upfront. Your subject matter, whether it is a landscape or an object, should be serious, grand in some way, dramatic, or all of the preceding, which definitely applies to the footage you'll be using for this technique. The story you tell with your footage, inclusive of mood, place, time, and point of view, determines whether your video looks amateurish or like a Hollywood production. In this technique, you build a sequence of clips that set a dramatic stage for a compelling narrative. The transitions and effects you apply to these clips, combined with the dramatic vast panoramas, help set the tone of the story as it begins, luring the audience into the movie. The first clip (see **Figure 18.1**) introduces viewers to the vast beauty of Yosemite Valley. After viewing a lush waterfall in the second clip, the third clip introduces viewers to the "Yosemite High Country" when they see the gnarled skeleton of a Jeffrey pine (see **Figure 18.2**) that crowns the summit of Sentinel Dome. The cinematic effects you apply in this technique are perfect for dramatic scenes like these.

iMOVIE

In this movie, the footage has been filmed with a "motion picture" perspective in mind. When the clips are dragged to the Clip Viewer, the cut between each transition is a little too choppy to carry off that cinematic look. A Fade In and Fade Out transition is used in this technique to begin and end the scene and to set the tone of the movie. Fade In and Fade Out transitions work well for beginning and ending a scene because they gently open and close the story by transitioning from black to an image and vice versa. Overlap transitions are used in between clips in this movie to gracefully fold one clip into another. To finish the movie off, a light fog is dropped onto the tree clip to give a dream-like atmospheric quality to the scene. With some careful planning of your shoot and the proper transitions and effects, you can raise the bar on the quality of your output.

STEP 1: START A NEW PROJECT

First you need to organize the clips on the timeline.

- Begin a new project and save the project on your hard drive.
- Choose **File ➢ Import** from the menu, navigate to the Clips folder on the CD-ROM, and select **MacClip026.mov**, **MacClip027.mov**, and **MacClip028.mov**. Drag the clips from the Clip pane into the Movie Track. Now you will add an effect.

STEP 2: ADD AN EFFECT

Here you apply a fog effect on the last clip in the Movie Track (**MacClip028.mov**) to create a slow moving steam over the mysterious Jeffrey pine tree.

- Click the last clip in the Movie Track and then click the Effects tab. In the Effects list, click the Fog effect. Note the results of the effect in the preview thumbnail.
- At the bottom of the Effects pane, there are three adjustments that can be made to the Fog effect. You can change the amount of fog, the direction the wind blows the fog (left or right), and the color of the fog (see **Figure 18.3**). Drag the Amount slider button to the middle, the **Wind** slider all the way to the right, and the **Color** slider button right, toward the White setting, as shown in **Figure 18.3**.

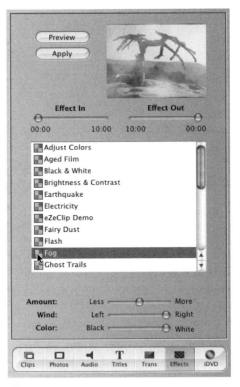

18.3

■ Click the **Apply** button in the **Effects** pane. After the clip renders, press the **Home** key and the **spacebar** to review the results of applying the fog effect.

STEP 3: ADD TRANSITIONS

Next, the Fade In, Fade Out, and Overlap transitions will be applied in between clips.

■ Click the first clip in the Movie Track. Then click the Trans tab at the bottom of the Shelf and from the Transitions list, click Fade In. In the preview thumbnail, note how the clip gradually transforms from total black to the movie, resulting in a soft, dramatic introduction (see **Figure 18.4**).

■ In the Transitions pane, drag the **Speed** slider all the way to the right toward the 04:00 setting. Doing this makes the Fade In transition period between a black frame and the gradual appearance of the first clip last longer (see **Figure 18.5**).

■ Drag the **Fade In** transition to the left of the first clip.

■ Repeat this process by clicking on the **Fade Out** transition from the Transitions list to the end of the last clip in the Movie Track (tree). Note a plus (+) sign appears to the right of your pointer, indicating you are adding a transition before a clip or in between clips and the clip(s) is long enough to hold the transition.

■ Now, drag an **Overlap** transition from the Transitions list in between the first and second and the second and third clips. The final Movie Track should resemble **Figure 18.6**.

■ Press the **Home** key and the **spacebar** to play the movie. Note the beginning, and in between subtlety the Fade In, Fade Out, and Overlap transitions give to the movie.

18.4

18.5

18.6

FILM VERSUS VIDEO

You can make your video appear more "film-like" in quality for that cinematic look. Some camcorderes offer settings that can help your video appear more cinematic. For example, the Canon GL-2 DV camcorder has a Movie Mode that works by changing the normal DV NTSC frame rate (29.97 fps) to that of film (24 fps). Some videographers achieve a film-like effect by adjusting their camcorder to a lower depth of field. Film tends to look flatter than video so this technique can suggest a cinematic look. Lastly, software applications and plug-ins such as DigiEffects CineLook and CineMotion (www.digieffects.com) can simulate a cinematic appearance in the post-production process, but they are costly and only available as an add-on to such applications as Final Cut Pro or Adobe After Effects.

WINDOWS MOVIE MAKER

To achieve dramatic effects with your movies, your initial preview is often your first inkling of the type of clips with which you have to work. Many Hollywood producers use a straight cut from one clip to another. However, when the subject matter differs greatly between clips, a straight cut is often too jarring and a transition is needed. Your goal as a moviemaker is to draw attention to your subject matter, not the coolness of your transition. Therefore, the transition should be seamless and not readily apparent to viewers of the finished movie.

STEP 1: START A NEW PROJECT

For this technique, you'll be working with video effects, a task that is easier to achieve when you work in Storyboard mode.

- Launch Windows Movie Maker and choose **File ➤ New Project**.
- Choose **File ➤ Import Into Collections**. Navigate to the CD-ROM that accompanies this book, select **WinClip023.wmv**, **WinClip024. wmv**, and **WinClip025.wmv**, and then click **Import**. Windows Movie Maker creates a collection for each clip.
- Click the **Show Storyboard** button if you're not already working in storyboard mode.
- Drag each clip from its respective collection and drop it in its respective slot on the storyboard in numerical order (see **Figure 18.7**).

18.7

STEP 2: APPLY THE EFFECTS

This technique requires two effects. The sequence begins with the first clip fading out. You'll apply the Hues, Cycles Entire Color Spectrum effect to the middle clip, making it appear as though the waterfall is being viewed through a lens that changes colors and then the clip fades out. The final clip also has the Hues, Cycles Entire Color Spectrum effect applied and at the end fades out, which is an excellent way to segue to ending credits.

- Select the first clip (**WinClip023.wmv**), right-click, and then choose **Fade Out** from the shortcut menu.
- Select the second clip (**WinClip024.wmv**), right-click, and then choose **Fade Out** from the shortcut menu.
- Select the third clip (**WinClip025.wmv**), right-click, and then choose **Fade Out** from the shortcut menu.
- Select the first clip and then click the **Play Storyboard** button. Windows Movie Maker plays the movie, which you can preview immediately in the Preview pane (see **Figure 18.8**).

> **TIP**
>
> While working in storyboard mode, you can see which video effects you've applied to a clip by holding your cursor over the Video Effects icon that looks like a star in the lower-left corner of a clip. After a few seconds a tool tip appears listing the effects in the order you've applied them.

Notice how the transition from one clip to the next is subtle thanks to the Fade Out option, which is the same as the Fade Out, To Black video effect. The Movie Maker programmers at Microsoft decided this effect deserved a position of prominence on the shortcut menu.

STEP 3: ADD EFFECTS

The movie looks good as it is, but can be improved by applying video effects to the second and third clips.

- Click the **Tasks** button if the Movie Tasks pane is not currently displayed.
- Click **View video effects** from the Edit Movie section of the Movie Tasks pane.

18.8

- Select the **Hues, Cycles Entire Spectrum** effect and drop it on the **second clip** (**WinClip024.wmv**).
- Select the **Hues, Cycles Entire Spectrum** effect and drop it on the third clip (**WinClip025.wmv**).
- Select the first clip and then click the **Play Storyboard** button to preview the movie (see **Figure 18.9**).

As you preview the finished movie, notice how the last two clips appear more compelling, thanks to the addition of the video effects. When you want to create your own "Cinematic" movies, experiment with different effects and choose one or more that adds some visual punch to your movie. If the clips in your movie are different subject matter, add a Fade Out as you've done in this example. If your clips are similar, you can transition from one clip to the next using a video transition that compliments the clips. However, when you use video transitions on a movie that consists of several clips, stick with one video transition. When you mix video transitions, the end result doesn't look professional.

18.9

ANTIQUING A MOVIE

19.1

19.2

ABOUT THE VIDEO

The videos for this clip were shot in Tijuana, Mexico, a city rife with sidewalk vendors, colorful murals, and the sound of singing senoritas and strumming guitars. Even though Tijuana's only a short walk across the border from southernmost California, you know you're in a different country. The video was shot using a JVC GR10-DVF-U and captured to PC using a IEEE 1394 host controller connected to a Sony DCR-TRV27. The clips were trimmed in Windows Movie Maker.

You may ask yourself why you would want to make footage you filmed three days ago (**Figure 19.1**) look like it was filmed half-a-century ago (**Figure 19.2**). The answer is twofold: because you can and because the end result is cool. iMovie and Windows Movie Maker 2 both provide you with more than enough effects to convert digital footage into a reasonable facsimile of an old 8mm movie that's been buried in a shoebox for 30 years. And the good news is that you can do it in just a few minutes.

iMOVIE

With a little creativity, in iMovie you can give your production the look and feel of an old-time movie. iMovie offers an effect called Aged Film that gives the feeling of an old-time production. However, unlike an old movie which is in black and white, the Aged Film effect renders your clips in color. So if you combine the Aged Film effect with a Sepia Tone effect, the combination of these effects makes your movie look very old.

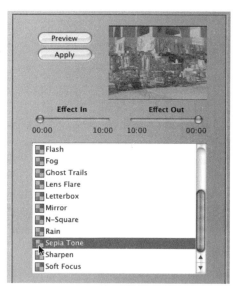

19.3

19.4

STEP 1: START A NEW PROJECT

■ Begin a new project and save the project on your hard drive.

■ Choose **File ➤ Import** from the menu, navigate to the Clips folder on the CD-ROM, and select **MacClip029.jpg**, **MacClip030.jpg**, and **MacClip031.jpg**. From the Shelf, drag these clips into the Movie Track in sequential order.

STEP 2: PREVIEW EFFECT ON CLIP

■ Click the first clip in the Movie Track and then click the **Effects** tab at the bottom of the Shelf. In the Effects list, click the effect named **Aged Film**. In the thumbnail preview, you can see that this effect adds dust, scratches, and degraded quality, comparable to the quality of an old movie.

■ At the bottom of the Effects pane, you can adjust the Exposure, Jitter, and the amount of scratches that appear in the effect. Maximum Exposure makes the clip appear washed out and Minimum Exposure makes the clip very dark. Jitter refers to the choppy movement of old film as it played in a projector.

■ Drag the **Exposure** slider to the center, as this will give you a medium exposure. Drag the **Scratches** and **Jitter** sliders to about a third of the way to the right. You see the results in the thumbnail preview, as shown in **Figure 19.3**.

Next, you can preview a second effect on top of the first.

TIP

You can also animate the Aged Film effect by adjusting the Effect In and the Effect Out sliders at the top of the Effects Shelf. For example, if you wanted the aged film effect to gradually disappear over time, you could make it do so by adjusting these settings.

STEP 3: ADD MULTIPLE EFFECTS

On some effects in iMovie you can add more than one to a clip. Fortunately, the Aged Film effect is one of those effects you can do this with. In this step, you preview a Sepia Tone effect on top of the Aged film effect. If this looks okay, you can apply them.

- Click the **Sepia Tone** effect. Notice in the thumbnail preview that it blends in well with the Aged film effect. The two effects used together do a better job of suggesting old film than either of these effects used singularly (**Figure 19.4**).

Because the effects look good in preview, you can now apply them both.

STEP 4: APPLY EFFECTS

You want these effects to reside on all three clips. Rather than apply each one separately, you can apply the effects to all three clips at once.

- Select all three clips in the Movie Track by Shift-clicking on all three.
- In the Effects pane, click the **Aged Film** effect and click the **Apply** button. Next, click the **Sepia Tone** effect and click the **Apply** button again. iMovie applies both effects to all three clips simultaneously, saving you a lot of rendering time (**Figure 19.5**).
- Now it's time to preview the movie. Press the **Home** key and then press the **spacebar** to play the movie. The movie now looks like it's circa 1920.

19.5

You can also apply the Black & White effect to obtain a similar antique effect. But instead of having a sepia cast, the film appears in black and white.

WINDOWS MOVIE MAKER

If you've ever watched old documentaries on educational television, you know that moviemaking equipment has come a long way. The footage you create with your digital camcorder can even rival the best results of the old Hollywood moviemakers if you use a tripod and the right lighting. When you follow the steps in this technique, you can make your footage appear as though it were filmed with vintage equipment.

STEP 1: START A NEW PROJECT

- Launch Windows Movie Maker and choose **File ➤ New Project**.
- Choose **File ➤ Import Into Collections**. From the CD-ROM that accompanies this book, select **WinClip026.wmv**, **WinClip027.wmv**, and **WinClip028.wmv**, and then click **Import**. Windows Movie Maker creates a new collection for each clip.
- Click **Show Storyboard** to switch to storyboard mode.
- Arrange the clips in numerical order on the storyboard.
- Click the **Play Storyboard** button to preview the clips. The clips are interesting, but the man in the large hat engaged in mock battle with his friend looks like it's out of a scene from yesteryear. This footage would definitely benefit from a bit of antiquing.

STEP 2: APPLY THE EFFECTS

If you've ever viewed vintage 8mm or 16mm movies, you know that they're anything but pristine. The moving image is degraded by dust and scratches that have built up on the film over the years, and bounces around a bit due to the fact that the film doesn't always align perfectly with the projector sprockets. Windows Movie Maker provides three effects that you can use to simulate aged film.

- Click the **Tasks** button and then click **View video effects** in the Edit Movie section.
- Select the **Film Age, Older** effect and then drag it onto the first clip (WinClip026.wmv). Windows Movie Maker places a blue highlight on the star at the lower-left corner of the clip indicating you've applied an effect to the clip.
- Select the **Sepia** effect and then drag it to the first clip (WinClip026.wmv). Windows Movie Maker updates the Preview pane in real time, giving you a preview of the effects you've applied (see **Figure 19. 6**).

19.6

STEP 3: COPY THE EFFECTS

When you become proficient with Windows Movie Maker, you'll end up making movies out of a large number of clips. When you're working with 20 or 30 clips, applying the same effects to each clip can be tedious. Fortunately, you don't have to do that when you apply effects in storyboard mode.

- Click the star in the lower-left corner of the first clip (WinClip026.wmv). A black rectangle appears around the icon.
- Right-click and choose **Copy** from the shortcut menu. Alternately, you can press **Ctrl+C**.
- Click the star in the lower-left corner of the second clip (WinClip027.wmv), right-click, and then choose **Paste** from the shortcut menu. Windows Movie Maker pastes the effects you copied from the first clip.
- Click the star in the lower-left corner of the third clip (WinClip028.wmv), right-click, and then choose **Paste** from the shortcut menu. The effects are applied to all clips, as shown in **Figure 19.7**.
- Select the first clip and then click the **Play Storyboard** button. Welcome back to yesteryear.

While you've still got all the clips on the storyboard, you might consider experimenting with the other Film Age effects to see what level of coolness you can achieve with them. You can also add your favorite transition between scenes to put the finishing touches on the movie.

19.7

DISINTEGRATING A SCENE

20.1

20.2

ABOUT THE VIDEO

The video for this technique was filmed at the 2003 12 Hours of Sebring automobile race. This clip shows the high-speed run from Turn 1, culminating at Turn 3, a sharp left-hander that bunches the cars up and always produces action. Filmed with a Sony DCR-TRV 27 digital camcorder, this clip was captured to PC with a FireWire connection.

This technique shows you how to add interest to a scene (see **Figure 20.1**) by making the scene appear to disintegrate as it ends, as shown in **Figure 20.2**. This technique works well when you apply it to footage of fast-moving objects and also works well with technical scenes. This technique could also generate visual interest when segueing from a crowded city scene to a pastoral country setting. And, of course, it works great if you want to make your home videos look like a sequel to *Star Wars*.

iMOVIE

Although no effect is specifically used to achieve a disintegrating technique in iMovie, something can always be pulled out of our bag of tricks to resemble footage in the process of turning to nothingness. In this technique, we're going to use a plug-in by CSB, specifically, the Solarization effect. You can download this plugin from `www.csb-digital.com`. Follow the instructions on how to load it into iMovie. When you are done, the effect will appear in

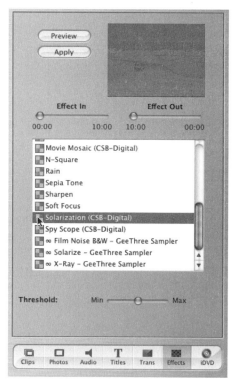

20.3

20.4

your effect list. If you have not loaded the CSB plug-ins yet, please do so. When you see these effects in action, you will be delighted at the additional versatility they provide you when trying to come up with creative ideas for movies. First, begin a new movie.

STEP 1: START A NEW PROJECT

- Begin a new project and save it on your hard drive.
- Choose **File ➢ Import**. From the menu, navigate to the Clips folder on the CD-ROM, and select **MacClip18.mov**. Technique 14 also requires this clip, so you may recognize it.
- Drag the clip to the Movie Track.

STEP 2: PREVIEW AND ADJUST THE SOLARIZATION

For this technique, you will experiment with the Solarization effect from CSB Digital. When turned up to full volume, this effect makes your clip appear as if the sun has turned the clip to an etched piece of metal. In iMovie, you can make the effect build up over time. Test the effect first so you can familiarize yourself with the results it will yield.

- Click the clip in the Movie Track, and in the Shelf click the **Effects** tab. Navigate through the Effects list until you find the Solarization effect from CSB Digital. Click it and watch the clip take on a metallic solarized appearance when you do so (see **Figure 20.3**).
- To adjust the effect so the clip starts out normal and the solarization builds up in time, we can adjust the Ease In and Ease Out sliders in the Effects pane. For **Effect In,** slide the slider button to the right, all the way to a setting of 10:00. For

Effect Out, slide the slider button again, all the way to the right, to a setting of 00:00. Doing this causes the effect to gradually appear over time.

■ For the Solarization effect, a **Threshold** slider is on the bottom of the Effects pane. The higher the threshold setting, the more solarized and metallic the effect appears. Drag the **Threshold** slider all the way to the right, toward the Max setting. You see the results of the settings in the thumbnail preview.

STEP 3: APPLY THE SOLARIZATION

Now it's time to apply the effect.

> **TIP**
>
> For a variation on the effect, use the Ease Out effect instead of the Ease In effect.

> **TIP**
>
> You can make the effect gradually disappear over time by reversing the settings on the Ease In and Ease Out sliders.

> **TIP**
>
> If you enjoy working with effects, you can purchase hundreds of interesting effects for iMovie from the vendors who have so kindly given us a sampling of their goods on the companion CD-ROM.

■ Click the **Apply** button in the Shelf.

■ To preview the transition, press the **Home** key and then the **spacebar**. Note the gradual changing from a normal clip to an etched metallic plate, as shown in **Figure 20.4**. If you think that the effect is too severe, try changing the **Threshold** setting. When you're done, click the **Apply** button to reset the effect.

WINDOWS MOVIE MAKER

As a moviemaker, the last thing you want tc happen is to have a scene fall apart on you. But you can disintegrate a scene to add visual interest to a movie. To disintegrate a scene with Windows Movie Maker, you use two effects: Ease In and Pixelate.

STEP 1: START A NEW PROJECT

When you apply this technique to a movie clip, you don't want the whole scene to disintegrate, just the end of it. After you import a clip, you need to split it where you want the disintegration to begin.

■ Launch Windows Movie Maker and choose **File ➤ New Project**.

■ Choose **File ➤ Import Into Collections**. Browse to this book's companion CD-ROM, select **WinClip017.wmv**, and then click **Import**.

■ Select the clip and then press the **spacebar** to view the clip in the Preview pane.

■ Press the **spacebar** when the clip reaches about 4 seconds (0:00:04.00), as shown in **Figure 20.5**. Note that if you don't cue a clip at exactly the point where you want to edit it, you can use the controls in the Preview pane to advance the clip a frame at a time, or step back to previous frames a frame at a time.

■ Click the **Split** button. Windows Movie Maker splits the clip at the 4-second mark.

STEP 2: APPLY THE EFFECTS

The disintegration part of this scene is a rather short clip. When you use this technique on your own footage, select the footage towards the end of a scene where the footage may not be as dramatic as the frames that open the scene. Even though you're splitting clips when you use this technique, there's no need for a transition because the two clips are actually one scene.

■ Drag the clips from their collection and arrange them in order on the timeline, or storyboard if you're working in that mode.

■ Click the **Tasks** button and choose **View video effects** from the Edit Movie section.

■ Select the **Ease In** effect and then drag it to the last clip.

■ Select the **Pixelate** effect and then drag it onto the last clip. The Preview pane updates to show the effects you've applied.

■ Select the first clip and then click the **Play Timeline** (or **Play Storyboard** if you're working in that mode) button to preview the technique (see **Figure 20.6**).

20.5

20.6

MIRRORING A CLIP

21.1

21.2

ABOUT THE VIDEO

The video for this technique was filmed in Torrey Pines, just north of LaJolla, California. The colorful flowers were recorded with a GR10-DVF-U and captured to PC using a FireWire card connected to a Sony DCR-TRV27.

When you're working with short clips of colorful scenery or foliage and there's not a lot of action, you can add action by mirroring the clip. Your viewers see a change when the clip mirrors itself, and they have the added benefit of seeing your steady camcorder work a while longer.

iMOVIE

Scenes with a field full of flowers are a perfect backdrop for the Mirror effect in iMovie. The flowers are colorful and they move ever so slightly, resulting in an effect akin to the old kaleidoscopes we used to have when we were kids. Here we apply the effect to all three scenes and gently adjust the settings to see what kind of result it yields.

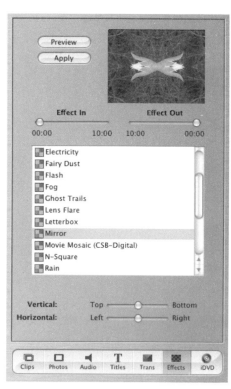

21.3

21.4

STEP 1: START A NEW PROJECT

- Begin a new project and save it on your hard drive.
- Choose **File ➤ Import**. From the menu, navigate to the Clips folder on the CD-ROM, and select **MacClip032.mov**, **MacClip033.mov**, and **MacClip034.mov**.
- Drag the clips to the Movie Track.

STEP 2: PREVIEW AND ADJUST THE MIRROR

First, you should preview the effect.

- Select all clips in the Movie Track by **Shift+clicking** on all of them. Select the **Effects** tab in the Shelf. Then, scroll through the Effects list and click the **Mirror** effect from the list. Note that in the preview thumbnail, the flower appears as a kaleidoscope, with multiple prisms replicating the flower.
- You can adjust the settings on the Mirror effect in a few different ways. Aside from being able to adjust the Ease In and Ease Out as you can do on many other effects, you can also adjust the horizontal and vertical position of the mirror. At the bottom of the Effects pane, click the **Vertical** slider and drag it to the middle so that the flowers will be vertically centered (see **Figure 21.3**).
- Now click and drag the **Horizontal** slider button to the middle, so the flower mirror appears in the center of the frame horizontally. You're ready to apply the effect to all three clips.

STEP 3: APPLY THE MIRROR

- Select all three clips in the Movie Track, and click the **Apply** button to apply the Mirror effect to all three clips.

When all three clips finish rendering, press the **Home** key and then the **spacebar** to play the movie. **Figure 21.4** shows how the Mirror effect creates some very exciting effects on each clip that change as the flowers sway in the wind.

If you want to go back and adjust the settings on the clips, click the clip, change the **Vertical** and **Horizontal** sliders again, and click the **Apply** button again.

TIP

For a variation of the effect, add the Mirror, Vertical effect to the second clip.

WINDOWS MOVIE MAKER

If you're working with clips that you want to display a while longer, you can always use the Slow Down, Half effect. This effect works fine if you've got some action in the clips, but if your clips are already a bit lethargic, the way to go is to place two instances of the clip on the timeline and use the Mirror, Horizontal effect.

STEP 1: START A NEW PROJECT

■ Launch Windows Movie Maker and choose **File ➢ New Project**.

■ Choose **File ➢ Import Into Collections**. Navigate to the CD-ROM that accompanies this book and select the file **WinClip029.wmv**. Click **Import** to create a collection for the clip.

■ Select the clip and drag it to the timeline.

■ Drag the clip to the timeline again. You now have two instances of the movie clip on the timeline (see **Figure 21.5**).

STEP 2: ADD THE EFFECT

When you mirror a clip, you really don't need a transition, because the clips are the same footage with the

exception being that the copied clip is mirrored. When you preview the movie after applying the effect to the second clip, it appears to be part of the same footage. However, if you're working with longer footage than the clips supplied for this technique, you may want to consider adding one of the transitions discussed in Chapter 3.

■ Click the **Tasks** button and then choose **View video effects** from the Edit Movie section.

■ Select the **Mirror, Horizontal** effect and then drag it onto the second clip. Windows Movie Maker creates a mirror image of the first clip. You might say the clip is beside itself (see **Figure 21.6**).

■ Select the first clip and then click the **Play Timeline** button to preview your handiwork.

21.5

21.6

CHAPTER 5

CREATING VINTAGE MOVIE EFFECTS

Many home moviemakers are also movie buffs who enjoy classic movies such as *Gone with the Wind, The Maltese Falcon,* and *Casablanca.* Other digital filmmakers enjoy the antics of Charlie Chaplin or The Three Stooges. If you enjoy any of these genres, or classic movies in general, you're bound to find a technique you'll like in this chapter. We begin by showing you how to convert some funny video clips into a hysterical slapstick comedy. If you enjoy the classic noir mystery movies of the '40s and '50s, you'll want to try Technique 23, where we show you how to replicate this look with your own footage. Chaplin fans will enjoy Technique 24. If you're a card-carrying baby boomer, or you watched your parents' 8mm home movies, Technique 25 shows you how to simulate this look. If you want to give your home movies a dreamy, glamorous look, you'll enjoy Technique 26, which can also be used to make wrinkles disappear for an instant digital facelift.

CREATING A SLAPSTICK COMEDY

22.1

22.2

ABOUT THE VIDEO

The clips used to make "Slapstick" were shot with a Canon GL-1 perched on a Bogen 3001TN tripod using automatic settings. The footage was then captured in iMovie, and trimmed in iMovie and Windows Movie Maker.

P eople do the strangest things when you aim a camcorder at them. If you are lucky, you capture really funny footage. When that happens, you can leave well enough alone, or you can take the footage to the next level by dabbling with video effects in iMovie or Windows Movie Maker. If you've ever watched a *Three Stooges* short, you know how much fun slapstick can be. Now we're not suggesting you ask your subjects to poke fingers in each others' eyes or whack someone with a two-by-four while you film them; what we're suggesting is you apply this technique to your funny videos to make them even funnier.

iMOVIE

The tools in iMovie enable you to approach slapstick in many ways. Classic slapstick movies from the early part of this century were always filmed in black and white because color film was not yet invented. Also, the frame rate for film during the silent film slapstick era was much faster than

121

today's 24 frames per second. To capture the flavor of a slapstick comedy on this technique, you're going to add a black-and-white effect, and speed up the frame rate of the clips. These techniques, combined with a subject willing to ham it up for the camcorder, can produce some pretty silly results.

STEP 1: START A NEW PROJECT

First you organize the clips on the Movie Track.

- Begin a new project and save the project on your hard drive.
- Choose **File ➢ Import** from the menu, navigate to the CD-ROM, and select the clips named **MacClip035.mov**, **MacClip036.mov**, and **MacClip037.mov**.
- Drag the clips from the **Shelf** into the **Movie Track Viewer**. To make certain that your clips are being viewed in this mode, click the **Movie Track Viewer** icon (clock) in the top left of the Movie Track.

STEP 2: INCREASE THE CLIP SPEED

The first step in the editing process involves speeding up the clip. When you speed up a clip, you actually shorten the clip's duration.

- While holding down the **Shift** key, click on all three clips in the Movie Track.
- At the bottom of the slider, locate the **Faster/Slower** slider. This slider has a rabbit icon to the left and a turtle to the right (see **Figure 22.3**).

The default setting is in the middle indicating a normal clip speed (30 fps). Drag this slider all the way to the left toward the rabbit icon to speed the clips up. (Conversely, dragging the slider toward the right would slow the clips down.) The clips in the Movie Track shrink to reflect their new, shorter length (**Figure 22.4**).

- Press the **Home** key and then the **spacebar** to play the movie. The chef is now performing her cooking at lightning speed.

STEP 3: APPLY A BLACK AND WHITE EFFECT

Now you make the clips black and white by adding a simple effect. This effect desaturates the color in the clip and reduces it to grayscale.

- With all clips selected in the Movie Track, click the **Effects** tab. Click the **Black & White** effect in the Effects list, as shown in **Figure 22.5**. Note also that the thumbnail preview shows you the results of the effect. Click the **Apply** button to simultaneously render the clips.
- Press the **Home** key and then the **spacebar** to see the results.

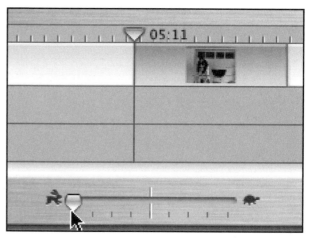

22.3

22.4

STEP 4: DUPLICATE CLIPS

Depending on the contents of your movie, another effective way to simulate old slapstick antics is to duplicate some of the clips and use them over and over again in the Movie Track. Duplicating clips can help heighten the silliness of your movie, and it's very easy to do.

■ Click the second clip in the Movie Track and then choose **Edit ➢ Copy** (see **Figure 22.6**).

> **TIP**
>
> To delete an effect in iMovie, simply click the clip in the Movie Track and then press the **Delete** key. The clip remains, but the effect is removed from it. Be warned that if you repeat this process, and no more effects are left on a clip, the clip will be deleted from the Movie Track. To bring the clip back to the movie, you have to reimport it from the folder in which it resides.

■ Drag the **Playhead** in the Movie Track to the tail of the second clip and choose **Edit ➢ Paste**. The clip duplicates, and the head of the new duplicate butts with the tail of the previous clip.

■ **Figure 22.7** shows the Movie Track (in Clip view) as it now appears with the duplicate clips added.

> **TIP**
>
> If you plan to speed up a clip, make certain that the length of the clip is long enough to support a shorter duration after you speed it up. In other words, if a clip is ten seconds in duration, and you plan on making the speed double, the clip will then last for five seconds — half it's original length. Keep this in mind when you capture the footage.

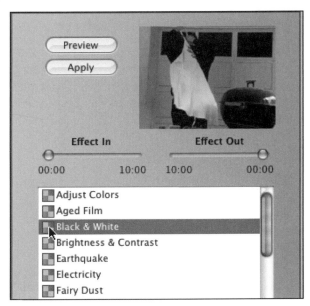

22.5

22.6

22.7

- Press the **Home** key and then the **spacebar** to play the movie from the beginning. The chef goes about her business in ultra-fast mode. The triplication of the second clip where she's attempting to light the grill accentuates her problem and makes the act of lighting a grill seem like it's a pretty funny exercise in futility.

WINDOWS MOVIE MAKER

If you've ever watched a classic slapstick movie, you know that many of the scenes have been sped up to achieve the comic effect. The fact that a scene was sped up was readily evident because the soundtrack went in triple time as well. When you use Windows Movie Maker to create your slapstick movies, you can mute the audio track and add some funny music to the Audio/Music track using one of the techniques in Chapter 7. And, of course, you want the movie to be in black and white.

STEP 1: START A NEW PROJECT

To create a slapstick movie, you apply lots of video effects to each clip. You can add transitions if you like, however, in this technique you focus on adding video effects to make the "World's Greatest Chef" the world's funniest chef. Well, almost. . . .

- Launch Windows Movie Maker and choose **File ➢ New Project**. Windows Movie Maker gives you a blank canvas with which to work.
- Choose **File ➢ Import Into Collections**. Navigate to the CD-ROM that accompanies this book, select **WinClip030.wmv, WinClip031.wmv, WinClip032.wmv,** and **WinClip033.wmv,** and then click **Import**. Windows Movie Maker creates a new collection for each clip.

- Click the **Show Storyboard** button if you're currently working in timeline mode, and then arrange the clips in numerical order on the storyboard.

STEP 2: APPLY THE EFFECTS

To turn some funny footage into a slapstick classic, you've got to speed up each clip. In Windows Movie Maker, you can apply multiple effects to a clip. In fact, you can use the same effect twice, as we do here to make our super chef a supersonic chef.

- Click the **Tasks** button and then select **View Video Effects**.
- Select the **Speed-Up Double** effect, drag and drop it to the first clip (WinClip030.wmv) on the storyboard, and then apply the effect again. One application of this effect is just not enough to pull off the slapstick effect. When you use this effect on your own clips, make sure that the clips are at least eight seconds in duration.
- Select the **Grayscale** effect and then drag and drop it on the first clip (WinClip030.wmv). Windows Movie Maker updates the clip in the Preview pane in real time (see **Figure 22.8**).

STEP 3: DUPLICATE THE EFFECTS

When you're working with several clips to which you want to apply the same effects, you can easily do so in Windows Movie Maker, especially when working in storyboard mode.

- Click the blue **Video Effects** icon in the lower-left corner of the first clip (WinClip030.wmv).
- Right-click and then choose **Copy** from the shortcut menu.
- Click the gray **Video Effects** icon in the lower-left corner of the second clip (WinClip031.wmv). This icon is gray until you add one or more video effects to the clip.

■ Right-click and choose **Paste** from the shortcut menu. Windows Movie Maker pastes the copied video effects to the second clip (WinClip031.wmv).

■ Paste the copied effects to the remaining clips.

■ Click the **Play Storyboard** button to preview the effect (see **Figure 22.9**).

TIP

Hold your mouse over a Video Effects icon that is highlighted in blue and a tool tip appears, noting the effects you've applied.

TIP

When you create a slapstick movie, you copy a clip and place several instances of it in your movie for comic effect. With the sample clips provided for this technique, try adding a few copies of the clip of our super chef tossing the match on the fire to your production. Do this with your own movies and speed up the clips to make it appear as though your subject's task is never-ending and seemingly impossible, which makes the finished movie even more comical.

22.8

22.9

ACHIEVING A CLASSIC FILM NOIR EFFECT

23.1

23.2

ABOUT THE VIDEO

The videos for this clip were filmed in Ybor City, a Spanish community in Tampa, Florida, that gained fame in the early 1900s when Teddy Roosevelt and the Rough Riders staged there before the Spanish American war. The footage was filmed with a Sony DCR-TRV27 and captured into Windows Movie Maker through a FireWire card. The map images were scanned using a Hewlett Packard ScanJet 5370C, cropped and optimized in an image editing program, and saved in the TIFF format.

The classic noir movies of the 1940s were dark tales about mysterious characters. The predominate characteristics of the genre was dark or high-contrast lighting. If you have film clips that are have high contrast with a wide range of darks and lights, or were shot in dark places, they are perfect candidates for a modern day noir movie. You can flesh out these clips if you have a friend or family member who's a bit of a ham, like the subject in **Figures 23.1** and **23.2**. The Windows version of this technique features another staple of early movies, an animated map to signify your lead character's travels.

iMOVIE

All the old great film noir movies, like *Casablanca* and *Diabolique*, were shot in black and white. The absence of color helped evoke a sense of deep mystery, foreboding, and suspense. Contemporary films of this genre often use black and white effects to capture that old film noir feeling. In iMovie, you can apply a Black & White effect to help give your movie a film noir effect.

STEP 1: START A NEW PROJECT

First, organize the clips on the Movie Track.

- Begin a new project and save the project on your hard drive.
- Choose **File ➢ Import** from the menu, navigate to the CD-ROM, and select the clips named **MacClip038.mov**, **MacClip039.mov**, **MacClip040.mov**, **MacClip041.mov**, and **MacClip042.mov**.
- Drag the clips from the Shelf into the Movie Track in Clip Viewer mode. To make certain your clips are being viewed in this mode, click the **Clip Viewer** icon (film icon) in the top left of the Movie Track.

STEP 2: ADD THE BLACK & WHITE EFFECT

- Press the **Shift** key and select all the clips in the Movie Track.
- Click the **Effects** tab and in the Effects list, click the **Black & White** effect. A preview of the effect displays in the preview thumbnail (see **Figure 23.3**).

TIP

To successfully achieve a film noir technique, your footage (like the movie we use in this example) needs to set the stage for impending suspense. When shooting the footage, use locations such as dark alleys, seedy bars, and long, dark corridors that viewers can interpret as mysterious and sinister. Scouting out locations for certain effects is an important part of the overall success of your final production.

- Click the **Apply** button to apply the effect to all five clips.
- Press the **Home** key and then the **spacebar** to play the movie. Notice that by removing the color from the movie, the tone of the movie has changed from a current, everyday event to an old suspense thriller.

STEP 3: FINISH THE MOVIE WITH TRANSITIONS

Rather than have the clips cut harshly from one scene to another, you're going to add some transitions to help create a sense of time passing. At the beginning and the end of the movie you'll be placing a **Fade In**

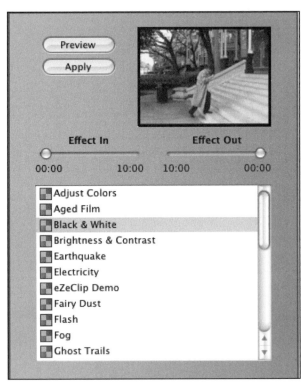

23.3

and a **Fade Out** transition, respectively. Fade transitions used at the beginning and end of a movie can help give the movie a narrative story feeling, as if you're about to curl up on the couch and become absorbed in a compelling mystery.

- Click the **Trans** tab to display the list of transitions.
- Click the first clip in the Movie Track and, in the list of transitions, click **Fade In.** Drag the **Speed** slider all the way to the right so the time in the thumbnail preview reads 04:00. The transition now lasts for four seconds. The length of the clip is 10:26 seconds, which more than accommodates a 4-second transition.
- Drag the transition to the head of the first clip in the Movie Track.
- Now that the Fade In is applied, click **Fade Out** in the transitions list and drag it to the tail of the last clip. Doing this makes the movie gradually fade to black at the end.
- To make the other clips more gradually transition into one another, click the **Cross Dissolve** transition in the transition list. Set the **Speed** slider to 02:00, so the transition lasts for two seconds.
- Drag a **Cross Dissolve** transition in between the first and second clips, the second and third clips, and the third and fourth clips. In the Movie Track, there should be a transition in between each clip as well as a transition at the beginning and end of the movie to give you a total of six transitions (see **Figure 23.4**).
- Press the **Home** key and then press the **spacebar** to play the movie. You see the combination of black-and-white video in combination with the transitions have transformed the feeling of this movie from a current event to an old-time film noir.

23.4

> **NOTE**
>
> When you change the speed of a Fade In and Fade Out transition, the new speed becomes the default speed until you change it again.

WINDOWS MOVIE MAKER

After you decide which clips to use for your noir movie, your first step is to make them look like they were shot in the 1940s, read black and white, or for your purists, grayscale. If any of your clips are excessively bright, you may want to add a bit of mystery using the Brightness, Decrease video effect.

- Launch Windows Movie Maker and choose **File ➤ New Project**. Windows Movie Maker gives you a blank canvas with which to work.

■ Choose **File ➢ Import Into Collections**. Navigate to the CD-ROM that accompanies this book, select **WinClip034.wmv**, **WinClip035.wmv**, **WinClip038.wmv**, **WinClip39.wmv**, and **WinClip040.wmv**, and then click **Import**. Windows Movie Maker creates a new collection for each clip.

■ Click the **Tasks** button and in the Capture Video section of the Movie Tasks pane, select **Import Pictures** and select **WinClip036.tif** and **WinClip037.tif** from the CD-ROM that accompanies this book. Windows Movie Maker adds the images to the current collection.

■ Click the **Show Storyboard** button and arrange the clips in numerical order.

STEP 2: ADD THE VIDEO EFFECTS

When you use this technique on your own footage, the amount of video effects you use will depend on your actual footage. If you've dressed a character for the part and filmed your production in low light, or at night, you'll only have to convert the footage to grayscale. Our sample clips were filmed during bright daylight, so we'll have to do a bit of tweaking to make them look more mysterious.

■ From the Movie Tasks pane, click **View video effects**. Windows Movie Maker displays the available video effects in the Tasks pane.

■ Click the **Brightness, Decrease** effect and then drag it onto the first clip (WinClip034.wmv).

■ Select the **Grayscale** effect and then drag it onto the first clip (WinClip034.wmv). Windows Movie Maker updates the Preview pane. The clip's starting to look more like a 1940s movie rather than something filmed in the year 2003 (see **Figure 23.5**).

■ Click the **Video Effects** icon in the lower-left corner of the first clip (WinClip034.wmv), right-click, and then choose Copy from the shortcut menu.

■ Click the second clip (WinClip035.wmv), right-click, and then choose Paste from the shortcut menu. As you may remember from previous techniques, you can also click the **Video Effect** icon to add or paste effects to a clip.

■ Paste the copied video effects to the other clips on the storyboard.

After you add the video effects to your clips, you need to animate the second map image to signify the character's travel from Ybor City to the University of Tampa.

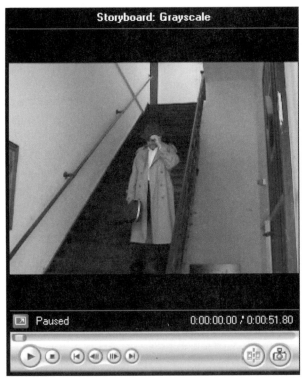

23.5

STEP 3: PUTTING THE MAP IN MOTION

If you've ever watched the classic movies from the '40s and '50s, or for that matter, some of the more modern movies set in that era, you know that producers would signify travel by showing a map with a line moving across it. You can achieve the same effect in Windows Movie Maker by using the appropriate transition.

- In the Edit Movie section of the Movie Tasks pane, click **View Video Transitions**. Your available video transitions are displayed in the Tasks pane.
- Click the **Inset, Down Left** transition and drag it into the slot between the two map image clips (WinClip036.tif and WinClip037.tif).
- Click the **Play Storyboard** button to preview your production. As the movie plays, you'll see the line on the second map gradually appear as the first image transitions into the second. By default, Windows Movie Maker displays images for five seconds. Combined with the default three-and-one-half-second duration of scene transitions, the effect is pulled off seamlessly, as if someone were drawing a line across the map (see **Figure 23.6**).

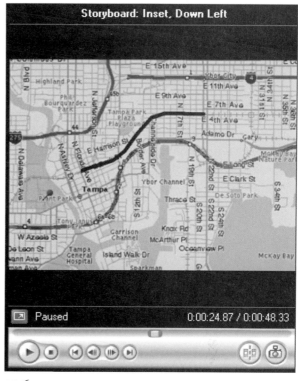

23.6

STEP 4: APPLY THE FINISHING TOUCHES

As you previewed the clips in the previous step, you probably noticed the final clips were a tad dark. With the exception of the maps, there are no transitions. Moviemakers in the 1940s liked to fade beginning scenes in from white and fade ending scenes out to white.

- Select the next-to-last clip (**WinClip39.wmv**), right-click, and then select **Video Effects** from the shortcut menu. Windows Movie Maker displays the Add or Remove Video Effects dialog box (see **Figure 23.7**).

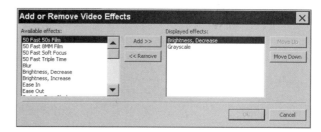

23.7

■ Select Brightness, Decrease from the Displayed Effects window and then click **Remove**.

■ Click **OK** to exit the Add or Remove Video Effects dialog box.

■ Select the final clip (WinClip40.wmv) and remove the Brightness Decrease effect as outlined previously. From the Available Effects window, click **Fade Out, To White** and then click **Add**. Windows Movie Maker adds the effect to the Displayed Effects list.

■ Click **OK** to exit the Add or Remove Video Effects dialog box.

> **TIP**
>
> You can also use this transition for your vacation footage. Scan a map that shows all the destinations along your route and save it as a JPEG or TIFF image. Remove the map from the scanner and trace your route with a felt-tip marker. Scan the map with your route and save this image as a JPEG or TIFF file. Follow the previous steps to animate the line, but choose the proper transition for your direction of travel. For example, if your route goes from south to north, choose a transition that wipes in from the bottom of the clip to the top.

CREATING A CLASSIC SILENT MOVIE

24.1

24.2

The clips for this technique, shown in **Figures 24.1** and **24.2**, were filmed in historic Ybor City, a community on the outskirts of Tampa, Florida. The clips were filmed with a Sony DCR-TRV27 in auto exposure mode and captured to PC with a FireWire card.

T he silent movies of the early 1900s were characterized by the superb antics of actors such as Charlie Chaplin, some text, background music, and some comical sound effects. The movies were in black and white, and the action took place at a frenetic pace. If you've got some clips of friends or relatives engaged in everyday activities that may be a little — ahem — boring, you can add some interest by converting them to classic silent movies. If you have some budding actors in your circle of acquaintances, give them some props, shoot some footage, and take the clips over the top by applying the steps described in this technique.

iMOVIE

The trick to achieving a silent movie feeling is in the combination of the effects you choose and the adjustments you make to these effects. In the iMovie version of this technique, you work with the Black & White effect, which you may be familiar with from Technique 23. You also speed up the sequences and add an aged film look to the clips.

STEP 1: START A NEW PROJECT

First you organize the clips on the Movie Track.

- Begin a new project and save the project on your hard drive.
- Choose **File ➤ Import** from the menu, navigate to the CD-ROM, and select the clips **MacClip043.mov**, **MacClip044.mov**, **MacClip045.mov**, and **MacClip046.mov**.
- Drag the clips from the Shelf into the Movie Track. Click the **Timeline Viewer** icon (clock) in the top left of the Movie Track to view your clips as a timeline.

STEP 2: ADD THE BLACK & WHITE EFFECT

Next, you apply the Black & White effect to all the clips in the Movie Track to help make the movie appear old.

- While holding down the **Shift** key, click all the clips in the Movie Track to select them.
- Click the **Effects** tab. In the effects list, click the **Black & White** effect. A preview of the effect displays in the Preview thumbnail.
- Click the **Apply** button to apply the effect to all five clips.
- Press the **Home** key and then the **spacebar** to play the movie. The movie now plays in black and white.

STEP 3: CHANGE CLIP SPEED

To simulate an old-time movie, you speed up the clips in the Movie Track a little. The frame rate of silent films was much faster and erratic compared to the films of today.

- While holding down the **Shift** key, click all four clips in the Movie Track. At the bottom of the Movie Track, locate the **Faster/Slower** slider. Drag this slider to the left two notches to speed up the clips a little (see **Figure 24.3**).
- Press the **Home** key and then press the **spacebar** to play the movie. The footage maintains a pace similar to that of an old movie.

STEP 4: APPLY THE AGED FILM EFFECT

iMovie has an effect that gives your video dust, scratches, and noise. *Noise* refers to a spattering of irregular pixels that transparently overlay a clip, giving it a distressed look, as if it has sat on a shelf for many years. Apple calls the effect Aged Film. You apply it to your clips to add the finishing touch to your silent movie production.

- With all the clips selected in the Movie Track, click the **Effects** tab. In your Effects list, click the **Aged Film** effect. The Preview thumbnail gives you a sample of the Aged Film effect.
- Press the **Home** key and then press the **spacebar** to review the results of the effect.

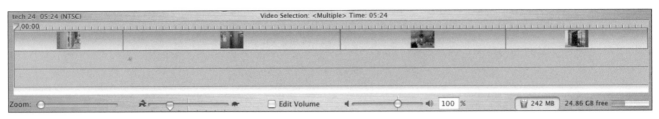

24.3

STEP 5: ADJUST THE AGED FILM EFFECT

On the bottom of the Effects pane, three adjustment sliders enable you to change the parameters of the Aged film look. The sliders are Exposure, Jitter, and Scratches. The Exposure slider enables you to adjust the brightness of the effect. The Jitter slider enables you to adjust the steadiness of the clip. Silent movies often appeared jittery because the film never perfectly aligned with the sprockets in old projectors. The Scratches slider enables you to change the frequency, amount, and size of dust, hairs, and other artifacts that traditionally collected in old film projectors. These three settings give you tremendous flexibility in getting the movie to look just right for your own vision of a silent movie.

24.4

- With all the clips in the Movie Track selected, drag the **Exposure** slider to the middle, in between Min and Max.
- Drag the **Jitter** slider about a quarter of the way to the right, as shown in **Figure 24.4**.
- Drag the **Scratches** slider to the left about a quarter of the way into the slider. Click the **Apply** button to set the effect with the adjustments.
- Press the **Home** key and then the **spacebar** to preview the movie. If you want to see more and longer jitters and scratches, select the clips, drag the sliders more to the right toward Max, and click the **Apply** button again.

WINDOWS MOVIE MAKER

When you create your own silent movies, make sure that your clips are at least eight seconds in duration. This technique relies on the ability to speed up the action for comic effect. When you try to do this with clips shorter than eight seconds, the converted clips are ineffective because they're over almost before they begin. The actor for the clips in our technique took his time getting from Point A to Point B. As a result, the footage was perfect for this technique.

STEP 1: BEGIN A NEW PROJECT

- Launch Windows Movie Maker and choose **File ➤ New Project**. You're now ready to import the clips for your production.
- Choose **File ➤ Import Into Collections**. Navigate to the CD-ROM that accompanies this book and then select **WinClip041.wmv**, **WinClip042.wmv**, **WinClip043wmv**, **WinClip044.wmv**, and **WinClip045.wmv**. Click **Import** to have Windows Movie Maker create a new collection for each clip.
- Click the **Show Storyboard** button and arrange the clips in numerical order.

STEP 2: APPLY THE EFFECTS

After you assemble your clips on the storyboard, you get the chance to be creative and tweak the footage by applying effects. Color film hadn't been invented when silent films were made. Therefore, your first step is converting the clips to grayscale. Then you speed up the clips and apply a film-aging effect to add the right amount of jerkiness to the footage.

- Click the **Tasks** button and then choose View Video Effects.
- Click the **Grayscale** effect and drag it onto the first clip (WinClip041.wmv).
- Click the **Film Age, Old** effect and drag it onto the first clip (WinClip041.wmv).
- Select the **Speed Up, Double** effect and drag it onto the first clip (WinClip041.wmv).
- Apply the **Speed Up, Double** effect to the first clip (WinClip041.wmv) again. After you add the last effect, Windows Movie Maker updates the clip in the Preview pane (see **Figure 24.5**).

STEP 3: COPY THE EFFECTS TO OTHER CLIPS

If you've worked through some of the other Windows Movie Maker techniques, you know how easy it is to copy effects from one clip to another. However, if you jumped to this technique before reading any of the others, you can copy effects to other clips as follows.

- Select the first clip (WinClip041.wmv) on the storyboard and then click the **Video Effects** icon in the lower-left corner of the clip.
- Right-click and then choose Copy from the shortcut menu.
- Click the **Video Effects** icon in the lower-left corner of the second clip (WinClip042.wmv).
- Right-click and then choose Paste from the shortcut menu.
- Repeat the Paste command for the other clips on the storyboard, making sure that you first click the **Video Effects** icon.
- Click the **Play Storyboard** button to view your handiwork in the Preview pane (see **Figure 24.6**).

You can achieve some interesting movies using this technique. If you have any footage of birthday parties, anniversaries, or other family occasions that need a bit of help, apply this technique to the clips and then add a humorous soundtrack, a title, and ending credits using the techniques presented in Chapters 7 and 8.

24.5

24.6

SIMULATING A FIFTIES HOME MOVIE

25.1

25.2

ABOUT THE VIDEO

The action in this video takes place at the famous White Manna Diner in Hackensack, NJ. It was shot on a rainy evening, at dusk, so the early evening sky was full of the rich blue tones shown. This miniature diner appeared in the 1939 Worlds Fair before being transported to New Jersey. Considered a classic diner, it is included in many nostalgic books and serves as the backdrop for many movies, music videos, and commercials. The video was shot with a Canon GL-2 and captured in iMovie and trimmed in iMovie and Windows Movie Maker. Auto focus and auto exposure was used.

If you've ever viewed old home movies shot with an 8mm or 16mm camcorder, you know that they are inferior to what you can achieve with modern camcorders. Old home movies are lint magnets, and after they've been run through the sprockets of a projector a few hundred times, you see noticeable lines and the film appears a bit jerky. The color is also off a little after being subjected to the intense light of the projector bulbs. Sometimes it's desirable to add these flaws to your modern home movies; for example, if you visit a nostalgic place such as your birthplace, your grandparents' home, or a historical building. You can transform your pristine digital video into a 1950s home movie by following the steps in this technique. The clips we have chosen for you to work with are perfect for this effect because diners are traditionally associated with burgers, fries, and sodas, the mainstay of teens in the 1950s. **Figure 25.1** depicts the diner before the footage was adjusted. **Figure 25.2** represents the results of applying effects that suggest an old home movie effect.

iMOVIE

If you've ever looked at pictures in the 1950s, they always seem to be tinted with warm orange, yellowish film. 8mm home movies of this era tended to lean toward warmer hues rather than the rich, realistic color we are accustomed to seeing in today's movies. In this technique, you are going to play off of the qualities of home movies in the fifties and make our sample clips appear as if they were shot over 50 years ago.

STEP 1: START A NEW PROJECT

First you organize the clips on the Movie Track.

- Begin a new project and save the project on your hard drive.
- Choose **File ➤ Import** from the menu, navigate to the CD-ROM, and select the clips **MacClip047.mov**, **MacClip048.mov**, **MacClip049.mov**, and **MacClip050.mov**.
- Drag the clips from the Shelf into the Movie Track. For this technique, you want to view the Movie Track in the Clip Viewer. To do this, click the **Clip Viewer** icon (film icon) in the top left of the Movie Track.

25.3

STEP 2: APPLY THE EFFECTS

Instead of using the traditional effects in iMovie, you're going to apply some QuickTime effects that become available during the export process. There are over 20 additional effects in the iMovie export dialog box, and many of these effects are different then the standard iMovie effects.

- Choose **File ➤ Export** from the menu to export your movie.
- In the iMovie Export dialog box, select **To QuickTime** in the Export list (see **Figure 25.3**). In the Formats list, select **Expert Settings**. Next, click **Export**.
- In the Save exported file as dialog box, navigate to the location on your hard disk where you want to save the movie.
- In the Export list, select **Movie To QuickTime Movie** and click the **Options** button. The Movie Settings dialog box appears (see **Figure 25.4**).

25.4

STEP 3: ADJUST THE EFFECTS

In the Movie Settings dialog box, you can set custom parameters for the movie you are exporting. Among these parameters are compression type, filter, and size. The filters offer several effects not available in the standard iMovie Effect selections. In this step, you select your own custom settings, one of which makes the movie appear old.

■ In the Movie Settings dialog box, click the **Settings** button to display the Compression Settings dialog box. In the pop-up compression list, select **Sorenson Video 3**. Sorenson 3 compression gives you a combination of well compressed file size with high quality output. Drag the **Quality** slider to High, as shown in **Figure 25.5**. Next, select **Millions of Colors**+ in the Depth pop-up list to ensure the best image quality for the High setting. Click the **OK** button to close the Compression Settings dialog box.

■ Back in the Movie Settings dialog box, click the **Filter** button. The Choose Video Filter dialog box contains a plethora of different filters, or effects, in the list to the left. Click the **Special Effects** arrow, and in the expanded list click **Film Noise**. Selecting this filter results in an effect similar to the iMovie Aged Film effect. In the QuickTime effect, however, you can make additional adjustments to a movie; one adjustment in particular facilitates the 1950s look.

■ At the top of the dialog box, select **Dust and Film Fading** from the pop-up list. Next, select **1930's color film** from the Film Fading pop-up list, as shown in **Figure 25.6**. Adjust the **Dust Density** and the **Dust Size** sliders accordingly. You can preview the results of your adjustments in the preview thumbnail at the bottom right. Click the **OK** button.

■ Back in the Movie Settings dialog box, click the **Size** button. In the **Export Size** dialog box, click the **Use custom settings** button. For Width, type in **320**. For Height, type in **240**. Click the **OK** button. Back in the Save Exported File As dialog box, click the **Save** button.

25.5

25.6

STEP 4: VIEW YOUR EXPORTED MOVIE

■ Navigate to the movie you just exported and open it by double-clicking in the file icon.

■ Back in the Movie Settings dialog box, click the **OK** button to export your movie. As you will see, the effects do a pretty good job of simulating an old home movie.

> **NOTE**
>
> The only downside of using QuickTime Effects is you don't have many options for previewing an effect before you export the movie. In the Choose Video Filter dialog box for QuickTime Effects, there is a very small thumbnail in the bottom left, but this thumbnail is static and low resolution. It only gives you a fleeting idea of what results the effect might yield. In contrast, the iMovie Preview Effects thumbnail gives you a larger and animated preview, which gives you a much better idea of what the effect is going to look like on the clip.

> **NOTE**
>
> Because digital video clips are very large, clips are generally compressed to make them easier to manage. In a nutshell, compression works by eliminating unnecessary color information in a file, thus reducing the file size. A reduction of color also means diminished quality, depending on which compression scheme you choose. Popular compression formats for Mac QuickTime files are Cinepak, Sorenson, and Sorenson 3. QuickTime Version 6 and newer also offers MPEG-4 Video compression, which provides a nice balance of quality versus size for files being downloaded via the Web.

> **TIP**
>
> In the Choose Video Filter dialog box, try adjusting the Hairs and the Scratches from the pop-up list. When clicked, they reveal their own custom settings that can sometimes be quite useful.

WINDOWS MOVIE MAKER

Windows Movie Maker has effects to age film, but none of them resemble the look of a vintage color movie played through an 8mm projector. As a workaround, we have created some video effects and included them on this book's CD-ROM.

STEP 1: ADD THE 50 FAST VIDEO EFFECTS TO WINDOWS MOVIE MAKER

Windows Movie Maker is set up to recognize XML files within a folder named AddOnTFX as video effects and adds these effects to the Video Effects pane. The effects for this technique are included in a file called 50FastEFX.xml. Before you can apply the effects, you must add them to Windows Movie Maker as follows:

■ In Windows, choose **Start** ➤ **All Programs** ➤ **Accessories** ➤ **Windows Explorer**.

■ Navigate to **C:\Program Files\Movie Maker\1033**. (This path will vary if you installed Windows Movie Maker on a different drive or renamed the folder.)

■ Choose **File** ➤ **New** ➤ **Folder**.

■ Rename the new folder to **AddOnTFX**. You can rename a new folder by typing a name and then pressing **Enter**. If you deselect the folder prior to renaming it, select the new folder, right-click, choose **Rename** from the shortcut menu, and then enter the new folder name.

■ Select the **50FastEFX.xml** file from the CD-ROM that accompanies this book and copy it into the new folder (see **Figure 25.7**).

STEP 2: BEGIN A NEW PROJECT

- Launch Windows Movie Maker and choose **File ➤ New Project**.
- Choose **File ➤ Import Into Collections**. Navigate to the CD-ROM that accompanies this book, select **WinClip046.wmv**, **WinClip047.wmv**, **WinClip048.wmv**, and **WinClip049.wmv**.
- Click **Import,** and Windows Movie Maker creates a new collection for each clip.
- Click the **Show Storyboard** button and arrange the clips in numerical order.
- Click the first clip (**WinClip046.wmv**) to display it in the Preview pane (see **Figure 25.8**). The clip is definitely of a 1950s-era diner, but it looks too modern and cutting edge through the lens of a digital camcorder. You'll fix that by applying the filters we've created for you.

STEP 3: ADD THE VIDEO EFFECTS

To mimic the flaws in a 1950s-style 8mm movie, we've created two effects, one of which duplicates the dust and lines you see on an old home movie and another that changes the color balance to give the movie that yellow-orange, slightly washed-out look home movies get after they've been run through a projector many times.

- Click the **Tasks** button and then choose **View video effects** from the Edit Movie section of the Tasks pane. You should see seven new effects labeled 50 Fast at the top of the Video Effects pane. If you do not see these new effects, save the project, close Windows Movie Maker, and then review Step 1 to make sure that you've added the file to the proper folder.
- Click the **50 Fast 8MM Film** effect and then drag it onto the Video Effects icon of the first clip (WinClip046.wmv).
- Click the **50 Fast 50s Film** effect and then drag it onto the Video Effects icon of the first clip (WinClip046.wmv).

After applying these two effects to the first clip, it definitely takes on the look of a 1950s home movie. Now all you need to do is copy the effect to the remaining clips.

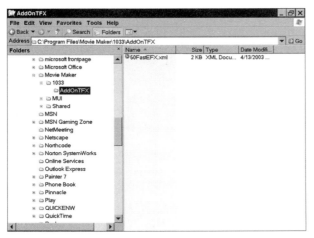

25.7

25.8

STEP 4: COPY THE EFFECTS TO OTHER CLIPS

After adding the custom effects to the movie clips, all you need to do is copy them to the other clips on the storyboard. Then you can take a step back in time and view a 1950s home movie on your PC.

- Click the **Video Effects** icon in the lower-left corner of the first clip (WinClip046.wmv).
- Right-click and then choose **Copy** from the shortcut menu.
- Click the **Video Effect**s icon in the lower-left corner of the second clip (WinClip047.wmv).
- Right-click and then choose **Paste** from the shortcut menu.
- Paste the video effects to the remaining clips, making sure you click the **Video Effects** icon before choosing the **Paste** command.

TRANSFORM 8MM MOVIES TO DIGITAL VIDEO

If you or a relative has a shoebox of old 8mm movies, you can have them converted to digital format and then edit them within your computer. You can locate several companies on the Internet that will clean your old 8mm movies and then capture them to MiniDV tapes, or perhaps you can find a company in your hometown. After your movies are transferred to MiniDV tapes, capture them into your computer and you can edit them by using the techniques from this book. After compiling the movies into digital format, burn them to a DVD disc and share them with your family. The DVDs can be enjoyed for generations to come; long after the 8mm tapes become too brittle to run through an antique projector.

- Click the **Play Storyboard** button. Presto — it's yesterday once more (see **Figure 25.9**)!

TIP

If you've worked with XML files before, and you'd like to take a crack at creating your own effects and transitions, log on to the Internet and point your Web browser to the following URL where you'll find detailed information on creating new Windows Movie Maker video effects: `http://msdn.microsoft.com/library/default.asp? url=/library/en-us/dnwmt/html/moviemakersfx.asp?frame=true&hidetoc=true.`

25.9

SOFTENING FOCUS FOR A GLAMOROUS LOOK

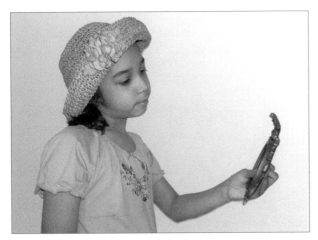

26.1

26.2

ABOUT THE VIDEO

The video was shot inside a photo studio using professional studio lighting. The camcorder used in this technique was a Canon GL-2 perched atop a Bogen fluid head tripod. The camcorder was set to auto exposure and manual focus was used. The video was then captured in iMovie and trimmed in iMovie and Windows Movie Maker.

Glamour photographers are famous for using soft focus to give their subjects a "dreamy" look, as shown in **Figure 26.2.** The optics of old-fashioned video equipment produced a dreamy, slightly out-of-focus effect as well. If you shoot some video and the sharp focus of your camcorder's lens is less than flattering to your subject, or you want to give your subject a more glamorous look, you can do so in iMovie and Windows Movie Maker with a little help from video effects. You can also use this technique to make your subject appear younger by giving him a digital facelift.

iMOVIE

The Soft Focus effect in iMovie offers a few different settings, which can work perfectly to achieve that ethereal, yesteryear effect. Here, you are going to apply this effect to some footage, which portrays a turn-of-the-century girl gazing into a mirror.

STEP 1: START A NEW PROJECT

First, you organize the clips on the Movie Track.

- Begin a new project and save the project on your hard drive.
- Choose **File ➤ Import** from the menu, navigate to the CD-ROM, and select the clips **MacClip051.mov** and **MacClip052.mov**.
- Drag the clips from the Shelf into the Movie Track.

STEP 2: ADJUST AND APPLY THE EFFECT

This effect is quite easy to apply. The trick to a successful result is adjusting the parameters of the effect the right way.

- While holding down the **Shift** key, click all the clips in the Clip Viewer to select them.
- Click the **Effects** tab. In the Effects list, click **Soft Focus**. When you do so, note that in the thumbnail preview, the slide sample appears to blur and glow.
- At the bottom of the Effects list are three parameters you can adjust for the Soft Focus effect. These include Softness, Amount, and Glow. Drag the **Softness** slider approximately to the middle of the slider. Drag the **Amount** Slider three quarters of the way to the right, toward the Lots setting. Drag the **Glow** slider closer to the None setting (see **Figure 26.3**). Notice that the glow part of the effect almost acts as a strong fill light, creating a radial illumination to one side of the subject.

- When you are satisfied with the adjustment, click the **Apply** button in the Effects pane. Press the **Home** key and then the **spacebar** to see the effect in action.

> **TIP**
>
> Each time you drag an adjustment slider or click the effect again, a thumbnail preview appears in the Effects window.

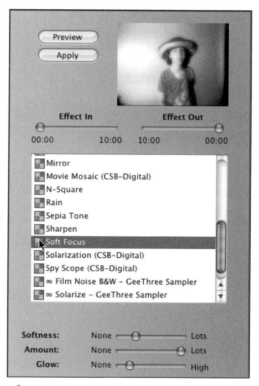

26.3

The Soft Focus technique works better on footage that tends to be on the darker side. In addition, if your output is QuickTime, make sure you use a high quality setting when compressing. Because the Soft Focus blurs your image a little, the overall image quality could be compromised with a low resolution compression setting.

WINDOWS MOVIE MAKER

Windows Movie Maker has a blur effect which works well on subjects such as moving cars, bikes, and athletes in motion. When you're trying to achieve a dreamy "yesteryear" look, however, the effect takes too much of the sharp edge off your subject. Therefore, we created a 50 Fast Soft Focus effect for Windows Movie Maker. If you haven't installed the 50 Fast Video Effects yet, refer to Step 1 of Technique 25 to learn how.

STEP 1: BEGIN A NEW PROJECT

- Launch Windows Movie Maker and choose **File ➤ New Project**.
- Choose **File ➤ Import Into Collections**. Navigate to the CD-ROM that accompanies this book, select **WinClip050.wmv** and **WinClip051.wmv**, and then click **Import**. Windows Movie Maker creates a new collection for each clip.
- Click the **Show Storyboard** button and arrange the clips in numerical order on the storyboard.
- Click the **Play Storyboard** button to preview the clips. Notice that the clips are in sharp focus. In the next step, you'll apply a video effect to transform the clips.

STEP 2: APPLY THE 50 FAST SOFT FOCUS EFFECT

Now that you have the clips arranged on the storyboard, it's time to soften the focus on the subject to achieve a softer look.

- Click the **Tasks** button and then choose **View video effects** from the Edit Movie section of the Tasks pane.
- Click the **50 Fast Soft Focus** effect and drag it onto the first clip (WinClip050.wmv).
- Click the **50 Fast Soft Focus** effect and drag it onto the second clip (WinClip051.wmv).
- Click the **Play Storyboard** button to preview the movie (see **Figure 26.4**).

26.4

CHAPTER 6

GOING HOLLYWOOD WITH YOUR MOVIES

If you've suffered through home movies that ramble on and on with uncut footage and no apparent direction, you would do your aspiring filmmaker friends a big favor by teaching them how to edit videos, or better yet, suggest they purchase a copy of this book. But sometimes even concise editing isn't enough to make the end product worth viewing. In this case, you need to add special effects. If you dissect the movies that attract the most attention at the box office, you know that the formula for success equals compelling footage plus a judicious sprinkling of special effects. Hollywood producers are famous for spicing up their movies with special effects, which is why we used Hollywood in the chapter title. In this chapter, you learn techniques to add Hollywood-style pizzazz to your productions. If your clips contain action, you can raise the excitement to a fever pitch by mastering Technique 27. If you have clips of a friend or loved one involved in a moment of quiet contemplation, you can flesh out the clips into a finished production by using the "dream sequence" technique. And if

you've ever wanted to turn back the hands of time, you'll love Technique 30. After you work through the techniques in this chapter, try adding your own creative touches to these techniques to put your stamp of originality on the finished clips.

MONTAGING ACTION CLIPS

27.1

27.2

ABOUT THE VIDEO

We shot these clips in many different locations in New York City and at a serene lake in Central Florida. We used a Canon XL-1, a Canon GL-2, and a Sony DCR-TRV27 to shoot the scenes, primarily on automatic exposure. A UV filter was used on the GL-2. Video was then captured in iMovie and Windows Movie Maker. Still shots of New York City were photographed with an Olympus Camedia 4-megapixel digital camera set on automatic exposure to catch the action. Flash was activated for underground subway shots. Still shots were then imported to iPhoto for review and exported in JPEG format. They were then edited on the Mac in Adobe Photoshop, and saved in the JPEG format. Lastly, the JPEG pictures were imported into iMovie.

A montage is a sequence of still images and video clips that tells a story in a compelling manner as the images and video clips are rapidly flashed before the audience in a sequence. In this technique, we bombard the timeline with a series of short clips and still pictures of New York City to evoke a sense of fast paced frenzy in the streets of Manhattan (see **Figure 27.1**). These actions clips are juxtaposed with a bucolic scene of water birds at dusk, on a lake (see **Figure 27.2**). The contrast between the frenetic and the serene engages the audience and leaves them wondering what will unfold next. Use this technique whenever you've got a collection of short clips with a lot of action. You can apply this technique to several clips to make a short video or use the technique on some short clips in a longer production when you need to change the pace.

iMOVIE

The montage clips you use in this technique are trimmed short, resulting in quick bursts of images that flash on the screen. Just when the viewer grasps the meaning of an image, another image replaces it. Each clip in this technique lasts less than a second, and a combination of editing procedures was used to prepare the clips for this technique. These include short captures, short trims, and changing the clip duration in some cases. Because the clips are already prepared for you, your first task is to import them into the Movie Track.

STEP 1: START A NEW PROJECT

First you organize the clips on the Movie Track.

- Begin a new project and save the project on your hard drive.
- Choose **File ➢ Import**, navigate to the Clips folder on the CD-ROM, and select the files **MacClip053.mov, still_1.jpg, MacClip054.mov, MacClip055.mov, still_2.jpg, MacClip056.mov, MacClip057.mov, still_3.jpg, MacClip058.mov, MacClip059.mov, still_4.jpg, MacClip060.mov,** and **MacClip061.mov**. Drag the clips from the Shelf into the Movie Track in the same order as you imported them, with the exception of MacClip061.mov. (You add this clip to the Movie Track in a later step.) Refer to **Figure 27.3** to see how the Movie Track should be set up. Note that in this figure, the Movie Track is in the Clip Viewer mode so the clips appear as pictures. For this action montage to be effective, you imported a significant number of clips and still pictures into the project. Amazingly enough, when you play the Movie Track, they fly by in a manner of seconds.
- At the bottom left of the Monitor window, click the **Timeline Viewer** button (clock icon). In order

to adjust the duration of the clips in the next step, you need to view the Movie Track in the Timeline view.

STEP 2: ADJUST THE DURATION OF CLIPS

Although most of the clips are immediately usable, you can augment the suggestion of time passing by changing the duration on some of the clips.

- Press the **Home** key and then the **spacebar** to play the movie clips at their normal speed and duration.
- Click the **MacClip057.mov** clip in the Movie Track. At the bottom of the window, which is now displayed in the Timeline Viewer mode, drag the **Duration** slider all the way to the left toward the hare icon to speed up the clip.
- Click the **MacClip058.mov** clip and drag the **Duration** slider two notches to the left to speed up the cab movement in the clip a bit.
- To slow down the last clip (**MacClip060.mov**), click it in the Movie Track, and then drag the **Duration** slider three notches to the right toward the turtle icon, as shown in **Figure 27.4.**

27.4

27.3

ADDING SOUND TO YOUR MONTAGE

The New York City montage doesn't need sound because the visuals create an imagined noise all their own. However, adding sound can help you create a certain mood. Playing this montage may remind you of a favorite tune of yours. In the next chapter, you will examine various techniques you can use to add sound to your busy creation.

STEP 3: DUPLICATE CLIPS

To make this montage last a little longer, you can duplicate some clips and paste them at the end of the Movie Track.

- While holding down the **Shift** key, click the first clip in the Timeline Viewer (**MacClip053.mov**) and the second-to-last clip (**still_4.jpg**). This action selects the two clips you clicked and all those in between them.
- From the menu, choose **Edit ➢ Copy** (see **Figure 27.5**). Position the Playhead after the last clip and choose **Edit ➢ Paste**. The copied clips appear on the Timeline Viewer.
- Drag the **MacClip062.mov** clip (which you haven't used yet) from the Shelf pane into the last position in the Movie Track.
- Click the last clip and then drag the **Duration** slider three notches to the right, toward the turtle icon, to slow down the last clip.
- Press the **Home** key and then the **spacebar** to play the movie from the beginning. Notice the contrast between the fast pace and the slow pace of clips in this montage. Changing the speed of clips in a montage helps create a visual tempo, almost like a silent beat of its own.

Edit	Advanced	Window	Help

Undo	⌘Z
Redo	⇧⌘Z
Cut	⌘X
Copy	⌘C
Paste	⌘V
Clear	
Select All	⌘A
Select None	⇧⌘A
Crop	⌘K
Split Video Clip at Playhead	⌘T
Create Still Frame	⇧⌘S

27.5

WINDOWS MOVIE MAKER

When you want to convey a sense of urgency or create viewer excitement, you can easily do so in Windows Movie Maker by either trimming or speeding up clips. When you use this technique on your own clips, you can alter the speed of short clips and then relieve viewer tension with a scenic clip with little action. This Windows Movie Maker technique contains no still images, because Windows Movie Maker has no provision to pan and or zoom images. When you use this technique on your own footage, you can experiment by adding still images to add another dimension to the finished movie. You can achieve a pseudo-zoom with the Ease-In and Ease-Out effects.

STEP 1: CREATE A NEW PROJECT

- Launch Windows Movie Maker and choose **File ➤ New Project**.
- Choose **File ➤ Import Into Collections**. Navigate to the CD-ROM that accompanies this book and select the files **WinClip052.wmv, WinClip053.wmv, WinClip054.wmv, WinClip055.wmv, WinClip056.wmv, WinClip057.wmv, WinClip058.wmv,** and **WinClip059.wmv**.
- Click **Select**. Windows Movie Maker creates a collection for each clip.
- Click the **Show Storyboard** button.
- Drag all the clips to the storyboard in numerical order, with the exception of WinClip059.wmv. The first three slots of your storyboard should resemble **Figure 27.6**.

STEP 2: APPLY THE EFFECTS

When your goal is to create visual excitement by creating a montage of several short clips, you can raise the excitement level a notch or two by altering the speed of a few clips. In this example, you speed up two clips and slow down the last clip in the sequence to change the pace of the movie.

27.6

- Click the **Tasks** button and in the Edit Movie section, click **View video effects**.
- Click the **Speed Up, Double** effect and drag it to the fifth clip (WinClip056.wmv) on the storyboard.
- Click the **Speed Up, Double** effect and drag it to the sixth clip (WinClip057.wmv) on the storyboard.
- Click the **Slow Down, Half** effect and drag it to the seventh clip (WinClip058.wmv) on the storyboard.
- Click the **Play Storyboard** button to preview the movie (see **Figure 27.7**).

As you can see, the assembled clips with effects applied does a good job of conveying excitement as the first clips play and then relaxes viewers when the quixotic heron ponders what to catch for dinner. In the next step, you duplicate the action clips to pique viewer interest.

STEP 3: DUPLICATE THE CLIPS

- Click **WinClip052.wmv** on the storyboard; then, while holding down the **Shift** key, click the sixth clip, **WinClip057.wmv**.
- Choose **Edit ➤ Copy**, or if you prefer keyboard shortcuts, press **Ctrl + C**. Windows Movie Maker copies the selected clips to the clipboard.

TIP

When you hold down the Shift key you can select a range of clips by clicking the first and last clips you want to select.

- Click the eighth slot in the storyboard and then choose **Edit ➢ Paste** (or press **Ctrl+V**). Windows Movie Maker pastes the copied clips and applied effects to the storyboard.

STEP 4: ADD THE LAST CLIP

To finish the movie, you add another scenic clip and slow it down. This releases viewer tension and is a fitting end to an action sequence.

- In the Edit Movie section of the Movie Tasks pane, click **Show collections**.

- Click **WinClip059.wmv** and drag it to the next available slot in the storyboard.
- In the Edit Movie section of the Movie Tasks pane, click **View video effects**.
- Click **Slow Down, Half** and drag it onto the clip you just added to the storyboard.
- Click the **Play Storyboard** button to preview the movie (see **Figure 27.8**).

When you preview the finished movie, notice how the excitement rises with the frenetic New York City clips, wanes when the heron appears, increases when the duplicate clips play, and ends on a serene note as three ducks make a graceful landing on a calm lake.

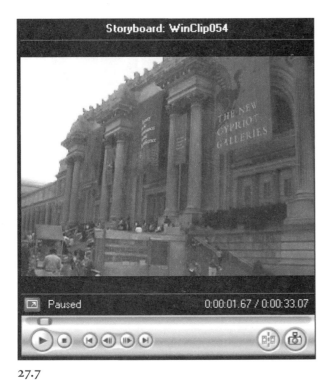

27.7

27.8

CREATING A DREAM SEQUENCE

28.1

28.2

ABOUT THE VIDEO

This video was created in a beautiful botanical garden on a sunny spring afternoon. We shot the footage with a Canon GL-2 using automatic exposure focus. It was then captured in iMovie and trimmed in iMovie and Windows Movie Maker.

Dream sequences are one of the most common techniques used in film and video. They are generally used to depict a surreal moment in time from the perspective of the character. Dream sequences can be silly or serious, depending on the genre of your story. Both iMovie and Windows Movie Maker give you tools you can use to create such an effect. In our video, we chose to add an element of comedy to the child's grueling homework routine (see **Figure 28.1**). The little girl imagines a place and time where she would rather be, and her dream sequence takes the viewer on a trip to that place, shown in **Figure 28.2**. You can use this on any clips where you've filmed a friend or relative relaxing or in deep contemplation. For the dream sequence, you can use just about any footage you can imagine. Your subject can be engaged in a dream of faraway places, or perhaps your dream sequence involves your subject reliving a scary experience that you concoct using Technique 31, which you'll find later in this chapter.

iMOVIE

When telling a story in a video, you need to think about things that might be obvious to you as the director, but not to your audience. In this technique, the little girl falls asleep on a table, providing the perfect entry to the dream she is about to have. To help communicate to the audience that you are depicting a dream, you will apply a Soft Focus effect along with a Ghost Trail. The Ghost Trail effect creates a transparent trail behind moving objects in the clip. When the girl is running, the Ghost Trail follows her movement for a brief time.

STEP 1: START A NEW PROJECT

First you organize the clips on the Movie Track.

- Begin a new project and save the project on your hard drive.
- Choose **File ➢ Import** from the menu, navigate to the Clips folder on the CD-ROM, and select the files **MacClip062.mov, MacClip063.mov, MacClip064.mov, MacClip065.mov, MacClip066.mov,** and **MacClip067.mov.** Drag the clips from the Shelf into the Movie Track in the same order as you imported them.

STEP 2: ADD SOFT FOCUS TO DREAM CLIPS

Soft Focus is very effective for suggesting an ethereal state in your video. You will preview, adjust, and add this effect to the clips in the dream, starting with the second clip.

- While holding down the **Shift** key, click **MacClip063.mov** and **MacClip066.mov** in the Movie Track. iMovie selects these two clips and the clip sequence in between them.

- Click the **Effects** tab to display the Effects pane. Scroll through the list to find the Soft Focus effect and select it.
- At the bottom of the Effects pane, drag the **Softness** slider so that it is almost all the way to the left, closer to the None setting. Drag the **Amount** slider so that it is in the middle of the slider. Drag the **Glow** slider close to the None setting, directly beneath the Softness slider button. The settings should appear as they do in **Figure 28.3**

STEP 3: ADD GHOST TRAIL TO DREAM CLIPS

With some effects in iMovie, you can add more than one to a single clip. In this step, you add a Ghost Trail effect to a couple of the clips in the dream sequence to make the clip look as if a ghostly trail follows any movement in the clip. It adds a bit of a surreal feeling to the dream.

- While holding down the **Shift** key, click the **MacClip063.mov** and **MacClip064.mov** clips in the Movie Track.
- Make certain that the Effects pane is displayed, and in the Effects list, scroll through and select the **Ghost Trails** effect (see **Figure 28.4**). A sample of the effect appears in the top right thumbnail preview. At the bottom of the Effects pane, you can adjust the Trail, Steps, and Opacity of the effect.
- Drag the **Trail** and the **Steps** sliders almost all the way to the right, toward the Long and Large settings.

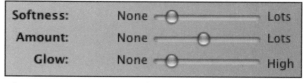

28.3

■ Drag the **Opacity** slider to the middle. The settings should look like those in **Figure 28.4**.

■ After the effects render, press the **Home** key and then the **Spacebar** to play the Movie Track. The combination of the two effects on the middle clips gives the footage a heavenly, dreamlike quality.

To finish off this short dream segment, in the next step you apply a couple of transitions to imply that the girl is gradually falling asleep and gradually awakening.

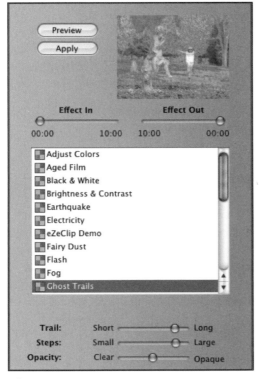

28.4

STEP 4: ADD TRANSITIONS BETWEEN CLIPS

Two perfect transitions to begin and end a dream sequence with are the Wash In and Wash Out effects. In this step, you use the Wash In and Wash Out effects together, in between the first and second clips. Then you repeat this process on the last two clips using both transitions together. The Wash transitions appear smoother in between clips (they generally are used at the beginning and end of a movie) if you use both the Wash In and Wash Out butted up against each other. The girl appears to softly fall into her dream and softly awake from it. To finish the movie off, you'll apply a Cross Dissolve in between the other dream clips.

■ Click the **Trans** tab at the bottom of the Pane window to access the Transitions pane.

■ Scroll to the transition named Wash Out. Drag the transition in between the first two clips. Drag a **Wash In** transition to the left of the Wash Out transition.

■ Click and drag a **Wash In** transition in between the last two clips in the Movie Track. To the right of this transition, drag a **Wash Out** transition.

■ In the **Transitions** list, scroll to the Cross Dissolve transition. Drag a copy of this in between the second and third clips, the third and fourth clips, and the fourth and fifth clips in the Movie Track. The Movie Track should now resemble the Movie Track in **Figure 28.5**.

After the transitions render, press the **Home** key and then the **spacebar** to play the movie. You have now created a full-fledged dream effect with the help of multiple transitions playing softly on one another.

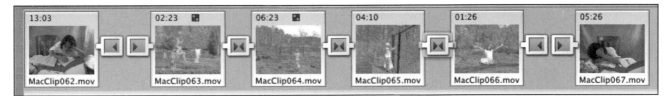

28.5

EDITING IN QUICKTIME PRO

If you want to expand the capabilities of iMovie, it's definitely worth investing in the QuickTime Pro update. QuickTime Pro enables you to finesse iMovies you export in QuickTime format. You can create some pretty sophisticated techniques, such as putting movies within your movies, masking effects, alpha channels, titles, and all sorts of other sophisticated effects generally associated with higher-end applications. To get QuickTime Pro, launch your QuickTime Player and in the menu, choose **QuickTime Player** ➢ **Preferences** ➢ **Registration**. In the dialog box, click the Online Registration button to connect your computer to the Apple site from which you can download the upgrade to your current QuickTime Player. It will add all sorts of additional features to your QuickTime Player utility. As of this writing, the Pro upgrade (from the free Player that shipped with your Mac) costs $29.95.

WINDOWS MOVIE MAKER

If you've ever been working away and all of a sudden a thought pops into your head and you drift off into La-La land, you've experienced real-time what you're going to digitally reproduce here. When you're having a good daydream, you're oblivious to the world around you, quite often blocking off all ambient sounds until you're wakened from your reverie with a sharp tap on the shoulder. You can't digitally reproduce the sharp tap on the shoulder — at least not yet — but you can do the next best thing with Windows Movie Maker effects we've created for you.

STEP 1: CREATE A NEW PROJECT

If you get a spark of creative energy after shooting some footage of a friend or loved one gazing off into the distance, you can put this technique to use to turn the footage into something special. After you capture the footage to your PC and preview the clips in Windows Movie Maker, put on your moviemaker maven director's cap, and get to work.

- Launch Windows Movie Maker and choose **File** ➢ **New Project**.
- Choose **File** ➢ **Import Into Collections**. Navigate to the CD-ROM that accompanies this book and select the files **WinClip060.wmv**, **WinClip061.wmv**, **WinClip062.wmv**, **WinClip063.wmv**, **WinClip064.wmv**, and **WinClip065.wmv**.
- Click **Import**. Windows Movie Maker creates a collection for each clip.
- Click the **Show Storyboard** button if you're currently working in timeline mode.
- Arrange the clips on the storyboard in numerical order.

STEP 2: APPLY THE EFFECTS

When moviemakers create dream sequences, they apply filters to the clips that make it appear as though the scene was being viewed through a haze or fog, thus suggesting a dreamlike state. Windows Movie Maker doesn't have any filters that simulate this, so we created a custom effect for this technique. If you haven't loaded the 50 Fast Effects into Windows Movie Maker, read Technique 25 for more information.

- Click the **Tasks** button.
- In the Movie Editing section, click **View video effects**. Windows Movie Maker displays the available effects.
- Click the **Fade Out, To White** effect and drag it onto the first clip (WinClip060.wmv).
- Click the **Fade In, From White** effect and drag it onto the last clip (WinClip065.wmv).
- Click the **50 Fast Soft Focus** effect and drag it onto the second clip (WinClip061.wmv).

■ Click the **50 Fast Ethereal Glow** effect and drag it onto the second clip (WinClip061.wmv). Windows Movie Maker updates the Preview pane to reflect the effects you've applied (see **Figure 28.6**).

Notice the soft glow around the young girl in **Figure 28.6**. You see this type of dreamy look in Hollywood movies. Now all you need to do is apply the same effects to the rest of the dream sequence clips.

STEP 3: COPY THE EFFECTS

To complete the dream sequence technique, you need to apply the same effects to the remaining clips of the girl's dream. You could fine-tune the movie by applying transitions between clips. However, you may notice that a lot of Hollywood movies with special effects just cut straight from one scene to the next.

Sometimes less is more, as in the case of the dream sequence technique.

■ Click the **Video Effects** icon (a blue star when effects have been applied to a clip) on the second clip (WinClip061.wmv), right-click, and then choose Copy from the shortcut menu.

■ Click the **Video Effects** icon (a gray star when no effects have been applied to a clip) on the third clip (WinClip062.wmv), right-click, and then choose Paste from the shortcut menu.

■ Follow the preceding instruction to paste the copied video effects to the fourth clip (WinClip063.wmv).

■ Click the **Play Storyboard** button to preview the movie. As the movie plays, notice how nicely the technique adds a dreamy glow around the young girl as she finishes her dream (see **Figure 28.7**).

28.6

28.7

CREATING A PSYCHEDELIC TIE-DYE EFFECT

29.1

29.2

We shot this video with a Sony DCR-TRV11, using the zoom function and automatic settings. We shot the footage on a fine spring day in New Jersey during late afternoon — which, by the way, is a wonderful time to shoot your movies because the sun dapples everything with a golden hue as opposed to the harsh midday sun. Early to mid-morning also offers excellent lighting. The footage was then captured in iMovie and trimmed in iMovie and Windows Movie Maker.

The 1960s was a very colorful decade in more ways than one. Some of you may remember lava lamps and tie-dyed t-shirts. In the Sixties, rock bands wore colorful tie-dyed t-shirts and used all sorts of abstract bleeding color effects to create primitive versions of today's music videos. If you're a card-carrying ex-flower child or your parents are children of the Sixties, you can rekindle that spirit with your digital videos. With the spirit of the Sixties in mind, you can achieve an awesome psychedelic effect by adjusting the color on clips. After you work through this technique, examine some of your own footage for candidates for this effect. Scenes with a wash of colorful flowers (see **Figure 29.1**) and perhaps night scenes with glowing sodium vapor lights are perfect clips on which to apply the technique. **Figure 29.2** shows the result of applying this technique on floral footage.

iMOVIE

The Brightness and Contrast effect can be used to achieve many different color and brightness-related effects. In this technique, you use Brightness and Contrast to eliminate midtone colors, thereby reducing the levels of color in the clips. The only colors that remain are harsh saturated "psychedelic" colors, reminiscent of the '60s. To top off this psychedelic technique, you add a Fairy Dust effect on the last clip to suggest something mystical is taking place in a mundane scene.

STEP 1: START A NEW PROJECT

First you organize the clips on the Movie Track.

- Begin a new project and save the project on your hard drive.
- Choose **File ➤ Import** from the menu, navigate to the Clips folder on the CD-ROM, and select the files **MacClip068.mov**, **MacClip069.mov**, and **MacClip070.mov**. Drag the clips from the Shelf to the Movie Track in the same order as you imported them.

STEP 2: APPLY EFFECTS TO CLIPS

Now you add the Brightness & Contrast effect and adjust the settings to change the color levels, resulting in psychedelic colors.

- Select all clips (**Shift+click**) in the Movie Track and click the **Effects** tab to display the Effects pane.
- In the Effects list, click **Brightness & Contrast**. At the bottom of the pane, you can adjust the brightness and contrast to achieve a multitude of different results on your output.
- Drag the **Brightness** slider to the middle of the slider. Drag the **Contrast** slider all the way to the

right toward High (see **Figure 29.3**). Check the thumbnail preview to see the results of your adjustments.

- This will create an extreme contrast in colors on the clip.
- When you are satisfied with the results, click the **Apply** button. The effect then renders on all three clips.
- Click the last clip in the Movie Track. To add an amusing twist to the psychedelic effect, in the Effects list, click **Fairy Dust**. As you can see in the thumbnail preview, a twinkling light travels from the bottom left of the thumbnail to the top right (see **Figure 29.4**). Click the **Apply** button to apply this effect.

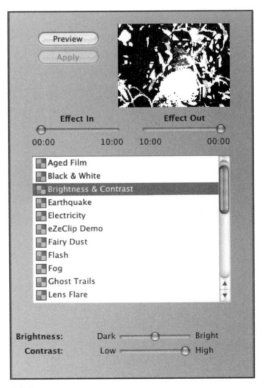

29.3

TIP

You can also change the settings of the Fairy Dust effect. At the bottom of the Effects pane, you can adjust the Direction and the Trail (length) of the fairy dust trail via two adjustment sliders. To make these adjustments, simply drag the sliders and check out the results in the preview thumbnail.

STEP 3: APPLY TRANSITIONS

To make the clips fold into one another softly, you now add a transition in between clips.

■ Click the first clip in the Movie Track and then click the **Trans** tab to display the Transitions pane. Click **Overlap** in the Transitions list. This

transition overlaps the first clip as the movie cuts to the next clip. For a brief moment, the last frame on the first clip pauses and fades out for a very dramatic effect. Check out the effect in the thumbnail preview.

■ Drag the **Speed** slider under the thumbnail preview to a setting of 2 seconds, as shown in **Figure 29.5**.

■ Click and drag the **Overlap** transition in between the first and the second clips and also in between

TIP

If you want to play back the movie in full screen mode, after you rewind the movie, click the **Play Movie Full Screen** button at the bottom of the Monitor window.

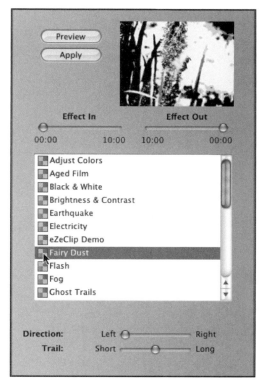

29.4

29.5

the second and third clips. When the transitions are finished rendering, press the **Home** key and then the **spacebar** to play back and see the results of the transitions. Now you apply the effects.

WINDOWS MOVIE MAKER

If you've got some clips of colorful scenery or wildlife, such as the flowers, butterfly, and bee in these clips, you can use this technique to create a compelling, eye-popping production. When you consider your own clips for use with this technique, select clips with vibrant colors from every spectrum of the rainbow. Colorful sunsets can be turned into something quite abstract and surreal with this technique. This technique does not work as well on clips with muted colors.

STEP 1: CREATE A NEW PROJECT

When you begin any new project, the first step is to choose your assets and arrange them on the timeline or storyboard.

- Launch Windows Movie Maker and choose **File ➢ New Project**.
- Choose **File ➢ Import Into Collections**. Navigate to the CD ROM that accompanies this book, and select the following files: **WinClip066.wmv**, **WinClip067.wmv**, and

WinClip068.wmv, and then click **Import**. Windows Movie Maker creates a new collection for each clip.

- Click the **Show Storyboard** button if you're currently working in timeline mode.
- Arrange the clips on the storyboard in numerical order.
- Click the **Play Storyboard** button to preview the clips (see **Figure 29.6**).

29.6

The clips in this movie are colorful and easy on the eyes. With the application of an effect, you can change these clips into footage reminiscent of a light show at a '60s rock concert.

STEP 2: APPLY THE EFFECT

To "psychedelicize" the sample clips, you apply the Threshold effect. To add a little extra pop to the clips, you also increase the brightness. The Threshold effect exaggerates all the colors in a clip to which it is applied. You can use this technique on any clip that contains vibrant colors that you want to exaggerate.

- Click the **Tasks** button to access the Movie Tasks pane.
- In the Edit Movie section, click **View video effects**. Windows Movie Maker displays the available video effects.
- Click the **Threshold** effect and drag it onto the first (WinClip066.wmv), second (WinClip067.wmv), and third (WinClip068.wmv) clips.
- Click the **Brightness** effect and drag it onto the first (WinClip066.wmv), second (WinClip067. wmv), and third (WinClip068.wmv) clips.

- Click the **Play Storyboard** button to preview the technique (see **Figure 29.7**).

As you can see, the effect really adds a lot of punch to the movie. The colors are vibrant, and the resulting video is quite surreal. Can you say Salvador Dali?

29.7

Technique 1 | Coping with Adverse Lighting

When you record subjects in heavy shade with your camcorder set to automatic exposure, subtle details such as facial features are often lost.

You can bring back the details of a shaded subject by manually adjusting your camcorder's exposure.

Technique 3 | Creating a Makeshift Dolly

Many common household items, such as the baby carriage used in this technique, can be used to create a makeshift dolly. Using a dolly while tracking an object allows you to smoothly capture the movement of the object.

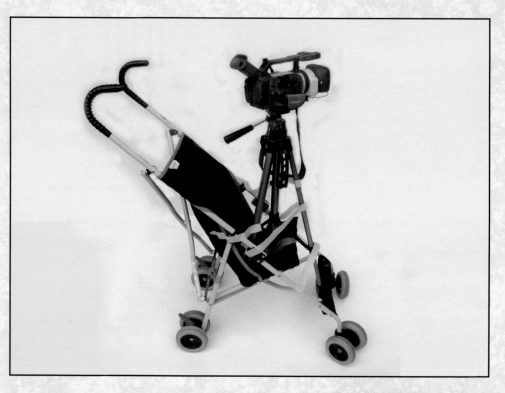

When you record scenes with diverse lighting using automatic exposure, areas of your scene may be too dark.

You can restore detail in dark areas, by brightening dark footage with an effect.

Technique 10 | Creating a Cross Fade

In this example, a cross fade is used to transition a clock scene into a fire scene. In the middle of the transition, the two scenes overlap for a moment, suggesting that time has passed.

When you create a movie with no transitions, one clip starts when the other stops, which can be visually jarring if the content of the clips differs.

You can add visual interest to your movies by using a transition such as the page curl between scenes.

Technique 12 | Wiping One Clip into Another

Wipe and Push transitions work well for movies attempting to evoke a sense of time speeding by. In this example, a close-up clip of the subway train coming to a stop forcefully pushes/wipes off the stage the clip of the subway train entering the station.

A straight cut from one scene to the next doesn't work well when your subject fades into the distance before the next scene begins.

You can direct viewer attention to beginning of the new scene by using a transition that highlights your distant subject.

Technique 14 | Changing Scenes with a Radial Wheel Transition

When a scene changes from bright daylight to night, your viewing audience may be momentarily confused.

With the effective use of a transition, your audience knows that a change is about to occur.

Technique 15 | Changing Scenes in Slow Motion

Some noteworthy action moments can pass by too quickly. By cutting a clip into several pieces, the segment with the action can be slowed down, allowing the viewer to savor every moment of the event.

Technique 16 | Posterizing a Movie

Colorful clouds and scenic lakes are great subjects for home movies, but sometimes even colorful scenes may seem a bit mundane.

You can add pop to colorful, but otherwise humdrum scenes and create artistic home movies by posterizing a clip.

In addition to movie clips, still photographs and digital pictures alone can be used to build an entire movie. In this example, we used special effects to zoom in and out of areas of pictures, making the still pictures appear as if they were animated.

Technique 19 | Antiquing a Movie

Digital camcorders faithfully record a scene capturing every subtle nuance and detail, which may not be appropriate for scenes like this.

You can make footage appear as though it were filmed 50 years ago when you use the "Antiquing a Movie" technique.

Viewer interest may wane at the end of a long scene.

You can pique viewer interest and anticipation for the next scene when you disintegrate a scene.

Technique 21 | Mirroring a Clip

Scenes with colorful wildflowers can add interest to your home movies.

You can pique viewer interest by placing two instances of a colorful clip in a movie and then mirroring the second instance.

This example captures a comedic moment caught on tape and turns it into an old-time slapstick movie. Speeding up silly footage lets viewers know that this movie is strictly for fun.

When you record interesting people in scenic places, you have excellent footage for a movie.

You can transform the footage into a "noir" classic by applying Technique 23.

Sleek diners often bring to mind the Fifties.

Effects were applied to these clips resulting in dust, scratches, and a bland yellow tint. These effects can be used to simulate footage from an old 16 mm home movie from this era.

Dream sequences can easily remove a subject from the mundane, and transport them into a surreal world. In this effect, the suggestion that the girl is dreaming is augmented with a transition that fades from white.

Multiple blur, glow, and trail effects are applied to clips, resulting in a dreamlike feeling.

Technique 29 | Creating a Psychedelic Tie-Dye Effect

Applying effects that reduce the levels of color on a clip brings out bold colors that eliminate midtones. In this technique, effects are applied that give the flower a posterized look. These effects are perfect for bringing out psychedelic colors in a subject.

Technique 30 | Creating an Ethereal Flashback Sequence

When you have no transitions between scenes, viewers assume the scenes play in the order in which you filmed them.

You can use the Ethereal Flashback technique to introduce a scene from the past.

Many independent filmmakers enjoy weaving spooky tales in their movies. To amplify the suspense in this narrative, multiple effects, such as a "spy scope" and an electrical bolt, are used.

Technique 32 | Creating a Painterly Movie

Scenes with colorful foliage are often subjects for an artist's canvas.

You can turn your footage into a moving work of art by using Technique 32.

Technique 33 | Controlling Clip Volume

When you record scenes with loud subjects such as racecars, the loud audio track often distracts viewers from the motion and your artistic composition.

You can direct your viewer's interest to the motion in your scene by reducing the volume of a loud audio track.

Technique 35 | Fading Sound in and Out

The sound volume in both iMovie and Movie Maker can be adjusted over a period of time during the editing process.

In this technique, the amplitude of the subway train is gradually lowered as the train pulls into the station.

When you record scenes in historic places, you experience the ambience and historical significance of the scene.

You can convey a sense of drama and excitement to your viewer when you narrate a movie.

Technique 40 | Superimposing a Title Over a Clip

Titles and subtitles can be added in both iMovie and Windows Movie Maker, and the properties of titles can easily be customized.

Titles are often displayed on top of clips, allowing viewers to read titles and not miss out on any action.

When your movie begins with dramatic footage, the effect might be ruined if you display title text over the beginning scene.

You can generate viewer interest by introducing your movie with an animated title over a solid background before the first clip plays.

Technique 42 | Adding a Layered Title

A colorful scene is an excellent way to begin a movie about your vacation.

You can add interest to the start of your vacation movie by adding a layered title over a colorful, but otherwise static scene.

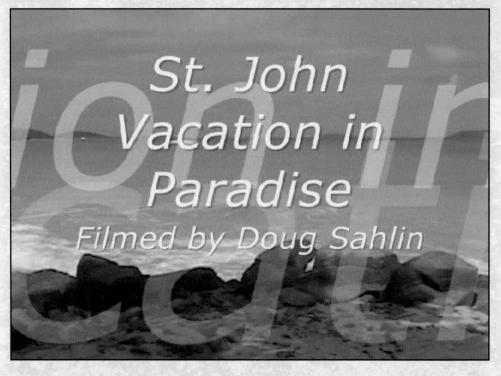

Colorful sporting events are wonderful subjects for video productions.

You can convey the enthusiasm you feel while recording an event by creating a title that wows your audience.

LATE EDITION

A DAY AT THE RACES

LOREM IPSUM

VOLUME 1, NUMBER 4

March 16, 2003

Lorem ipsum silliam covol gu monja. Mis cullum on tubo so quinwe marz romo. Cheekalu yom jarvus yallo. Rubu som ekoumn humo iroue ti.

Lorem ipsum silliam covol gu monja. Mis cullum on tubo so quinwe marz romo. Cheekalu yom jarvus yallo. Rubu som ekoumn humo iroue ti.

Lorem ipsum silliam covol gu monja. Mis cullum on tubo so quinwe marz romo. Cheekalu yom jarvus yallo. Rubu som ekoumn humo iroue ti.

Lorem ipsum silliam covol gu monja. Mis cullum on tubo so quinwe marz romo. Cheekalu yom jarvus yallo. Rubu som ekoumn humo iroue ti.

Lorem ipsum silliam covol gu monja. Mis cullum on tubo so quinwe marz romo. Cheekalu yom jarvus yallo. Rubu som ekoumn humo iroue ti.

Lorem ipsum silliam covol gu monja. Mis cullum on tubo so quinwe marz romo. Cheekalu yom jarvus yallo. Rubu som ekoumn humo iroue ti.

Lrem ipsum silliam covol gu monja. Mis cullum on tubo so quinwe marz romo. Cheekalu yom jarvus yallo. Rubu som ekoumn humo iroue ti.

Lorem ipsum silliam covol gu monja. Mis cullum on tubo so quinwe marz romo. Cheekalu yom jarvus yallo. Rubu som ekoumn humo iroue ti.

Lorem ipsum silliam covol gu monja. Mis cullum on tubo so quinwe marz romo. Cheekalu yom jarvus yallo. Rubu som ekoumn humo iroue ti.

Lorem ipsum silliam covol gu monja. Mis cullum on tubo so quinwe marz romo. Cheekalu yom jarvus yallo. Rubu som ekoumn humo iroue ti.

Lorem ipsum silliam covol gu monja. Mis cullum on tubo so quinwe marz romo. Cheekalu yom jarvus yallo. Rubu som ekoumn humo iroue ti.

Lorem ipsum silliam covol gu monja. Mis cullum on tubo so quinwe marz romo. Cheekalu yom jarvus yallo. Rubu som ekoumn humo iroue ti.

Lrem ipsum silliam covol gu monja. Mis cullum on tubo so quinwe marz romo. Cheekalu yom jarvus yallo. Rubu som ekoumn humo iroue ti.

Technique 45 | Ending Your Movie with Pizzazz

When you record colorful scenes and then edit them to create an interesting movie, you should end the production on a high note and take credit for your efforts.

Incorporating motion and graphical elements enables you to end your movie with pizzazz, as described in Technique 45.

Florida Restaurant Guide

Filmed By
Doug
Sahlin

CREATING AN ETHEREAL FLASHBACK SEQUENCE

30.1

30.2

ABOUT THE VIDEO

The clips for this technique were filmed at a triathlon in Clermont, Florida. The event started in the early morning when the ambient light dapples the landscape with golden hues and finished around noon when the overhead light isn't especially flattering. Sometimes events take place in poor lighting conditions, as in **Figure 30.1**, and you have to go with the flow and compose your shots artistically. The event was filmed with a Sony DCR-TRV 27 mounted on a Stitz tripod. The footage was captured to PC through an IEEE 1394 host controller.

Many filmmakers tell a story in the sequence in which the events occurred. However, you can add significant interest to your movies if you jump from point to point in the story's timeline. For example, you can begin your movie at the end of the story and flash back to tell the story. Hollywood filmmakers have used flashbacks for decades. To understand how this is done, you begin this technique by using footage of an athlete crossing the finish line after swimming 1.5 miles, biking 25 miles, and running 6.2 miles. After crossing the finishing line, the athlete relives the triathlon by flashing back to each segment of the event, as shown in **Figure 30.2**. After you learn this technique, you can use it to tell a story in reverse order. For example, when you are documenting a vacation, film family members as they get off the airplane or exit the car. This can be the jumping-off point for the flashback, employing footage from the places you visited in the next scene.

iMOVIE

Creatively altering the sequence of events in a narrative has become an increasingly popular form of storytelling in movies. It provides a welcome relief from the old, humdrum, linear storytelling style of old movies. In this technique, you create a movie that starts in the present tense and then flashes back and forth from past to present.

STEP 1: START A NEW PROJECT

First you organize the clips on the timeline.

- Begin a new project and save the project on your hard drive.
- Select **File ➢ Import** from the menu, navigate to the Clips folder on the CD-ROM, and select the files **MacClip071.mov, MacClip072.mov, MacClip073.mov, MacClip074.mov, MacClip075.mov, MacClip076.mov**, and **MacClip077.mov**.
- Drag the clips from the Shelf into the Movie Track in the same order as you imported them.
- In the Movie Track, change the view from Clip Viewer to Timeline Viewer by clicking the **clock** icon (see **Figure 30.3**). Adjusting the duration of clips can only be accomplished in the Timeline Viewer.
- Play the movie to see how it looks before adjusting the clips (press the **Home** key and then the **spacebar**). Your challenge is to create the illusion that the runner is sequentially rewinding the highlights of the event in his mind.

STEP 2: CHANGE THE DURATION OF CLIPS

The clips that show the athlete walking over the finish line currently have a duration of three seconds. To increase the drama of the moment, you can slow down this group of clips.

- Click **MacClip071.mov** and then drag the **Duration** slider two notches to the right, toward the turtle icon, as shown in **Figure 30.4**.
- Repeat the process of slowing down the duration of the next three clips, **MacClip073.mov, MacClip075.mov, MacClip077.mov**.
- Click **MacClip072** and then drag the **Duration** slider one notch to the left, toward the hare icon (see **Figure 30.5**).
- Repeat the process of speeding up the remaining triathlon clips using the same procedure as above.

Changing the duration helps imply a flashback, but to make the time tense change between clips more obvious to the viewer, you need to add some transitions.

STEP 3: APPLY TRANSITIONS

To facilitate the feeling of a flashback, you can use a Burst transition in concert with a Fade. Get the Burst transition from the GeeThree Sampler pack. You can download this sampler pack for free at `www.gee3.com`. The Burst works well for a subject thinking back on an event gone by. Because Fade Ins/Outs only transition to or from the clip they are associated with,

30.3

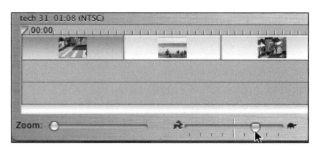

30.4

they generally are used at the beginning and end of movies. But because rules are meant to be broken, this example requires you to fade one clip into another simply because this flashback technique lends itself to a Fade In. Because this transition fades from a picture to black and then from black to a picture, it's a perfect effect for suggesting that someone is thinking. The

> **NOTE**
>
> iMovie does not ship with the Burst transition. You must download it from www.gee3.com. It is part of the Slick Sampler, which provides you with nine free sample effects. These effects are inclusive of a Drip, Radiator, Bar Doors, and different kinds of hearts. After you download the effect, follow the install directions.

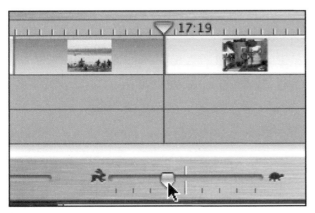

30.5

Fade In transition contrasts with the Cross Dissolve transition, which is more appropriate for moving along a scene to get the story told in a short amount of time.

- Click the first clip in the Movie Track and then click the **Trans** tab to display the Transitions pane.
- In the Transitions list, click **Burst-GeeThree Sampler**. Check out the results in the thumbnail preview and then drag the transition from the Transitions pane to in between the first and second clips in the Movie Track. The Burst transitions to the next clip with a small burst that gradually grows.
- Repeat the process, dragging the **Burst** in between the third and fourth and the fifth and sixth clips in the Movie Track.
- In the Transitions list, click the **Fade In** transition and drag it in between both the second and third clips and the fourth and fifth clips in the Movie Track. The Movie Track should resemble **Figure 30.6**.

> **TIP**
>
> When transitions appear in the Movie Track (in either Clip Viewer or Timeline Viewer mode), either a double or a single arrow appears on the icon. A double arrow represents a transition that affects the two clips between which it is sandwiched. A transition with a single arrow affects only one clip.

30.6

■ To give the movie a polished look, drag a **Fade In** transition before the first clip and a **Fade Out** transition at the tail of the last clip.

■ Play the movie (press **Home** and then the **spacebar**) to see the results of your efforts. Combining these techniques creates a pretty convincing flashback technique.

WINDOWS MOVIE MAKER

Even though the athlete began his recovery as soon as he crossed the finish line, the clip was rather short, because he had to move out of the way to make room for other athletes crossing the finish line. To cover each segment of the triathlon, the finishing line clip was divided into four segments, which will sandwich each leg of the event. If you've ever competed in an athletic event that tests your endurance, you know that time seems to stand still when you cross the finish line. To accentuate this, you slow down the athlete's finish line clips. You speed up the flashback segments as well as applying one of our 50 Fast effects to these clips.

STEP 1: CREATE A NEW PROJECT

■ Launch Windows Movie Maker and choose **File ➤ New Project**.

■ Choose **File ➤ Import Into Collections**. Navigate to the CD-ROM that accompanies this book and select the files **WinClip069.wmv, WinClip070.wmv, WinClip071.wmv, WinClip072.wmv, WinClip073.wmv, WinClip074.wmv,** and **WinClip075.wmv**.

■ Click **Import,** and Windows Movie Maker creates a new collection for each clip.

■ Click the **Show Storyboard** button if you're currently working in timeline mode.

■ Arrange the clips on the storyboard in numerical order.

■ Click the **Play Storyboard** button to preview the clips (see **Figure 30.7**).

When you initially preview a production, you'll have a good idea of what you need to do to create the desired impact on your viewing audience. In this case, use effects to make the transition between current time and the athlete's flashback more apparent.

STEP 2: APPLY THE EFFECTS TO THE ENDING CLIPS

When you apply effects to clips in Windows Movie Maker, you cannot apply the same effect to several

30.7

clips at once. When you use identical effects on multiple clips, however, you can copy effects from one clip and paste them to other clips one at a time.

- Click the **Tasks** button and in the Edit Movie section, click **View video effects**.
- Click the **Slow Down, Half** effect and drag it onto the first clip (WinClip069.wmv). Repeat this step to apply the effect a second time.
- Click the **Video Effects** icon in the lower-left corner of the first clip (WinClip069.wmv), right-click, and then choose Copy from the shortcut menu.
- Click the **Video Effect**s icon in the lower-left corner of the third clip (**WinClip071.wmv**), right-click, and then choose Paste from the shortcut menu. Paste the copied effects on the fifth clip (WinClip073.wmv) as well.

STEP 3: APPLY EFFECTS TO THE FLASHBACK CLIPS

When you create a flashback, you need to signify the passage of time, or otherwise alter the clips to signify to viewers that what they are viewing has occurred in the past. You can do this either with transitions or by applying effects to the clips. For this technique, we wanted the flashbacks to occur rapidly, and at the same time, appear slightly surreal. To achieve this, we created an effect that you've already added to Windows Movie Maker if you completed Technique 25 in Chapter 5. If you have not added the 50 Fast Effects to Windows Movie Maker, refer to step 1 of the Windows Movie Maker section of Technique 25.

- Drag the **50 Fast Eerie Yellow Glow** effect onto the second clip (WinClip070.wmv).
- Drag the **Speed Up, Double** effect onto the second clip (WinClip070.wmv).

- Click the **Video Effects** icon in the lower-left corner of the second clip (WinClip070.wmv), right-click, and then choose Copy from the shortcut menu.
- Click the **Video Effects** icon in the lower-left corner of the fourth clip (WinClip072.wmv), right-click, and then choose Paste from the shortcut menu.
- Paste the copied effects to the sixth clip (WinClip074.wmv). After pasting the effects to the clips, Windows Movie Maker updates the preview window, as shown in **Figure 30.8**.
- Click the **Play Storyboard** button to preview the technique.

When you use the flashback technique on your own clips, you can experiment with a combination of sound effects and transitions to signify the beginning of a flashback. For more information on adding sound effects to your movies, refer to Chapter 7.

30.8

CREATING SPOOKY MOVIES

31.1

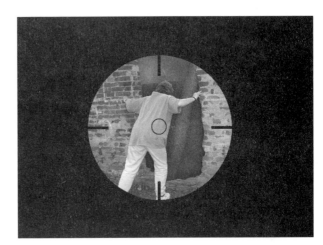

31.2

ABOUT THE VIDEO

Legend has it that the grounds and the mansion on which the scene shown in **Figure 31.1** was shot are haunted. The footage was shot with a Canon GL-2, set to auto focus, auto exposure, and captured in iMovie and trimmed in iMovie and Windows Movie Maker.

I f you've ever watched any of the low-budget movies created by independent filmmakers, you know that with the proper effects, they set the tone of the movie and imply impending horror without even showing the boogieman. When the footage you use for this effect was initially filmed, the intention was to create a scary scene. However, after the scene was captured and previewed, it looked more comical then scary. We attempted to change that with the judicious use of a couple of filters in iMovie and Windows Movie Maker (see **Figure 31.2**). The end result is this "Creating Spooky Movies" technique. You can use this technique on your own clips to make them scarier, for example, applying the technique to footage of a distant thunderstorm. You can also use this technique to convert mundane footage into something truly special.

iMOVIE

iMovie offers a myriad of effects that address many of the needs you will have as a moviemaker. However, sometimes you need to turn to third-party plug-ins to achieve a particular effect. For these clips, we used a third-party plug-in as well as an effect native to iMovie. On the first clip, we applied a Spy Scope effect from CSB Digital. The Spy Scope effect is part of the iPlugins2 pack offered by FXhome.com. Download the iPlugins2 pack from `www.FXhome.com/iplugins2` and install it before proceeding. Alternately, you can skip applying this effect and move on to the next. On the second clip, we employed the Electricity effect from iMovie. In the iMovie version of the haunted sequence, the order of the clips is the reverse of the Windows Movie Maker sequence simply because it was more effective this way in iMovie. As you can see from the movie sample on the CD-ROM, using this combination of effects can facilitate the creation of some very creepy footage.

STEP 1: START A NEW PROJECT

First you organize the clips on the Movie Track.

- Begin a new project and save the project on your hard drive.
- Choose **File** ➤ **Import** from the menu, navigate to the Clips folder on the CD-ROM, and select the files **MacClip078.mov** and **MacClip079.mov**.
- Drag the clips from the Shelf into the Movie Track in the same order as you imported them.

STEP 2: APPLY THE EFFECTS

You use a third-party plug-in for the scope effect (Spy Scope from CSB Digital), so make certain that you have downloaded and installed the third-party effects plug-ins from the CSB Digital website (`www.Fxhome.com/iplugins2`). Otherwise, this effect won't appear in your Effects list.

- Select **MacClip078.mov** and click the **Effects** tab. In the Effects pane, click the effect named **Spy Scope-CSB Digital**. Note that in the thumbnail preview, this effect creates a mask over the clip that resembles the viewfinder in a scope (see **Figure 31.3**). Click the **Apply** button to apply the effect to the first clip.
- Click **MacClip079.mov** and then, in the Effects pane, click the effect named **Electricity**. This effect creates a charge of electricity that originates in the center of the frame and points upwards as shown in **Figure 31.4**.
- Drag the **Rotate** slider button to the right toward CCW, as shown in **Figure 31.5**. In the

---

TIP

You can adjust the appearance of the Spy Scope at the bottom of the Effects pane by dragging the Scope Size and Crosshair slider buttons. Dragging them to the right increases the size of the scope and crosshair.

thumbnail preview, the electrical bolt appears to originate from the top northeast sky and penetrate the chest of the subject. Click the **Apply** button to apply the effect to this clip.

■ With the second clip still selected, click the **Flash** effect in the Effects list. As shown in the thumbnail preview, the Flash effect makes the electrical bolt appear as if it is sparking. At the bottom of the pane, drag the **Count** slider all the way to the left for one flash. Drag the **Brightness** slider three-quarters of the way toward Max to

TIP

If you want two bolts of electricity to zap a subject, simply apply the effect two times to a clip, and in the Electricity adjustments, change the rotation of each electrical bolt.

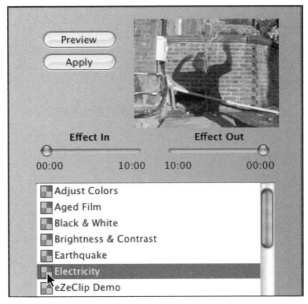

31.4

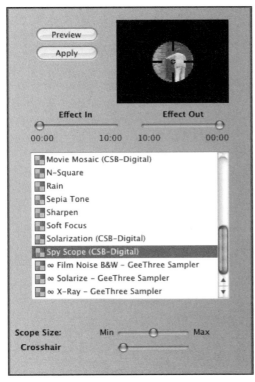

31.3

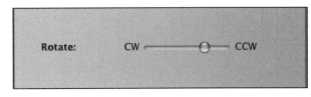

31.5

make the flash blinding. Lastly, drag the **Speed** slider button to the left toward Fast, so the flash happens quickly. See **Figure 31.6** for the suggested adjustments.

STEP 3: APPLY TRANSITIONS

To make the movie appear a little more finished, you will add a few transitions; one at the beginning, one at the end, and one in the middle of the movie to make the cuts from one scene to the next a little less rough.

- Click the **Trans** tab and in the Transitions list, select the Fade In transition. Drag it to the front of the Movie Track.
- Now, click the **Fade Out** transition and drag it to the end of the Movie Track.

- Click the **Cross Dissolve** transition and drag it in between the two clips. The Movie Track should resemble **Figure 31.7**.
- When the movie is finished rendering, press the **Home** key and the **spacebar** to play the movie. With the right footage, you can cast an ominous pall over a clip sequence.

> **TIP**
>
> To increase the sense of tension and suspense of your horror movie, try adding weird sound effects. iMovie ships with over 50 sound effects. Technique 37 explores the process of adding these effects. For a horror movie, you can use the Forboding, Suspense, Tire skids, or Footsteps sounds. In the sample movie provided on the CD for this technique, a spooky sound was added to the sound track. As such, there is no mistaking that this movie is scary.

31.6

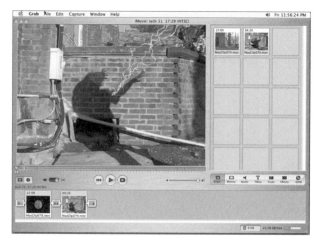

31.7

WINDOWS MOVIE MAKER

When you were a kid and saw things that glowed in the dark, you were probably frightened until you figured out what was glowing. And if you saw something that glowed during the day, you were even more frightened. Our attempts to use the available Windows Movie Maker video effects to get our character to glow in broad daylight proved unsuccessful, so we created our own effects. To successfully re-create this technique, you'll need to have the 50 Fast Effects installed in Windows Movie Maker. If you haven't already installed these, refer to Technique 25 for detailed installation instructions.

STEP 1: CREATE A NEW PROJECT

After you capture footage to Windows Movie Maker, you have a pretty good idea of what type of movie you can create. After you begin the project and arrange the clips in Windows Movie Maker, you have your first inkling of what you need to do to pull off the desired effect.

- Launch Windows Movie Maker and choose **File ➤ New Project**.
- Choose **File ➤ Import Into Collections**. Navigate to the CD-ROM that accompanies this book and then select the files **WinClip076.wmv** and **WinClip077.wmv**.
- Click **Import**, and Windows Movie Maker creates a collection for each clip.
- Click the **Show Storyboard** button if you're currently working in timeline mode.
- Arrange the clips on the storyboard in numerical order.
- Click the **Play Storyboard** button to preview the clips (see **Figure 31.8**).

As you preview the clips, you can see that our heroine made a valiant attempt to appear frightened, but the flailing hands don't seem natural, and the second scene. . . suffice to say, our actress won't be breaking any track records in the near future.

STEP 2: APPLY THE EFFECTS

When you edit your own videos, get in the habit of previewing the clips before adding any transitions or effects. After initially previewing these clips, we decided to subject our heroine to an evil spell from an unseen sorcerer that causes her to glow. To complete the effect, we sped up the clips.

- Select the first clip (WinClip076.wmv), right-click, and choose Video Effects from the shortcut menu. Windows Movie Maker displays the Video Effects dialog box.

31.8

- Select the **50 Fast Eerie Yellow Glow** effect and then click the **Add** button.
- Select the **Speed Up, Double** effect, click the **Add** button, and then click **OK** to exit the dialog box.
- Select the second clip (**WinClip077.wmv**), right-click, and choose **Video Effects** from the shortcut menu.
- Select the **50 Fast Edge Glow** effect and then click the **Add** button.
- Select the **Speed Up, Double** effect and then click the **Add** button. Windows Movie Maker adds the second effect to the clip (see **Figure 31.9**).
- Click **OK** to exit the Video Effects dialog box.

> **TIP**
>
> When working in the Video Effects dialog box, you can double-click a video effect to add it to a clip.

31.9

- Click **Play Storyboard,** and Windows Movie Maker plays the movie in the Preview pane (see **Figure 31.10**).

As you preview the movie, notice how the yellow glow makes it appear as though some evil spirit is causing the heroine to flail her hands in a valiant attempt to ward off evil. In the second scene, the evil sorcerer has had his way; the scenery and our heroine are all aglow as she flees for her life.

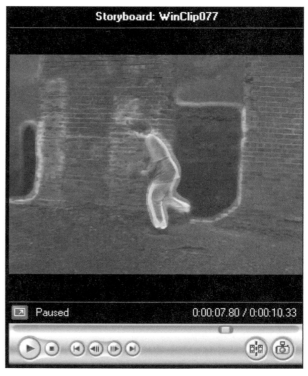

31.10

CREATING A PAINTERLY MOVIE

32.1

32.2

ABOUT THE VIDEO

The clips for this technique were filmed in the Henry B. Plant Park near the University of Tampa. The clips were filmed on a spring afternoon using a Sony DCR-TRV 27 in auto exposure mode. The clips were captured to PC through an IEEE 1394 hosting device (FireWire card) and trimmed in Windows Movie Maker.

When you capture and preview colorful footage like that shown in **Figure 32.1**, you can either let the footage stand on its own or turn your movie into something really special by adding effects to create a painterly movie. When you create a painterly movie, each frame looks like a work of art. iMovie and Windows Movie Maker have different effects to achieve this end. In fact, the authors modified one of the Windows Movie Maker effects to make the footage appear as though a master watercolor artist repainted each frame in the original clip (see **Figure 32.2**). Use this technique when your original footage is colorful, and you want to turn the edited movie into something truly special. When you master this technique, experiment by mixing the other available effects to achieve different painterly results.

32.3

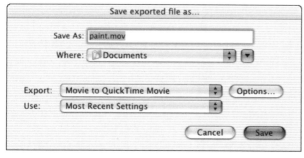

32.4

32.5

iMOVIE

Mac users often export their movies to QuickTime because QuickTime is the native video file format for the Mac platform. The good news for QuickTime users is that an Expert Settings option enables you to select from over 14 custom effects. These include such selections as Lens Flare, Blur, and Emboss, as well as many more. Each filter, as QuickTime calls them, has custom adjustment settings so the effect can be tweaked to look exactly the way you want. You can add these filters on top of any effects you may have added via iMovie. Unlike iMovie, where you can add multiple effects on clips in some cases, only one filter can be added to a movie via the QuickTime export process. In the iMovie version of this technique, you walk through the process of adding a QuickTime filter on export. Other QuickTime filters are also discussed in Chapter 5, Technique 24.

STEP 1: START A NEW PROJECT

First you organize the clips on the Movie Track.

- Begin a new project and save the project on your hard drive.
- Choose **File ➢ Import** from the menu, navigate to the Clips folder on the CD-ROM, and select the files **MacClip080.mov** and **MacClip081.mov**.
- Drag the clips from the Shelf into the Movie Track in the same order as you imported them. Your Movie Track and Monitor window should resemble **Figure 32.3**.

STEP 2: EXPORT THE MOVIE

Unlike other movies in previous techniques, this movie is a no-frills production with just two clips on the Movie Track. You apply the painterly effect, or filter, during the export process.

■ Choose **File ➤ Export** to activate the iMovie Export dialog box. Click **Export** and select **To QuickTime**. Click **Formats** and select **Expert Settings...** (see **Figure 32.4**). Then, click the **Export** button.

■ In the Save exported file as... dialog box, type a filename in the **Save As** text box. iMovie automatically assigns a filename, but you can customize it to your liking, as shown in **Figure 32.5**.

■ Click the **Save** button to open the Movie Settings dialog box (see **Figure 32.6**).

■ Click the **Filter** button. The Choose Video Filter dialog box appears. It contains many other settings related to exporting, such as movie size and

compression format, but in this technique we focus on the filters. For more information on exporting, see Chapter 9.

32.6

TIP

When you assign a filename in the **Save exported file as...** dialog box, in your naming convention, make certain you leave the **.mov** extension intact. This extension clearly defines the movie as a QuickTime file and will eliminate potential problems on multiple platform delivery.

EXPORTING IN QUICKTIME

When you export to QuickTime in iMovie, generally you would select a preset that would be determined by the final destination of the movie. For example, if you intended for your movie to be burned to CD-ROM, you would select a preset of CD-ROM. Other settings include e-mail, web, web streaming, and DV. You can also export for DVD in iMovie, but this function is performed using a different process (discussed in Chapter 9). Presets make all your decisions for you based on your preset selection. In the previous exercise, Expert Settings was selected as opposed to a preset. With Expert Settings, users must set their own compression scheme, file size, and color model. In the Mac sample movie for this technique, the file was exported in Sorenson Video 3 — which provides excellent quality and size ratio — and a file size of 320 x 240, which is half the size of a standard, full-screen QuickTime movie. See Chapter 9 for a more detailed discussion of the various export options.

■ Expand the Special Effects list by clicking the arrow associated with it, as shown in **Figure 32.7**. From the list, select Color Style. Three sliders appear in the right-hand side of the dialog box.

■ Drag the **Solarize Amount** slider to the right to 2. Leave the **Solarize Point** setting at 0. Drag the **Posterize Amount** slider to the right to a setting of 8. A thumbnail preview appears in the lower-left corner of the dialog box to show you what your adjustments look like.

■ When you are done, click the **OK** button. Doing this takes you back to the Movie Settings dialog box. Click the **OK** button to return to the Save exported file as... dialog box. Click **Save**, and iMovie exports the file. During export, a status bar appears in the iMovie workspace. When export is done, the bar disappears.

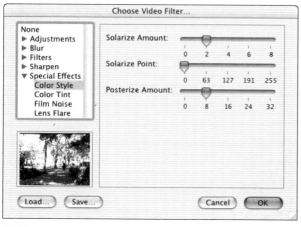

32.7

■ After the file has exported, navigate to the folder in which you saved the movie. Double-click the icon to display a QuickTime window and play the movie. The filter has changed the appearance of the movie beyond the iMovie dialog box.

WINDOWS MOVIE MAKER

The Windows Movie Maker Watercolor video effect intrigued us when we began laying out the groundwork for this technique. The effect worked well on many clips, but when we tried it on video clips with a lot of foliage, the effect was over the top, so we created a subtler effect for you to add to your toolkit. If you haven't already installed the 50 Fast Video Effects, refer to Technique 25 for detailed installation instructions.

STEP 1: CREATE A NEW PROJECT

■ Launch Windows Movie Maker and choose **File ➤ New Project**.

■ Choose **File ➤ Import Into Collections**. Navigate to the CD-ROM that accompanies this book, select **WinClip078.wmv** and **WinClip079.wmv**, and then click **Import**. Windows Movie Maker creates a collection for each clip.

■ Click the **Show Storyboard** button if you're currently working in timeline mode.

■ Arrange the clips on the storyboard in numerical order.

- Click the **Play Storyboard** button to preview the movie without the effects (see **Figure 32.8**).

When you preview the clips, notice the wonderful mix of green colors in the first clip and then the cerulean blue of the skies in the second clip. Scenes like these are often chosen as subjects for paintings.

STEP 2: APPLY THE VIDEO EFFECTS

To convert these clips to moving watercolor paintings, you apply our 50 Fast Watercolor Brush video effect. The Windows Movie Maker Watercolor effect is the basis for our effect, but ours is just a bit more subtle so that some of the beauty of the original footage shines through.

- Click the **Tasks** button to display the Movie Tasks pane.
- Click the **View Video Effects** button in the Movie Editing section of the Movie Tasks pane.

- Click the **50 Fast Watercolor Brush** video effect and drag it onto the first clip (WinClip078.wmv).
- Click and drag the **50 Fast Watercolor Brush** video effect onto the second clip (WinClip079.wmv).
- Click the **Play Storyboard** button, and Windows Movie Maker plays the clips in the Preview pane (see **Figure 32.9**).

TIP

If you've read this chapter from the start, you know that all of the techniques have used video effects. When you start using these techniques on your own footage, remember that you can add another level of interest by adding transitions between scenes. If you're in a creative mood, try applying a transition between these clips before previewing the technique.

32.8

32.9

CHAPTER 7

ADDING SOUND TO YOUR MOVIES

When you record scenes using a digital camcorder, you record audio as well as video. If you've recorded a few tapes with your digital camcorder, you know that the sound is sometimes distorted, and at other times, the sound is too loud. And then there are other situations where your movie would be better served with the addition of some nice background music. Adding sound effects is another way to take your productions to the next level. In this chapter, you'll learn to compensate for some of the deficiencies in the audio tracks of your home movies. You'll learn to set the volume of an audio track, mute the audio track as well as fade in and fade out an audio track. In Technique 36, you learn to extract music from a royalty-free music CD and use it as a soundtrack. In Technique 37, you get a sound effects baptism by fire when you apply multiple sound effects to one of our sample movies. You also learn to add "alien" sound effects to a movie for comic effect. If you're a historian and you like to add all the details of an event to a movie, you'll find Technique 39 of interest as we show you how to add narration to your movies.

CONTROLLING CLIP VOLUME

33.1

33.2

ABOUT THE VIDEO

The footage for this technique shows a gaggle of racecars approaching Turn 3 during the 2003 12 Hours of Sebring (see **Figure 33.2**). The video was filmed with a Sony DCR TVR 27 and the audio was captured using the camcorder's built-in microphone. The video and audio were captured to PC through an IEEE 1394 FireWire card.

If you've ever filmed an event with loud sounds, such as an auto race (see **Figure 33.1**), you know that the resulting audio track may distract from your footage, especially if members of your viewing audience have sensitive hearing. Most devices on which your movies will be viewed have some method for controlling the volume. However, you don't want your viewers rushing for the volume control if the audio is extremely loud. When you're assembling your movie, during your initial preview you'll know whether or not the clips are too loud. Sometimes you'll only need to adjust the volume on one or two clips. Alternatively, you may decrease the volume of all clips, for example, when you augment the movie with an audio soundtrack. You can easily control the volume of individual clips in both iMovie and Windows Movie Maker as shown in this technique.

iMOVIE

STEP 1: CREATE A NEW PROJECT

The thunder of cars racing can result in sound over-
load in your movie. Such is the case in the racing clip
you use in this technique. The car noise is way too
loud, to the point of distracting from the actual video
image. To remedy the excessive noise problem, you
lower the *amplitude,* or volume, of the clip. When you
lower the volume, the noise from the race becomes
more like background sound, enabling you to add a
narration, or an additional sound track that blends in
more pleasantly with the racecar noise.

- Begin a new project and save the project on
  your hard drive.
- Choose **File ➢ Import** from the menu, navigate
  to the CD-ROM, and select **MacClip082.mov**.
- Drag the clip into the Movie Track.
- Display the Movie Track in Timeline Viewer
  mode by clicking on the **Timeline** (clock) icon. In
  this view, additional audio tools, which allow you
  to adjust the volume level on a clip, become available (see **Figure 33.3**).

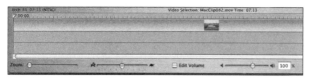

33.3

STEP 2: ADJUST THE CLIP'S VOLUME

In iMovie, you can adjust the volume of a clip in one
of two ways. You can use the **Volume Slider** at the
bottom of the Timeline view in the Movie Track, or
you can use **Volume Bars** on the audio clips. The
Volume Bars become visible when you click the **Edit
Volume** button at the bottom of the Timeline view in
the Movie Track. In this step, you adjust the volume
using the **Volume Slider**. In Technique 35, you get a
chance to experiment with the volume sliders.

- Select the clip in the Movie Track and then
  locate the **Volume Slider** at the bottom of the
  Movie Track. Dragging the button on the slider to
  the left lowers the amplitude of the sound and
  dragging the button to the right increases the
  amplitude on a selected clip. With the clips

TIP

In OS X, you can't see the audio tools at the bottom of the Movie Track in Timeline view when you
position your Dock at the bottom of your screen.
You can move your Dock to a different part of the
desktop (**Apple ➢ Dock ➢ Position on Left/
Right/Bottom**) or hide the Dock (**Apple ➢
Dock ➢ Turn Hiding On**). If you hide the Dock
and want to access it while hidden, simply position your pointer in the vicinity of the Dock's hidden location and it temporarily appears.

selected, drag the button to the left, so the volume percentage is at 30 percent (**Figure 33.4**).

■ Press the **Home** key and the **spacebar** to play the movie. Note that the volume has been lowered considerably. Keep in mind that lowering or raising the volume in iMovie is only relative to the volume settings on your computer. In other words, if your viewer's volume is turned way down, your clip, in turn, may seem inaudible on their system.

TIP

To change the volume on multiple clips in the Timeline, press the **Shift** key, click two or more clips to select them, and then adjust the **Volume Slider** accordingly.

TIP

You can tell a lot about a sound by looking at its waveform. A loud sound contains a tall waveform, and a soft sound contains a relatively short waveform. A waveform with high peaks and low valleys indicates that the audio clip contains very loud and very soft sounds, and a waveform with uniform height indicates that the clip volume is uniform.

33.4

WINDOWS MOVIE MAKER
STEP 1: CREATE A NEW PROJECT

When you capture your own video clips with Windows Movie Maker, you capture both the audio and video, unless, of course, you use an analog capture card and disable the hookup from your camcorder to your computer's sound card. Windows Movie Maker creates a timeline for captured video and audio for each new clip you add to a project. When you work with video effects and transitions, it's easier to do so in storyboard mode. However, the audio track is only visible when you work with the timeline.

■ Launch Windows Movie Maker and choose **File ➤ New Project**.
■ Choose **File ➤ Import Into Collections**. Navigate to the CD-ROM that accompanies this book, select **WinClip080.wmv** and then click **Import**. Windows Movie Maker creates a new collection for the clip.
■ Click the **Show Timeline** button if you're currently working in storyboard mode.
■ Drag the clip onto the timeline. The clip's waveform appears on the audio timeline (see **Figure 33.5**).

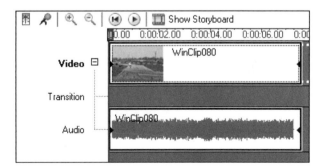

33.5

■ Click the **Play Timeline** button. Gentlemen, start your engines. As you preview the clip, you notice the engines are quite loud and can detract from a soundtrack or narration that you may add to your production.

STEP 2: MODIFY THE VOLUME

When you have a video clip with a very loud audio track, lowering the volume to an acceptable level is best. Windows Movie Maker makes it possible for you to change the volume of an audio track by dragging a slider.

TIP

To boost the volume of an audio track, select the track, open the Audio Clip Volume dialog box and drag the slider to the right.

■ Click the **clip's audio track** and then choose **Clip ➤ Audio ➤ Volume**. Windows Movie Maker displays the Audio Clip Volume dialog box (see **Figure 33.6**).

■ Drag the **slider** to the left to lower the clip volume.

■ Click the **Play Timeline** button. As you preview the clip this time, you notice the engines aren't quite as loud as they were with the unmodified clip. If you haven't lowered the volume sufficiently, repeat this step until the volume reaches an acceptable level.

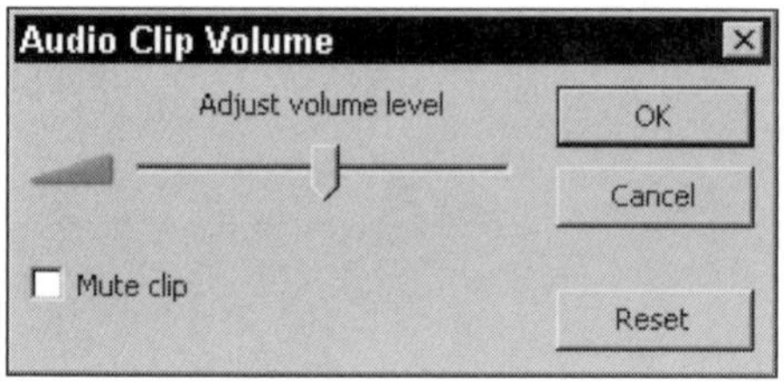

33.6

MUTING CLIP SOUND

34.1

34.2

The clip for this technique was filmed at a lake in Central Florida in the late afternoon. The golden colors of the sun combined with the white plumage of the swans provided enough visual interest to commit the scene to tape. The footage was recorded with a Sony DCR-TVR27 and captured into Windows Movie Maker through a FireWire card.

U nless you record your video clips in controlled conditions, you may end up with an unacceptable audio soundtrack. When you film outdoors, as shown in **Figure 34.1**, you have all manner of ambient noise with which to contend. For example, with wildlife in a bucolic setting, you don't want the intrusion of airplane noise or automobile traffic. If you shoot video in conditions with distracting ambient sounds, such as a great deal of wind noise, or if your audio track becomes garbled, you may have no alternative but to mute the sound track. After muting a soundtrack, you can add audio to the movie on the Audio/Music timeline using one of the upcoming techniques.

iMOVIE

Sometimes the ambient sounds that you pick up when filming a video can get in the way of the mood you are trying to create. In this technique, the background drone of a big gust of wind beating against the microphone on the camcorder shatters the vision of the beautiful swan floating peacefully in a lake. Rather than trash the footage, you can simply mute the sound on the video clip in iMovie.

STEP 1: BEGIN A NEW PROJECT

■ Begin a new project and save the project on your hard drive.

■ Choose **File ➢ Import** from the menu, navigate to the CD-ROM, and select **MacClip083.mov**.

■ Drag the clip to the Movie Track.

■ Display the Movie Track in Timeline Viewer mode by clicking on the **Timeline** (clock) icon. In this view, additional audio tools become available to you that allow you to edit the sound on a clip.

STEP 2: MUTE THE SOUND ON A VIDEO CLIP

■ Click the clip in the Movie Track. Press the **Home** key and then the **spacebar** to play the movie. Notice the annoying ambient wind sound that is audible about halfway through the video.

■ To the far right of the Movie Track you see the **Volume Icon**. Under this icon you have check boxes that correspond to the video track and subsequent audio tracks. Click the check box that corresponds to the first track (video track). When you do this, the check disappears, and clips on the track become mute. To turn the sound on, check the box again (see **Figure 34.3**).

■ Press the **Home** key and then the **spacebar** to play back the movie. The sound of the wind disappears.

NOTE

Deselecting the **Volume** check box makes all sound on that track mute. If you want to selectively adjust volume on clips, you need to check the **Edit Volume** box at the bottom of the timeline and use the Volume Slider. Technique 37 gives you details on how to edit individual audio clips on the same track. The same technique applies to sound on video clips in the video track.

34.3

WINDOWS MOVIE MAKER

In high-end video editing programs, such as Adobe Premiere and Vegas, you can simply delete an audio track if needed. If you try to delete an audio track with Windows Movie Maker, you'll also delete the video. Although you can't get rid of an unwanted audio track, you can mute it. In the case of the sample footage, the sound of passing traffic clashes with peaceful footage of the swimming swan.

STEP 1: CREATE A NEW PROJECT

■ Launch Windows Movie Maker and choose **File ➤ New Project**.

■ Choose **File ➤ Import Into Collections**. Select **WinClip081.wmv** from the CD-ROM that accompanies this book and then click **Import**. Windows Movie Maker creates a new collection for the clip.

■ Click the **Show Timeline** button.

■ Drag the clip onto the timeline. Notice that the clip's waveform appears on the audio timeline.

■ Click the **Play Timeline** button to preview the clip. As you preview the clip, you notice a lot of audio in the form of chirping birds, but you also hear the occasional rush of passing traffic, which doesn't seem natural. To rectify this problem, you simply mute the soundtrack. You can then add sound effects of birds chirping and water flowing by following the steps outlined in Technique 37.

STEP 2: MUTE THE SOUNDTRACK

■ Click the audio track to select it. When you work with video clips that have audio tracks, you must click the audio track to modify it. Although Windows Movie Maker highlights both tracks, you need to select the proper track in order to make it the active track.

■ Right-click and choose **Mute** from the shortcut menu, or if you prefer, choose **Clip ➤ Audio ➤ Mute**. Windows Movie Maker collapses the waveform to a single line, signifying a muted track (see **Figure 34.4**).

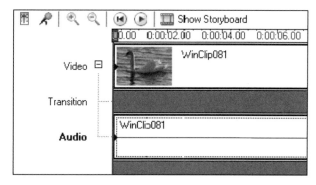

34.4

FADING SOUND IN AND OUT

35.1

35.2

When you have several video clips with audio tracks in a project, and use transitions between clips, Windows Movie Maker fades one audio clip into another. However, if you don't have a transition between scenes, the audio from the next scene starts in lockstep with the video, which can be jarring. iMovie and Windows Movie Maker enable you to begin an audio track with a fade in, and end it with a fade out. To demonstrate this technique, we use the jarring sound of a subway entering a station (see **Figure 35.1** and **35.2**) and alter the volume in time.

iMOVIE

In the last technique, you experienced the ease with which you can mute the soundtrack portion of a video track. In some scenarios, you may want the sound on a clip to fade from loud to soft or vice versa. iMovie gives you the flexibility to adjust clip volume over a period of time. Although this is a feature generally associated with more sophisticated applications like iMovie's big brother, Final Cut Pro, Apple thoughtfully includes a less sophisticated version of this tool in iMovie. In this technique, you make the volume of a passing subway car fade out as the car passes. To accomplish this, you use the Volume Edit tools.

STEP 1: BEGIN A NEW PROJECT

- Begin a new project and save the project on your hard drive.
- Choose **File ➢ Import** from the menu, navigate to the CD-ROM, and select **MacClip084.mov**.
- Drag the clips from the Clip Pane to the Movie Track.
- Display the Movie Track in Timeline Viewer mode by clicking the **Timeline** (clock) icon.

STEP 2: EDIT THE CLIP VOLUME OVER TIME

To fade the sound in and out over time, you must first activate the Edit Volume mode.

- Click the video clip in the Movie Track and press the **Home** key and then the **spacebar** to play the video. Listen to the sound of the subway as it approaches. You are going to gradually fade the volume of the subway sound to mute beginning in the middle of the clip.

MULTIPLE VOLUME ADJUSTMENTS OVER TIME

In this technique, you added one marker to adjust the volume on a clip. In addition, you can add as many markers as you want on a single clip. To do this, simply click another portion of the Volume Bar and then drag the new marker up or down. Dragging a marker up increases the volume while dragging a marker down decreases the volume. Dragging a marker horizontally (left or right) increases or decreases the duration of the edits on the Volume Bar. You can delete a marker by clicking it and pressing the Delete key.

- At the bottom of the Timeline, click the **Edit Volume** box. When you check this, video tracks (with sound) and audio tracks display a thin horizontal line down the middle of the clip. This is known as the Volume Bar (**Figure 35.3**).

Volume Bar

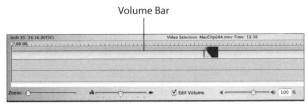

35.3

■ Click the **Volume Bar** on the tail of the clip. Notice that a yellow ball, known as a *marker*, appears where you clicked. The marker (the beginning) allows you to adjust the volume at a particular point in time. A short yellow line connects the marker with a small point designating the other end of the line. Between these two points on the Volume Bar is where your sound fades in time.

■ Click the point that connects the yellow line with the marker and drag the point all the way to the beginning of the Movie Track, as shown in **Figure 35.4**.

■ Now press the **Home** key and then the **spacebar** to play the movie again. Notice how the sound gradually recedes, following the downturn of the line curve on the Volume Bar.

WINDOWS MOVIE MAKER

When you have a clip with audio, or add an audio soundtrack to a project, you can start and end the audio track gradually by applying menu commands. You cannot, however, change the duration of the fade; Windows Movie Maker uses a preset percentage of the clip's duration to determine the length of each fade.

STEP 1: CREATE A NEW PROJECT

■ Launch Windows Movie Maker and choose **File ➤ New Project**.

■ Choose **File ➤ Import Into Collections**. Select **WinClip082.wmv** from the CD-ROM that accompanies this book and then click **Import**. Windows Movie Maker creates a new collection for the clip.

■ Click the **Play Timeline** button if you're currently working in storyboard mode.

■ Drag the clip onto the timeline. Windows Movie Maker snaps the clip to the 0:00:00.00 timecode and displays the track's audio waveform.

> **NOTE**
>
> If you prefer menu commands for editing audio, select the audio track you want to edit, choose **Clip ➤ Audio**, and then choose the desired command from the drop-down menu.

35.4

STEP 2: FADE THE AUDIO TRACK

- Click the **audio track** to select it.
- Right-click to open the **shortcut menu** and choose **Fade In** (see **Figure 35.5**).
- Right-click and then choose **Fade Out** from the **shortcut menu** (see **Figure 35.5**).
- Click the **Play Timeline** button and the clip begins playing in the Preview pane (see

Figure 35.6). Notice that the sound of the subway train gradually fades in as the clip begins and then gradually fades out as the clip ends.

✂ Cut	Ctrl+X
⧉ Copy	Ctrl+C
Paste	Ctrl+V
✕ Delete	Del
Select All	Ctrl+A
▶ Play Timeline	Ctrl+W
Mute	
Fade In	
Fade Out	
Volume...	Ctrl+U
Browse for Missing File...	
☑ Properties	

35.5

35.6

ADDING ROYALTY-FREE MUSIC AS A MOVIE SOUNDTRACK

36.1

36.2

Whenever you add a soundtrack to a movie, you heighten viewer interest by involving another sense as well as set the mood of a piece by choosing appropriate music to suit your clips and intended audience. For example, easy listening jazz music with a tropical beat is an excellent choice for the sample clips provided for this technique. You can, however, choose music that is 180 degrees opposite the type of clips you are assembling. For example, you can add upbeat music to offset somewhat somber footage shot in the dead of winter. Let your creative muse guide you in your search for the perfect soundtrack for your piece. In this technique, we extract music from a royalty-free CD.

iMOVIE

Images of an aqua ocean and blue sky evoke a sense of relaxation and a little music can help create that mood. Because everyone's concept of relaxing music is different, grab a CD that makes you feel good, and insert it into the

199

CD tray of your Mac. You will extract your favorite track from this CD and add it to the audio track in iMovie.

STEP 1: BEGIN A NEW PROJECT

- Begin a new project and save the project on your hard drive.
- Choose **File ➢ Import** from the menu, navigate to the CD-ROM, and select **MacClip010.mov, MacClip011.mov, MacClip17.mov,** and **MacClip085.mov**.

CAUTION

Although you are copying sound from a music CD in this lesson, beware of using CD music in any movie you plan to use in public. Unless you own the rights, copying and using music is generally illegal. Obviously, if you just use tracks from CDs to share with a small group of family and friends, there is no problem. But if you intend to submit independent productions to film festivals or place your videos on a Web site for a larger audience to view, be aware of music copyright laws. If you need to use music in your videos, try royalty-free music, which you can purchase and use wherever you want. Alternatively, you can make your own music with some inexpensive sound mixing and editing applications that are listed in Appendix B of this book.

- Drag the clips from the Clip Pane to the Movie Track.
- Display the Movie Track in Timeline Viewer mode by clicking the **Timeline** (clock) icon.

STEP 2: SELECT A SOUND TRACK FROM A CD

If you've listened to CDs on your Mac using QuickTime or iTunes, the interface in iMovie probably looks familiar to you. Here, you select and convert music from a CD to a digital file you can import into iMovie.

- With the music CD inserted into the tray of your computer, click the **Audio** tab to display the Audio Pane. The contents of the CD, including the name and length of each song, appear in the Audio Pane.

TIP

If you want to find out the new duration of the clip after splitting it and deleting the other half, click the clip and choose **File ➢ Show Info**. In the Clip Info dialog box, you can find or change the name of the clip and check out the new duration of the clip. Keep in mind that the original music is still intact and saved in your movie folder. If you decide that you split the clip incorrectly, delete the clip and import the music back in again by choosing **File ➢ Import**. The name of the clip becomes the name of the song you imported from the Audio Pane.

■ Sample tracks on the CD by clicking them and then clicking the **Play** control arrow at the bottom of the pane. When you find one that is appropriate for the video, drag the **Playhead** to the beginning of the timeline. Click the **Place at Playhead** button in the Audio Pane. The selected music track imports into the audio track.

■ In this movie, notice that the audio clip is of a longer duration than the video clips on the Movie Track, as shown in **Figure 36.3**. To shorten the new audio clip created from your CD, place the **Playhead** at the tail of the last video clip and from the menu, choose **Edit ➤ Split Selected Audio Clip at Playhead** as shown in **Figure 36.4**. Doing this splits the audio clip into two segments.

■ To delete the unwanted segment of audio clip, click the second segment and press the **Delete** key. Play the clip from the beginning and notice that the audio now stops where the video clips end.

TIP

In addition to splitting an audio clip, you can also adjust the length of a clip using the handles on either end of the clip. To do so, click and drag the clip inward, to the point where you want the audio clip to end. To sample a specific segment of audio so that you can determine what part of the audio you want to trim, click the audio clip and press the **spacebar** to play the movie. As the movie plays, the timecode displays. Jot down the points in time where you want the movie to begin and end. Move the handles at the head and tail of the audio clips to correspond with the timecode you recorded.

NOTE

This technique is for music CDs only. If the royalty-free CD you are using is a data disc, the music is already in digital format. Digital sound files that can import into iMovie will have an extension of AIF or WAV. To import music from a data disc, in iMovie, click **File ➤ Import**. In the File Import dialog box, navigate to the CD and select the sound file you want to import. Then click the Import button. The sound will appear on the iMovie sound track.

Edit	Advanced	Window	Help
Undo			⌘Z
Redo			⇧⌘Z
Cut			⌘X
Copy			⌘C
Paste			⌘V
Clear			
Select All			⌘A
Select None			⇧⌘A
Crop			⌘K
Split Video Clip at Playhead			⌘T
Create Still Frame			⇧⌘S

36.4

STEP 3: FADE OUT THE MUSIC

The music may end too abruptly at the end of your movie. In this step, you adjust the Volume Bar so that the music gradually fades out.

- At the bottom of the Movie Track, click the **Edit Volume** button.
- Click the **Volume Bar** at the end of the Movie Track to create a marker.
- Drag the endpoint on the horizontal adjustment line (on the opposite end of the marker) to the beginning of the Movie Track.
- Click the marker at the end of the movie and drag the marker down, as shown in **Figure 36.5**. The Volume Bar starts out high, gradually slopes, and then drops to the bottom of the audio clip at the end. Play the movie to test the fading out of the sound.

WINDOWS MOVIE MAKER

Windows XP ships with Windows Media Player. From within Windows Media Player, you can capture audio soundtracks from royalty-free music CDs in digital format and use them as soundtracks for your movies.

STEP 1: SELECT AN AUDIO CD-ROM

Windows Movie Maker supports soundtracks in the WMA (Windows Media Audio) audio format. Coincidentally, you can use Windows Media Player to export your favorite royalty-free music in WMA format.

- From within Windows choose **Start ➤ All Programs ➤ Windows Media Player.**
- Insert a royalty-free music CD in your CD-ROM player.
- Choose **File ➤ Copy ➤ Copy From Audio CD**. After choosing this command sequence, Windows Media Player searches your CD-ROM disc(s) for audio discs. After several seconds, the title of the album displays.
- Click the **album title** to display the playlist. If you're connected to the Internet, the Windows Media Player connects to a remote service and identifies the album by artist and lists each song, if the CD from which you are extracting songs is listed in the database. If you're not connected to the Internet, Windows Media Player lists each song by duration and track number (see **Figure 36.6**).

TIP

If you don't own any royalty-free music CDs, you can purchase them from several places on the Internet. Point your Web browser to `www.royaltyfree.com`, `www.musicbakery.com`, or `www.studiocutz.com`. If none of these sources suits your fancy, go to your favorite search engine and type **royalty-free music** in the search field.

36.5

STEP 2: CAPTURE THE SOUNDTRACK

When you display the play list, all songs are selected by default. To exclude a song from the selection, click the song's check box to deselect it.

■ Select the song you want to use as a soundtrack and then click **Copy Music**. When you copy music for the first time, Windows Media Player displays a dialog box asking whether you want to copy protect the copied music so it won't play on other devices. In addition, you must select a check box that acknowledges that the music you are copying is protected by copyright laws. Of course, this isn't a problem with royalty-free music. Windows Media Player also prompts you to select a compression setting. The default WMA compression works well in most cases.

■ After clicking **OK**, Windows Media Player copies the soundtrack to the My Music Folder. If you were connected to the Internet when you copied

the music, the copied tracks are saved with the path C:\Documents and Settings\Username\ My Documents\My Music\Artist name\Album title, where Username is your Windows logon name. The artist's actual name and the title of the album replace the Artist name and Album name listings

> **NOTE**
>
> This technique applies to music CDs only. If the royalty-free CD you are using is a data disc, the music is already in digital format. To import music from a data disc in Windows Movie Maker, click the Tasks button and from the Capture Video section choose Import Audio or Music.

> **NOTE**
>
> If the playlist is not visible, choose **View** ➤ **Now Playing Options**, and then choose the viewing options you want displayed from the drop-down menu.

> **WARNING**
>
> Make certain that you have the legal right to extract and use music from a CD. Copyright laws, among other things, prevent the illegal or unauthorized copying of music. In other words, you cannot copy a copyrighted song for your own use without the permission of the copyright owner. If you incorporate a song as an audio track for a movie for which you will be compensated, you should obtain permission to use the audio track from the copyright owner; otherwise, you may be in violation of copyright laws. Sometimes getting permission is as simple as contacting the publisher (such as ASCAP or BMI). Many publishers have fee schedules from which they quickly can provide you with a quote. Some fees are one-time fees, while others are per-use fees. The simplest approach, however, is just to use royalty-free music. You can purchase royalty-free music CDs in many music stores, or from Internet resources. You can also download royalty-free music from the Internet, which we cover in Techniques 37 and 38.

36.6

in the preceding path. If you did not log onto the Internet when you copied the tracks, the listing changes to unknown artist/unknown album.

STEP 3: CREATE A NEW PROJECT

■ Launch Windows Movie Maker and choose **File ➢ New Project**.
■ Click the **Play Timeline** button if you're currently working in storyboard mode.
■ Choose **File ➢ Import Into Collections**. Select **WinClip009.wmv, WinClip010.wmv, WinClip016.wmv. and WinClip083.wmv** from the CD-ROM that accompanies this book and then click **Import**. That's right; we're using clips from prior techniques. You'll also reuse your best clips when you create your own movies.
■ Drag the clips onto the timeline in numerical order. Windows Movie Maker snaps the first clip to timecode 0:00:00.00 and snaps each succeeding clip to the end of the preceding clip.

STEP 4: ADD THE SOUNDTRACK

■ Click the **Tasks** button and from the **Capture Movie** section choose **Import Audio or Music**. Windows Movie Maker displays the Import File dialog box.
■ Click **My Documents**, navigate to the folder in which your soundtrack has been saved, select the soundtrack, and then click **Import**. Windows Movie Maker adds the soundtrack to the current collection.

■ Drag the soundtrack onto the **Audio/Music** timeline. When you add a sound track to this timeline, Windows Movie Maker does not snap it to the beginning of the movie. You can drop the audio track in the desired position and move it as needed when fine-tuning your movie. For the purpose of this exercise, drag the soundtrack to the beginning of the movie timeline.
■ Trim the length of the soundtrack to suit the movie. Unless you're splicing lots of clips together to make a three- or four-minute movie, your soundtrack is probably longer than the movie. To trim the soundtrack clip, select it and move your cursor towards the end of the soundtrack. When it becomes a red double-headed arrow, click and drag left until the soundtrack is the same length as the movie (see **Figure 36.7**).
■ With the soundtrack still selected, right-click and select **Fade Out** from the shortcut menu. This step is optional, but if you trim the length of the soundtrack, your production seems more professional if the track fades out at the end of the movie.
■ Click the **Play Timeline** button to preview the movie. Windows Movie Maker plays the movie and your soundtrack at the same time.

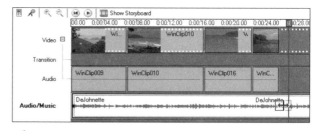

36.7

USING MULTIPLE SOUND EFFECTS

37.1

37.2

This video was shot in a classic New Jersey diner using a Canon GL-1. We captured the video to a Mac G4 using iMovie before trimming it in iMovie and Windows Movie Maker. Most sound effects were recorded directly on a Mac G4 using a Verse USB microphone. The sound was then edited in Bias Peak and exported to an audio file format (AIFF and WAV). The movie was captured in iMovie and trimmed in iMovie and Windows Movie Maker.

Y ou may have been lucky enough to capture great sound effects when you were shooting your video. If not, you can include sound effects in the postproduction process to add drama and new dimension to an otherwise ho-hum movie. Hollywood does this all the time. For example, you can't see the hooting owl, but the sound effect adds a sense of foreboding to the scene. You can also use sound effects to exaggerate or add a sense of comedy to your movies. For example, a bell gong on the audio timeline snaps your viewers to attention, or announces a new scene. You can download sound effects from many sources on the Internet. With a good microphone and a sound card, you can create your own.

iMOVIE

Although iMovie ships with over 35 different sound effects, in this technique, you add sound effects imported into iMovie from an external source. The process of importing sound into an iMovie is identical to that of

205

importing movie clips and still pictures. You also have the opportunity to adjust the volume level over time on individual clips. Although iMovie's audio capabilities are unsophisticated compared to an application such as Final Cut Pro or Adobe Premiere, it still offers an impressive array of basic audio adjustment tools.

STEP 1: BEGIN A NEW PROJECT

You begin by importing some clips into the Shelf. These clips may look familiar because you used them in an earlier technique. iMovie contains two audio tracks that reside under the Movie Track. Make sure you check the **Mute Toggle** button on each track so you can hear the audio when you import it.

■ Begin a new project and save the project on your hard drive.

■ Choose **File ➢ Import** from the menu, navigate to the CD-ROM, and select **MacClip047.mov**, **MacClip048.mov**, **MacClip049.mov**, and **MacClip050.mov**. Drag these clips from the Shelf to the Movie Track in sequence and display the Movie Track in the Timeline Viewer. To see and adjust the audio clips, you must work with the clips in the Timeline Viewer mode in the Movie Track.

STEP 2: IMPORT SOUND EFFECTS

In iMovie, audio clips import directly onto the audio track in the Timeline Viewer to the location of the Playhead.

■ Drag the Timeline Track **Playhead** to the beginning of the Movie Track. Choose **File ➢ Import** from the menu and navigate to the Clips folder on the CD-ROM. Select the following sound files: **ambient noise.aif, eat.aif, grease.aif, paper2.aif, short traffic.aif**, and **straw.aif**. The head of the clips imports to the current location of the Playhead.

STEP 3: ARRANGE THE AUDIO CLIPS ON AUDIO TRACKS

Now you must arrange the clips in order on the audio tracks, so the sound corresponds with the visuals in the video clips. You can move the clips from one location to another in the two audio tracks by clicking and dragging on them to their new location.

■ On the first audio track, place the clip named **short traffic.aif** under the first video clip. Drag the clips named **grease.aif** and **paper2.aif** under the second and third video clips. Under the fourth video clip, drag the audio clip named **straw.aif** and **eat.aif** to the first audio track. Refer to **Figure 37.3** for the proper positioning of all clips.

> **TIP**
>
> You can make your own sound effects using a microphone in iMovie. Technique 39 covers the process of attaching a microphone and recording sound directly into iMovie.

37·3

■ On the second audio track, drag the audio clip named **ambient noise.aif** all the way to the left, under the **short traffic.aif** audio clip. With the clip named **ambient noise.aif** selected, drag the **Playhead** to the tail of this clip. From the menu, choose **Edit ➢ Copy** and then choose **Edit ➢ Paste**. A copy of the clip appears at the location of the **Playhead**. Now drag the **Playhead** to the tail of the second clip (**ambient noise.aif**) and repeat the copy and paste process two times to generate a third and fourth copy of the clip adjacent to the previous clips. Refer to **Figure 37.4** to see how the Movie Track should look after you have all the clips in place.

■ Press the **Home** key and then the **spacebar** to rewind the Playhead and play the movie. At this point, if any of the sounds are out of sync with the video clips, simply drag them to the correct position. Notice that the last copy of the **ambient noise.aif** clip is too long. It actually hangs over the last video clip resulting in black footage for a moment at the end of the movie.

STEP 4: TWEAK THE SOUND EFFECTS

In iMovie you can shorten the length of a clip in one of two ways. You can split the clip to make it shorter (**Edit ➢ Split Clip at Playhead**), or you can drag the handles at the head and tail of the audio clip. In this step, you use the handle dragging method to shorten the last clip so that it ends where the last video clip ends. This eliminates the black footage at the end of the movie. In addition, you lower the volume on the clips on the second audio track.

■ In the second audio track, click the handle of the tail of the last clip named **ambient noise.aif**. Drag the handle to the right, so it ends where the video clip on the first track ends (**Figure 37.5**).

■ Because the clips on the second audio track (**ambient noise.aif**) are a little loud, you need to reduce their volume. Press the **Shift** key and click all four clips in the track named **ambient noise.aif**. Under the Movie Track, you see the **Volume Slider**. Click the **Volume Slider** button and drag it to the left, for amplitude of about 30 percent (**Figure 37.6**).

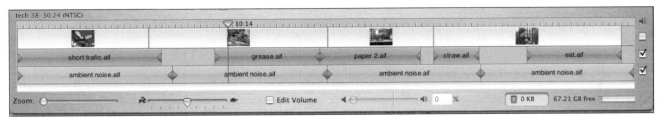

37.4

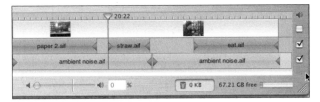

37.5

37.6

STEP 5: FADE OUT SOUND EFFECT

You can now edit the sound of the last **ambient noise.aif** clip on the second audio track so that it doesn't end so abruptly, but rather fades out gradually.

■ At the bottom of the Movie Track Timeline Viewer, click the **Edit Volume** button. When you do so, the Volume Bars (horizontal adjustment lines) appear in the clips.

■ Click the end of the Volume Level bar on the tail of the last **ambient noise.aif** clip. Drag the ball marker down and play back the movie to hear the results. Note that a point appears on the other end of the Volume Bar, representing where the volume gradually begins to fade out.

> **TIP**
>
> When clips do not butt up against one another in the Movie Track Timeline Viewer mode, a black area occurs in between the two clips. In the Clip Viewer, you see a black clip when the movie plays. Sometimes you may want a black clip to appear in between two clips. For example, if you wanted to use the Push transition and push from a black clip into a regular clip, creating a black clip by moving clips down in the Timeline View is an effective way of achieving this end.

■ If you find that the last ambient noise.aif clip still ends too abruptly, drag the opposite point on the Volume Bar to the left, toward the middle of the clip, as shown in **Figure 37.7**. Doing this extends the duration of the volume fade out.

■ Play the movie back. The last ambient noise.aif clip gradually fades out in time. You can go back and tweak the volume if necessary by repeating the process in this step.

> **TIP**
>
> If you decide that you don't want your sound to gradually fade out, just select the marker and press the **Delete** key.

> **NOTE**
>
> If you plan on importing sound into your movie, you need to know which audio file formats are compatible with iMovie. You can import AIFF, WAV, and MP3 file formats directly into in iMovie.

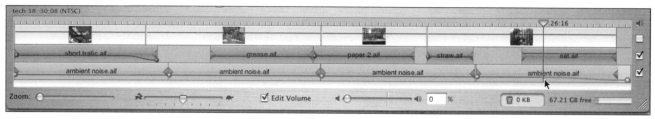

37.7

WINDOWS MOVIE MAKER

When you capture footage and the audio is garbled, or of poor quality, you can mute the audio as described in Technique 34, and add sound effects to the Audio\Music timeline. You can also use sound effects for a comic effect, as you learn in this technique. Typically, you preview clips at the beginning of a project, paying special attention to the quality of the audio and video, which helps you determine whether you need to mute the audio track, or augment it with sound effects. As most of the techniques in this book don't use audio, including the clips for this project, we have stripped the audio portion of the sample clips in order to conserve space on the book's CD-ROM.

STEP 1: CREATE A NEW PROJECT

■ Launch Windows Movie Maker and choose **File ➢ New Project**.
■ Choose **File ➢ Import Into Collections**. Navigate to the CD-ROM that accompanies this book, select **WinClip046.wmv, WinClip047.wmv, WinClip048.wmv**, and **WinClip049.wmv**, and then click **Import**. Windows Movie Maker creates a new collection for each clip.
■ Click the **Show Timeline** button if you're currently working in Storyboard mode. Remember, when you work in Storyboard mode, the audio timelines are not visible.
■ Arrange the video clips in numerical order on the timeline.

STEP 2: IMPORT THE AUDIO

When you decide to add sound effects to a movie, you can import audio clips in any of the following file formats: .AIF, .AIFC, .AIFF, .ASF, .AU, .MP3, .MPA, .SND, .WAV, and .WMA. You can mix different formats on the audio timeline. When you export the finished movie, Windows Movie Maker renders clips on the Audio/Music timeline to the applicable format for the selected compression codec.

■ Click the **Tasks** button and in the **Capture Video** section, choose **Import Audio or Music**. Navigate to the CD-ROM that accompanies this book, select **WinClip084.wav, WinClip085.wav, WinClip086.wav,** and**WinClip087.wav**, and then click **Import**. Windows Movie Maker imports the clips into the current collection.
■ Select **WinClip084.wav** and then drag it onto the Audio/Music timeline. Note that when you drag audio clips to the timeline, they do not snap to the beginning of the timeline, or the previous clip. Audio tracks stay where you drop them. In this case, you want the clip to start playing when the movie does, therefore, drop the audio track at timecode 0:00:00.00.
■ Select **WinClip085.wav** and then drag it to the Audio/Music timeline. Align it with the end of the audio clip you previously added to the timeline.
■ Select **WinClip086.wav** and then drag it to the Audio/Music timeline, releasing the mouse button when the end of the audio clip aligns to the end of the second video clip and overlaps **WinClip085. wav** (see **Figure 37.8**).

STEP 3: MIX THE SOUNDS

With only one Audio/Music timeline, you can't do a lot of sophisticated mixing of sounds. You can, however, overlap sounds as you did in the previous steps.

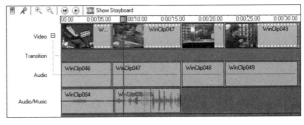

37.8

When you overlap sound clips, Windows Movie Maker mixes the sounds. You cannot, however, align the beginnings of two clips. When you try to do this, Windows Movie Maker bumps the first clip to the end of the second clip when you release the mouse button.

- Select **WinClip085.wav** and then drag it onto the Audio/Music timeline. Release the mouse button when the clip aligns to the end of the first instance of WinClip085.wav. Notice that this clip overlaps the clip on the video timeline. Also, the waveform at the end of this clip is a flat line (see **Figure 37.9**), indicating silence. You use this as a marker for aligning the next sound clip.

- Select **WinClip084.wav** and then drag it to the Audio/Music timeline, aligning it so that it overlaps the flat line in the waveform of WinClip085.wav.
- Select **WinClip087.wav** and then drag it to the Audio/Music timeline, aligning the clip so that it butts up to the end of the previous clip (see **Figure 37.10**).
- Click the **Play Timeline** button to preview the movie with the soundtrack. The movie plays along with the audio track and you hear ambient noises of traffic, burgers being wrapped, and a person enjoying a shake and a burger.

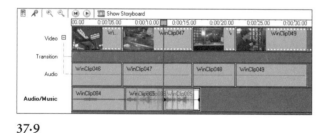

37.9

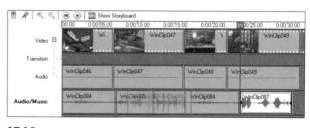

37.10

ADDING ALIEN SOUND EFFECTS

38.1

38.2

The sample clip for this technique was filmed at a pedestrian path on a scenic lake in Central Florida. You can find people exercising here at almost any hour of the day when the weather is clement. The skaters in this clip were filmed with a Sony DCR-TRV27 and captured to the PC through an IEEE 1394 card.

Whether you need to mute an audio track that is garbled, or you just want to spice up a production with some sound effects, you can add some alien sound effects to the Audio\Music track. The alien sound effects can be sounds like you'd hear in a sci-fi movie, or they can be everyday sound effects that are "alien" to the scene, for example a pretty girl smiling to the sound effect of a witch cackling. A multitude of sound effects are available. You can purchase sound effects collections at your local office supply store, or find them on the Internet. You can even find sound bytes of cartoon characters, such as Homer Simpson. However, if you use recognizable sound effects, make sure that you're not violating any copyright laws.

iMOVIE

Although you can easily find royalty-free sound effects on the Internet, you may never have to because iMovie comes with a pretty impressive array of sound effects. In this technique, you apply some to a video clip to create a creepy alien effect.

211

STEP 1: BEGIN A NEW PROJECT

- Begin a new project and save the project on your hard drive.
- Choose **File ➢ Import** from the menu, navigate to the CD-ROM, and select **MacClip086.mov**.
- Drag the clips from the Shelf to the Movie Track.
- Display the tMovie Track in Timeline Viewer mode by clicking on the **Timeline** (clock) icon.

STEP 2: NAVIGATE THE iMOVIE SOUND EFFECTS

Although you can find plenty of sound effects from all sorts of places on the Web or make your own, in a pinch, you can use the iMovie sound effects. In addition, you can blend effects together by placing them on the alternate audio track or by placing them right on top of each other.

- Click the **Audio** tab. At the top of the Audio Pane, click the pop-up menu and select **iMovie Sound Effects**. This displays a long list and variety of Skywalker sound effects and the sound effects native to iMovie. Skywalker sound effects were specially created for iMovie by Skywalker Sound, an Academy Award-winning sound studio. Browse through the list by clicking a sound and pressing the **Play** control button at the bottom of the sound effect list (see **Figure 38.3**).

STEP 3: APPLY iMOVIE SOUND EFFECTS

- Press the **Home** key to return the **Playhead** to the beginning of the Movie Track and drag the **Suspense** sound to the second audio track. On the **Suspense** sound effect, drag the handle on the tail to butt with the tail of the video clip, as shown in **Figure 38.4**.

38.3

- To make the sound fade out, click the **Edit Volume** button, click the end of the Volume Bar to create a marker, and drag down the marker.
- Adjust the point at the other end of the fade segment accordingly, as shown in **Figure 38.5**.
- Back in the sound effects list, click the **Bark** effect and drag it to the beginning of the Movie Track.

- Return to the sound effects list and drag a copy of the **Footsteps** sound effect to the audio track so it butts up against the **Bark** sound. Shorten the clip's duration by dragging the tail handle so it stops under the last video clip (see **Figure 38.6**).
- Play the movie to test your alien sounds. It sounds like aliens from another planet are stalking the rollerblading couple.

STEP 4: APPLY A VIDEO EFFECT

To make the clip a little scarier, you can add one of the free sample video effects available for download on the GeeThree Web site at `www.geethree.com/download.html`. Here, you can download free sample effects for iMovie (Slick Sampler). Make sure you download and install these effects before proceeding with this technique. Once installed, the effects appear in your Effects pane in iMovie.

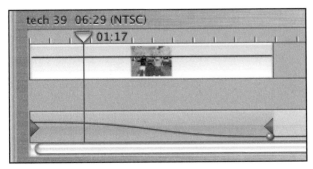

38.4

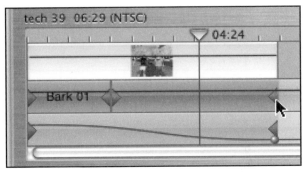

38.6

38.5

■ Click the video clip and click the **Effects** tab. From the **Effects** list, click the **X-Ray** effect from **GeeThree Sampler**. This is a free sample of one of their many wonderful and unique plug-ins. Note from the thumbnail preview, the effect creates a strange, eerie, x-ray effect, just right for our alien effect (see **Figure 38.7**).

■ Click the **Apply** button and play the movie to see the results. Your otherwise ordinary video clip now has an added element of suspense thanks to some sound effects and a third-party plug-in.

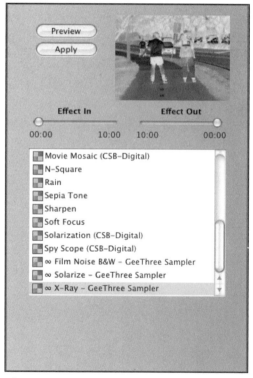

38.7

WINDOWS MOVIE MAKER

Windows Movie Maker does not provide sound effects for your movie projects. However, we've provided some sound effects for you to experiment with on the CD-ROM that accompanies this book. For this technique, you add some sound effects that aren't alien in nature, but are alien when you take into account the clip to which you apply them.

STEP 1: CREATE A NEW PROJECT

■ Launch Windows Movie Maker and choose **File ➢ New Project**.

■ Choose **File ➢ Import Into Collections**. Navigate to the CD-ROM that accompanies this book, select **WinClip088.wmv,** and then click **Import**. Windows Movie Maker imports a clip of two skaters into a collection.

■ Click the **Show Timeline** button if Windows Movie Maker is currently in Storyboard mode.

■ Drag the clip onto the timeline. Windows Movie Maker snaps the clip to timecode 0:00:0.00.

■ Click the **Zoom Timeline In** button twice. Zooming in on the timeline makes it easier to align audio clips.

STEP 2: ADD THE SOUND EFFECTS

■ Click the **Tasks** button and from the **Capture Video** section choose **Import Audio or Music**.

■ Navigate to the CD-ROM that accompanies this book, select **WinClip089.wav, WinClip090.wav,** and **WinClip091.wav,** and then click **Import**.

Windows Movie Maker adds the audio clips to the current selection (see **Figure 38.8**).

■ Drag **WinClip089.wav** onto the Audio/Music timeline, align it to timecode 0:00:00.00, and release the mouse button.

■ Drag two more instances of **WinClip089.wav** onto the Audio/Music timeline, aligning the clips end to end.

■ Drag **WinClip090.wav** onto the Audio/Music timeline, align it to the end of the previous clip, and release the mouse button.

■ Drag **WinClip091.wav** onto the Audio/Music timeline, align it to the end of the previous clip, and release the mouse button (see **Figure 38.9**).

After arranging the clips on the timeline, you can preview your handiwork by clicking the Play Timeline button. Before moving on to the next technique, try rearranging the clips for a different effect.

While the project is still open, import some of the sound effects from the CD-ROM that accompanies this book, let your creative child run amuck, and have some fun with sound.

SURFING FOR SOUNDS

There are a plethora of Web sites that feature sound effects. Some of the sites have free sound effects that you can download for non-commercial use. To locate Web sites with sound effects, log onto the Internet, point your Web browser towards a good search engine (www.google.com is favored by the authors of this book), and type "sound effects" in the search field. You'll wind up with several pages of results. In most instances you'll be able to use free sound effects for non-commercial productions. Before downloading any sounds, pay attention to any EULA (End User License Agreement) to be aware of any terms or conditions for use posted by the Web site owners. For example, the owners of the sound may request written credit in your production in exchange for use of the sound.

38.8

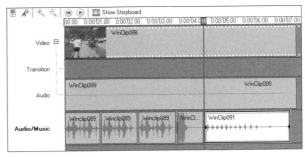

38.9

NARRATING A MOVIE

39.1

39.2

ABOUT THE VIDEO

The video clips for this technique were filmed at the University of Tampa, which was originally the Tampa Hotel, built in the late 1800s. The architecture is quite striking with several minarets peering up towards the sky. The footage was filmed with a Sony DCR-TRV27 set to auto exposure and auto focus and captured to PC through an IEEE 1394 card.

If you have a good microphone attached to your computer, you can narrate your movies. When you add a narration to your movies, the clips play so that you can synchronize your audio to key events such as a scene change. When you narrate a movie in this manner, you're telling your version of the story as it unfolds. With narration, you can create your own mini-documentaries, or simply add a greeting when creating a movie that you e-mail to a friend or relative. In the steps that follow, you add your own narration track to the sample clips we've provided. When you create narrations for your own movies, you may find it helpful to play the clips before adding the narration. If the narration is lengthy, you can create a cue card with key points and place it near your computer monitor. Remember if you get it wrong, you can always do another take. Oh yes, you can have your significant other or one of your children close a clapper with the take number to get you in a moviemaking state of mind.

iMOVIE

If you own a microphone for your Mac, you can easily record sound effects and narrations. In this technique, you narrate a movie while it plays. You can easily sync your narration with the actual clips so the movie doesn't end up looking like a badly dubbed foreign movie, where the sound is out of sync with the moving lips and actions of individuals and events.

STEP 1: BEGIN A NEW PROJECT

■ Begin a new project and save the project on your hard drive.
■ Choose **File** ➢ **Import** from the menu, navigate to the CD-ROM, and select **MacClip087.mov**, **MacClip088.mov**, and **MacClip089.mov**.
■ Drag the clips from the Shelf to the Movie Track.
■ Display the Movie Track in Timeline Viewer mode by clicking on the **Timeline** (clock) icon.

STEP 2: RECORD A NARRATIVE

In iMovie, you can record several segments of narration and place them at exactly the right point by moving the Playhead to another point in the Movie Track. When you record a sound in iMovie, the sound clip saves to wherever you place the Playhead. The length of your narration determines the length of the clip.

■ Plug the microphone into your Mac. If you use a PowerBook, you already have an internal microphone, so you won't have anything to plug in, unless you're looking for better sound quality than the built-in mic offers. In this case, you want to purchase an external microphone.
■ Click the **Audio** tab to display the Audio Pane. When you plug in a microphone, the red Record button in the Microphone portion of the pane becomes highlighted, indicating that the microphone is ready to record.
■ Press the **Home** key to return the **Playhead** to the beginning of the Movie Track and get ready to record. The Movie Track Timeline Viewer in **Figure 39.3** shows three clips of the University of Tampa, and you are providing a description of the architecture on campus. Click the **Record** button and record less than ten seconds of yourself talking into the microphone. To prevent creating muffled and unprofessional sound and to optimize sound quality, position yourself a good 6 inches from the tip of the microphone.
■ When you finish recording, click the red **Record** button to end the session and save the clips. The clip appears where you positioned the Playhead, and it syncs perfectly with the clip in the final movie if left in this position.

39.3

■ To record narrative for the next clip, move the **Playhead** to the beginning of the next clip and repeat the recording process. In **Figure 39.4**, there are individual narratives for all three clips.

■ Play the Timeline to test the results of your narrated movie.

STEP 3: MOVING SOUND AND AUDIO CLIPS

In the technique above, you always move the Playhead to the beginning of a video clip to record your narrative. In a real-life scenario, you record at a point in a video clip that is not as easy to find. In iMovie, you can lock an audio track to a video track; if clips move, the narration stays together with the video. Here, you lock the last audio clip to the last video clip.

■ Move the last audio clip (narrative you just made) on the audio track so it's aligned under the middle of the last clip in the Movie Track above. Make sure the **Playhead** is at the head of the audio clip.

■ From the menu, choose **Advanced ➤ Lock Audio Clip at Playhead**. A yellow pin marker appears on the video clip, and another on the audio clip. These pins indicate that the audio will still play at the same point you originally locked it, even if you move the video clip in the Movie Track (**Figure 39.5**). Try to slide the video to a different place and play the movie again. Although you moved the video clip, the audio still plays with it. This is a pretty useful feature when you have multiple narrations associated with multiple clips and then decide to delete some. The video won't get lost from its mother, the video clip.

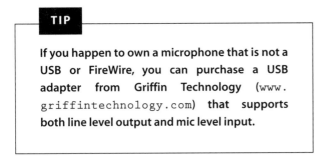

39.4

TIP

If you happen to own a microphone that is not a USB or FireWire, you can purchase a USB adapter from Griffin Technology (www.griffintechnology.com) that supports both line level output and mic level input.

Pin marker

39.5

WINDOWS MOVIE MAKER

Adding narration to a Windows Movie Maker project is similar to using your tape recorder. You click a button, begin speaking, and Windows Movie Maker records your voice. If you plan on doing a lot of movie narrating, you'll find a headset with a microphone is very useful. Such an accessory leaves your hands free to use the mouse. A headset microphone is generally unidirectional, meaning that it records your voice and not the ambient sounds in the room, such as your meowing cat or your computer's fan.

STEP 1: CREATE A NEW PROJECT

■ Launch Windows Movie Maker and choose **File ➢ New Project**.
■ Choose **File ➢ Import Into Collections**. Navigate to the CD-ROM that accompanies this book, select **WinClip092.wmv, WinClip093.wmv,** and **WinClip094.wmv,** and then click **Import**. Windows Movie Maker imports each movie clip into its own collection.
■ Click the **Show Timeline** button if Windows Movie Maker is currently in storyboard mode.
■ Arrange the movie clips in numerical order on the timeline.

STEP 2: RECORD THE NARRATION

If you have a good unidirectional microphone, you can start recording when you're ready. You may want to consider closing the windows because even a good unidirectional microphone may pick up loud sounds from outdoors. Closing the door to your work area is also a good idea, especially if you have a budding guitarist in the family who decides to launch into a techno-version of Purple Haze while you're narrating your prized footage from The Grand Canyon.

■ Move the Playhead to the point on the timeline where you want to begin recording. Position the Playhead several frames before the point where you want the narration to begin, so you don't have to begin speaking the instant you click the **Start Narration** button.
■ Position your microphone or don your headset.
■ Click the **Narrate Timeline** button that looks like a microphone. Windows Movie Maker displays the Narrate Timeline pane (see **Figure 39.6**).
■ Adjust the narration volume by speaking into the microphone. Speak in the same tone of voice you'll use to narrate the movie. As you speak, a blue line moves up and down in the Input window. Adjust the volume by dragging the **Input Level slider** up to increase volume or down to decrease volume. Your goal is to prevent the input level from going into the red. After adjusting the input, you're ready to record.

■ Click the **Start Narration** button and begin speaking. As you record, keep an eye on the Preview pane, which will give you the visual clues you need to properly synchronize your audio with the video. This prevents you from talking about Aunt Madge two seconds before she appears on screen.

■ Click the **Stop Narration** button to end recording. Windows Movie Maker displays the Save Window Media File dialog box. You must save the narration. Windows Movie Maker compiles the saved narration file with the video clips when you render your movie.

■ Name your narration and then click **Save**. Windows Movie Maker saves the narration and adds a waveform to the Audio/Music timeline (see **Figure 39.7**). A thumbnail for the narration appears in the current collection as well.

■ Click the **Play Timeline** button to preview the narrated movie. If the movie plays to your

satisfaction, you can render the movie using one of the techniques in Chapter 9. If the narration is unsatisfactory, you can delete it and record another. If the narration is satisfactory, but not synchronized perfectly, you can click and drag the clip to another location. When you need to resynchronize a narration, you'll find it helpful to zoom in on the timeline.

NOTE

You cannot pause the recording, but you can stop recording where desired, add a sound effect or musical clip to the Audio/Music timeline, and then record again further down the timeline.

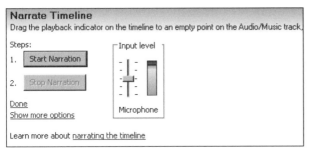

39.6

39.7

CHAPTER 8

CREATING COMPELLING TITLES AND CREDITS

W hen you use iMovie or Windows Movie Maker to edit footage that you shoot with your digital camcorder, you can create professional-looking movies by applying effects, transitions, and working with sound as you've seen in previous chapters. When you apply the techniques presented in this book to your clips, your production will have considerably more panache then most home movies. However, you can take your movies to the next level when you add a compelling title and ending credits. Combine titles and credits with narration or a soundtrack, and you've got a movie you can share with anybody. With a descriptive title, all your viewers need to do is cue up and view your finished production. If you've done a good job creating your title and ending credits, your viewing audience has all the information they need to know. The last four techniques in this chapter include an instruction to save the technique as a project. You will be using these projects in Chapter 9 to make movies files.

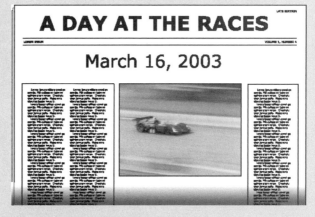

SUPERIMPOSING A TITLE OVER A CLIP

40.1

40.2

ABOUT THE VIDEO

We shot this video clip in the depths of the New York City subway system, using a Canon GL-2 on with the exposure manually increased to compensate for the darkness of the subway. We then captured the clip in iMovie and trimmed it in iMovie and Windows Movie Maker.

One of the biggest benefits of editing video in an application such as iMovie or Windows Movie Maker is the ability to add titles to your work. Sure, you can make a simple title on some consumer and prosumer DV camcorders but you don't have many options to control the appearance of the title. If you've watched your fair share of television shows and movies, you know there are a myriad of methods for displaying the title of a production. One technique is to display a title over the first clip of the movie to introduce your production. In iMovie and Windows Movie Maker, you can display either a static title or animated title over a movie clip. Neither application has a sophisticated superimpose track like higher-end applications. However, both iMovie and Windows Movie Maker offer a drag-and-drop interface that allows even a beginner to easily superimpose titles on top of clips. Use this technique when you want to give your viewers a preview of your movie while they're reading the title for the movie. When preparing clips for titles, make sure that the clip, which resides under the title, is at least 10 seconds long. This gives you plenty of time to display the title and the last few seconds of your movie's first clip. **Figure 40.1** shows a subway pulling into a station. **Figure 40.2** shows a frame from the same clip with a title superimposed over it.

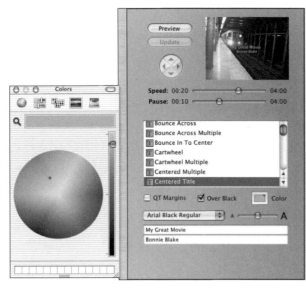

40.3

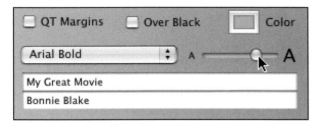

40.4

iMOVIE

STEP 1: BEGIN A NEW PROJECT

First you place a clip on the Movie Track, which the title will appear over.

■ Launch iMovie. In the New Project dialog box, type in a project name in the Save As box and then navigate to the folder where you want to save the project. Click the **Save** button.

■ Choose **File ➤ Import** from the menu.

■ In the Import dialog box, navigate to the CD-ROM and click **MacClip050.mov**.

■ Click the **Open** button. After the file imports into iMovie, drag the clip from the Shelf to the Movie Track.

STEP 2: ADJUST THE TITLE ATTRIBUTES

Creating a title which overlays a clip is a relatively easy process in iMovie. First you select the attributes of the title, inclusive of font, color, and size.

■ Click the **Titles** tab to display the Titles pane. In the Titles list, select the title named **Centered Title**. A thumbnail preview appears in the upper-right corner of the Titles pane with dummy text. Note that the first line reads **My Great Movie,** and the second line reflects your name. These lines are placement text that you select and type over to create your title. This default placement text also has default attributes, so if you don't feel like adjusting the text color, size, font, and so on, it will be chosen for you.

■ In the bottom half of the Titles pane, you can adjust the text settings. Click the **font** pop-up list and select a font from the menu. The fonts available here reflect the font selection available in your computer system.

■ If you want the text to be a color other than the default white, click the **Color** box (see **Figure 40.3**). Select a color for the text from the Color palette by clicking and dragging within the color wheel; the color in the Color box reflects the current color.

■ Drag the **Font Size** slider in the Title pane three-quarters of the length to the right, toward the large letter **A** to **increase** the size of the font (see **Figure 40.4**).

STEP 3: TYPE THE TITLE

iMovie offers a simple interface for creating text. Dummy text is used to define the placement and the look of the text. You have a good idea of what it's going to look like before you apply the text because you can see what it looks like in the thumbnail preview in the Titles pane.

- To type the text, select the first line of text (representing the main title) in the text box near the bottom of the Titles pane that says, My Great Movie and type in a line of text. In the example, we typed in **Mass Transit**, as shown in **Figure 40.5**.
- Next, select the second line of text (representing the subtitle) and type your subtitle. (Note the second line of text is smaller than the first.) If you only need a one-line title, delete the dummy text from the second line (name) so that it appears blank.
- To apply the title, click the title in the titles list and drag it to the head of the first clip. After the clip renders, press the **Home** key and then the **spacebar** to play the new movie with a title. Notice that your clip is now split in two on the Movie Track and that the new clip is given a new name to reflect the actual title you created (see **Figure 40.6**).
- The duration of the new title (indicated on the top of the clip in the Movie Track and at the bottom of the thumbnail preview) is based on the duration set in the **Speed** slider in the Titles pane (see **Figure 40.7**).

> **TIP**
>
> To change the adjustments you made on the title after you apply the title, simply select the new adjustments and press the **Update** tab at the top of the Title pane.

Mass Transit
New York City

40.5

40.7

40.6

STEP 4: ADD A FADE IN TRANSITION

To add a professional touch to the title that introduces your movie, try using a Fade In transition at the front of your clips. A Fade In transition fades in the title from black to the image resulting in a more dramatic entrance for the movie.

40.8

- Click the **Trans** tab to display the Transitions pane. In the Transitions list, click **Fade In**, as shown in **Figure 40.8**.
- When adding a transition before, after, or to a clip, always take note of the duration of the clip, so you will know how long to make the duration of the transition. The duration of the first clip in the Movie Track is 04:08, so our transition needs to be LESS than this amount to hold the transition. Drag the Speed slider in the Transitions pane to 02:00 (see **Figure 40.9**).
- Deselect all clips in the Movie Track by clicking in the gray vacant area to the right of the clip. Click the Fade In and drag it to the front of the first clip in the Movie Track, as shown in **Figure 40.10**. Press the **Home** key and then the **spacebar** to play the movie. Note the title now gradually fades in from black.

40.9

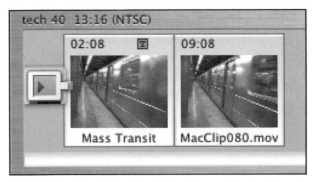

40.10

WINDOWS MOVIE MAKER

After you assemble a project on the timeline or storyboard, apply video effects, and add transitions, you'll have a pretty good idea of what type of title you want to use to introduce your movie. Windows Movie Maker gives you the necessary tools to add an interesting title to your production, to animate the title, and to format the title text.

STEP 1: CREATE A NEW PROJECT

■ Launch Windows Movie Maker and choose **File ➢ New Project**.

■ Choose **File ➢ Import Into Collections**. Navigate to the CD-ROM that accompanies this book, select **WinClip082.wmv**, and then click **Import**. Windows Movie Maker creates a collection for the clip.

■ Click the **Show Timeline** button if you're currently working in storyboard mode.

■ Drag the clip to the timeline. Windows Movie Maker snaps the clip to timecode 0:00:00.00.

STEP 2: ADD THE TITLE

When you create titles for your own movies, make sure to create a descriptive title that your audience can quickly understand. Doing this is especially important when you're displaying a title over a clip. Make the title short and simple. If you want to add your name as the moviemaker, you can always add this to the ending credits.

■ Click the **Tasks** button if the Movie Tasks pane is not currently displayed.

■ Click **Make titles or credits** in the Edit Movie section of the Movie Tasks pane.

■ Click **title on the selected clip** to display the Enter Text for Title section.

■ In the **Text window**, type the title for your movie. For the purpose of this example, type **New York City Mass Transit** (see **Figure 40.11**).

■ Click **Change the title animation** to display the Choose the Title Animation section. As you open this section, you notice many different ways you can animate a title. You can choose from a selection of one- and two-line title animations.

■ Click **Basic Title** from the Titles, One Line list, as shown in **Figure 40.12**. After you choose an animation, Windows Movie Maker displays the animated title over a preset image.

40.11

40.12

The title looks fine as it is, but can be tweaked by changing the font style. When you add titles to your movies, the initial preview helps you determine what text attributes, if any, you need to modify.

STEP 3: EDIT THE TITLE TEXT FONT AND COLOR

After you choose a title animation, you can accept the default font type and size or modify text attributes to suit the clips you are editing and your personal taste.

- Click **Change the text font and color** to display the Select Title Font and Color section.
- Click the **Font** drop-down menu and select a font. This list contains all the fonts installed on your system. Notice that you can also change the text alignment and apply styles to the text. These options are similar to what you find in word-processing applications.
- Choose **Verdana** from the **Font** drop-down menu. (If you don't have the Verdana font installed on your system, choose your favorite font from the list.)

TIP

You can add certain titles to a movie while working in storyboard mode; if you're working in timeline mode, however, you can use all of the Movie Maker's titles and credits. As an added bonus, you can trim the length of title clips while working in timeline mode.

- Click the large **A** icon to increase the text size (see **Figure 40.13**).
- Click **I** to italicize the text. Note that you can also boldface or underline the text. As with word-processing applications, you can apply more than one style to title text. Your working title is updated in real time in the Preview pane. You can preview the title over your first clip after you finish editing the title.
- Before adding a title to your movie, click the **Play** button in the Preview pane to preview the title clip over a preset Windows Movie Maker image. If you have any spelling errors or decide to change the title, click **Edit the title text** to display the Enter Text for Title section.

Notice the change text color option. For the purpose of this exercise, accept the default white color as the clip the title is being displayed over has predominantly dark colors.

Select Title Font and Color
Click 'Done' to add the title to the movie.

Font:
Verdana   B *I* U

Color: Transparency: 0%   Size: Position:

Done   Cancel

More options:
    Edit the title text
    Change the title animation

40.13

STEP 4: ADD THE TITLE TO YOUR MOVIE

After entering the title text and choosing the font attributes, your next step is to add the title to the movie and preview it.

- Click **Done, add title to movie** to exit the Add Titles or Credits pane.
- Click the **Play Timeline** button to preview the title on the sample clip (see **Figure 40.14**).

As the clip plays, the title is displayed for a duration of 4 seconds. When you add a title that displays over a clip, it appears on the Title Overlay timeline. You can change the title duration in the same manner as you trim clips on the timeline. Select the title clip and move your cursor towards the right side of the clip. When your cursor becomes a red double-headed arrow, click and drag the clip right to increase or left to decrease the duration of the title. By default, Windows Movie Maker snaps the beginning of the title overlay clip to the beginning of the clip to which you apply it. You can change this by clicking the center of the title overlay clip and then dragging it to the desired position.

40.14

ANIMATING A TITLE OVER A COLOR BACKGROUND

41.1

*Larry's
Great
Adventure*

41.2

ABOUT THE VIDEO

The sample clips you'll be working with was filmed at the Great Clermont triathlon in Clermont, Florida. The athlete crossing the finish line (see **Figure 41.1**) is exhausted after swimming 1.5 miles, biking 25 miles, and running 6.1 miles. The finished technique will display a title clip (see **Figure 41.2**) before the first clip plays. The footage was shot with a Sony DCR-TRV27 using automatic exposure and auto-focus. The footage was captured to the PC through an IEEE1394 FireWire card and trimmed in Windows Movie Maker.

When you edit footage that is recorded in bright lighting conditions, an overlay will be hard to see. You could choose a dark text color, but this might distract attention from the clip over which you are displaying the title. When this is the case, you can display an animated title over a solid color background. The title animation piques viewer curiosity for the clips that follow. Use this technique when you're editing footage that contains scenery you don't want hidden by a title overlay, or when the first scene in your movie is bright.

iMOVIE

In iMovie you can overlay a title on a black background but not on a color background. But this does not mean you can't do this. To achieve this effect, all you need to do is create a solid color background picture in an application such as Photoshop or any application that allows you to size files in pixels and export in a format that iMovie can recognize. iMovie can import PICT, JPEG, GIF, and PSD file formats. When you do import this solid-color background file, the file has to be sized as 640 x 480, the native QuickTime dimensions. After creating the color

233

background, you can import it into iMovie and use it as the underlay for your movie.

If you don't have an application in which to make a color background, you can use one of eight color background templates in the Color Backgrounds folder on the CD-ROM that comes with this book. You will use one of these backgrounds for this technique. And, if you like the color background templates on the CD-ROM for your backgrounds, you may never have to make your own.

STEP 1: BEGIN A NEW PROJECT

- Launch iMovie.
- In the New Project dialog box, type a name for the project in the **Save As** text box and then navigate to the folder where you want to save the project. Click the **Save** button.
- Choose **File ➤ Import** from the menu. The Import dialog box appears. Navigate to the CD-ROM, select **MacClip071.mov**, and then click the **Open** button.
- Choose **File ➤ Import** again. Navigate to the Color Backgrounds folder on the CD-ROM, open a color background file of your choice, and click the **Open** button.
- Drag the clips from the Shelf to the Movie Track, placing the color background clip as the first clip and **MacClip071.mov** as the second one (see **Figure 41.3**).

> **TIP**
>
> On the Mac, there is an easy way to import non-contiguous files located in the same folder. Press the **Command** key while selecting the files. You can save a lot of time selecting multiple files because you do not have to return to File ➤ Import for each new file.

- Under the Monitor window, click the **Timeline Viewer** icon (clock) to display the Movie Track in Timeline view. Timeline view enables you to adjust the duration of the clips.

STEP 2: LENGTHEN THE COLOR BACKGROUND

- iMovie has several cool animated titles to choose from. In this technique, you use the title named Bounce Across. This title gives the effect of the line of text riding on a fast moving roller coaster. This playful style is ideal for creating a light and fun introduction to your movie. Before creating the title, the duration of the background color picture needs to be extended to hold the title long enough for the viewer to read it.
- Click the first clip (color background) and then click the **Photos** tab to display the Photos pane. Drag the **Duration** slider to approximately 7 seconds and click the **Apply** button. Now the color background appears for 7 seconds, more than enough time for the title to display (see **Figure 41.4**).

41.3

STEP 3: CHOOSE THE TITLE ATTRIBUTES

Now you select the title and adjust the title attributes.

- Click the first clip in the Movie Track and then click the **Titles** tab to display the Titles pane. Navigate to the title named Bounce Across. The thumbnail preview shows you what the title looks like on the color background of the first clip (see **Figure 41.5**).
- In the Titles pane, select a font, size, and if you like, a font color.
- In the text box at the bottom of the pane, select the line of text that reads **My Great Movie** and type in a new title of your choice. Then select the second line and type in a subtitle of your choice over the placeholder text as shown in **Figure 41.6**. (If you do not need to type a second line of text, simply delete the placeholder text.)
- When you are done, drag the title from the Title list to the beginning of the first clip.
- Press the **Home** key and the **spacebar** to preview the effect. As you can see, this creates a fun, lyrical entrée to your movie.

As you can see from this technique, creating a color background for a title is relatively easy, even though iMovie does not offer you this option. Another variation of this technique would be creating color backgrounds that are a little more lively than just solid color. For example, you could make a gradient background and apply some of the great Photoshop filters to this gradient to give it some texture. You might even want to create your title in Photoshop and use Photoshop effects on your text that are not available in iMovie. Photoshop and many other photo editing applications offer effects that work well with text like an inner and outer bevel and emboss feature and drop shadow, just to name a few.

41.5

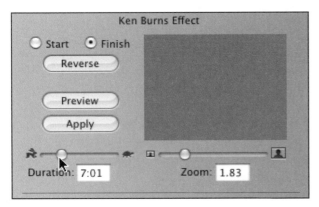

41.4

41.6

WINDOWS MOVIE MAKER

When you want to preserve the first scene of your movie and still display a title, the only alternative you have is to display a title over a solid background. You can do this easily in Windows Movie Maker by creating a title at the beginning of the movie as outlined in the following steps.

STEP 1: CREATE A NEW PROJECT

When you edit clips in Windows Movie Maker, you can add a title at any time. However, if you assemble the clips and preview the movie first, you'll have a better idea of which title animation will work best for your footage.

- Launch Windows Movie Maker and choose **File ➤ New Project**.
- Choose **File ➤ Import Into Collections**. Navigate to the CD-ROM that accompanies this book, select **WinClip069.wmv** and click **Import**. Windows Movie Maker creates a collection for the clip.
- Click the **Show Timeline** button if the storyboard is currently displayed.
- Drag the clip onto the **timeline**. Windows Movie Maker snaps the clip to timecode 0:00:00.00.

At this stage in a project, you'd add the rest of the clips to your production and preview it before deciding on a title.

STEP 2: ADD A TITLE

- Click the **Tasks** button.
- Click **Make titles or credits** from the Edit Movie section of the Movie Tasks pane. The Where Do You Want to Add A Title section opens.

- Click **at the beginning** to open the Enter Text for Title section.
- In the **Text** window type **Larry's Great Adventure**.
- Click **Change the title animation** to display the Choose The Title Animation section.
- Choose **Zoom, Up and In**. Windows Movie Maker displays the title clip in the Preview pane (see **Figure 41.7**).

When you choose title animations for your own movies, choose one that fits the subject matter. We chose the Zoom, Up and In animation for the sample clip because it mirrors the motion of the athlete crossing through the finish line archway.

41.7

STEP 3: CHANGE THE TITLE TEXT ATTRIBUTES

When you create a title at the beginning of a movie, it appears over a color background. You can choose a background color to suit the movie you are creating and modify the title text font, size, and color.

■ Click **Change the text font and color** to open the Select Title Font and Color section.
■ Click the **Font** drop-down menu and choose **Times New Roman**.
■ Click the **B** and **I** icons to boldface and italicize the text. When you create titles for your movies, apply styles to suit your taste. If you're using a font that looks like handwriting, you're probably better off applying no styles to the text.
■ In the Color section, click the **Change the background color** icon to open the Color window (see **Figure 41.8**).

TIP

If you want some of the background color to show through the title text, click and drag the Transparency slider. As you drag the slider, Windows Movie Maker updates the title text in the Preview pane.

■ Click a color to select it and then click **OK**. For the purpose of this exercise, choose one of the light blues.
■ Click **Done, add title to movie** to exit the Add Titles or Credits pane.

STEP 4: APPLY A TRANSITION

This step is optional depending on the length of the first clip in your movie. As a general rule, you shouldn't apply a transition when you've got a clip of short duration, but we're taking some liberty here to show how you can use a transition to smoothly segue into your first scene.

41.8

- Click the **Show Storyboard** button to switch to storyboard mode.
- Click **View video transitions** in the Edit Movie section of the Movie Tasks pane.
- Drag the **Fade** transition into the slot between the clips.
- Click the **Play Storyboard** button to preview the movie. As the movie plays, notice how the first scene fades from the title clip (see **Figure 41.9**).

TIP

You can quickly edit a title in the Add Titles or Credits pane by double-clicking the title clip.

41.9

ADDING A LAYERED TITLE

42.1

St. John
Vacation in
Paradise
Filmed by Doug Sahlin

42.2

The art of moviemaking is much like writing a novel. You grab the viewers' attention at the beginning of your work and don't let it go until your production is finished. One of the best ways to get your viewers to stand up and notice your work is with an interesting title. iMovie and Windows Movie Maker give you a plethora of choices for title animations. When you apply this technique to your movies, your viewers will see title text moving over your first scene. Use this technique when the first scene of your movie doesn't have a lot of action, otherwise the moving title will compete with the opening footage of your movie, and your viewers will have a hard time reading the title text.

Figure 42.1 shows the first scene of a movie. Figure 42.2 shows the same first scene with an added layered title.

iMOVIE

In this technique you use a Cross Through Center title. This title spins around on a two-dimensional axis, simulating a virtual 3D effect. On the center axis, the letters in the word cross over one another so at one point, all the letters in each line of text are on top of one another. Halfway into the movie, a second title appears that gives text information on the remaining footage. To create this text, you split the clip and add a subtitle. This technique provides a solid explanation on how to use more than one title on a single clip.

STEP 1: BEGIN A NEW PROJECT

- Launch iMovie.
- In the New Project dialog box, for **Save As**, type in a name for the project and then navigate to the folder where you want to save the project. Click the **Save** button.
- Choose **File ➤ Import** from the menu.
- In the Import dialog box, navigate to the CD-ROM and select **MacClip010.mov**.
- Click the **Open** button. After the file imports into iMovie, drag the clip from the Shelf to the Movie Track.
- Under the Monitor window, click the **Timeline Viewer** icon (clock) to display the Movie Track in Timeline view. Working in Timeline view allows you to split the clip in the Movie Track, which you cannot do in Clip view.

STEP 2: SPLIT THE CLIP

To accommodate the second title, you need to split the clip into two. Then you place the second title on the new clip segment.

- In the Movie Track Timeline view, position the **Playhead** halfway through the clip.

- From the menu, choose **Edit ➤ Split Video Clip at Playhead** (see **Figure 42.3**). iMovie splits the clip into two segments.

STEP 3: ADD A TITLE TO THE FIRST CLIP

- Click the first segment and then press the **Titles** tab. In the Titles list, click the **Cross through Center** title. The thumbnail preview demonstrates how the title works.
- From the **Font** list, select a font such as **Arial Black** that works well with the title. This font works well for titles because it is heavy and simple.
- Drag the **Font Size** slider a little to the right of the middle to make the title size a little larger.
- Click the **Colors** box and then click and drag in the color wheel until you find a color you like.
- In the **Text Input** box, highlight the first line of placement text and input your new text. Repeat this process for the second line of placement text (see **Figure 42.4**).
- Make sure that the **Over Black** box is deselected because this title will overlay the video clip, not a black background.

42.3

■ When you are satisfied with the adjustments you have made to your title, drag the title from the Titles list to the front of the timeline.

STEP 4: ADD A TITLE TO THE SECOND CLIP

Because the last title acts as a supplemental subtitle, its text should be smaller and less intrusive.

■ Click the second clip segment (not counting the new title clip at the front of the timeline) and in

42.4

42.5

the Titles list, navigate to the title named **Subtitle**. As you can see from the thumbnail preview, the subtitle is small and it appears toward the bottom of a clip.

■ Repeat the process of selecting a **font, font size**, and **color** for the subtitle. In addition, repeat the process of highlighting the first and second lines of placement text in the text box, then type in the replacement text (see **Figure 42.5**).

■ Press the **Home** key and the **spacebar** to see the results. The first title turns on a 3-D axis and then stops a few seconds into the clip. About halfway into the clip, the subtitle appears. By splitting the clip, you can place a title wherever you want within a movie sequence.

WINDOWS MOVIE MAKER

When you want to tease your viewers with a preview of your movie while rolling the titles, you can use this technique to good effect. What better way to whet your viewers' appetites than displaying title text over the first clip of the movie?

STEP 1: CREATE A NEW PROJECT

■ Launch Windows Movie Maker and choose **File ➤ New Project**.

■ Choose **File ➤ Import Into Collections**. From the CD-ROM that accompanies this book, select **WinClip010.wmv,** and then click **Import**. Windows Movie Maker creates a collection for the clip.

■ Click the **Show Timeline** button if you're currently working in storyboard mode.

■ Drag the clip onto the timeline. Windows Movie Maker snaps the clip to timecode 0:00:00.00.

■ Click the **Play Timeline** button. Windows Movie Maker plays the clip in the Preview pane.

The clip looks like the perfect vacation getaway, especially if you live in the northern United States and you're reading this in the dead of winter. Now that you've got the clip on the timeline, you need to add a compelling title.

STEP 2: SELECT A TITLE ANIMATION

When you begin a movie with a clip 10 seconds or longer, you can use a title overlay to good effect. An animated title is always a good choice when you have interesting footage in your first scene. The equation for an interesting movie is eye-catching footage plus an effective animated title.

- Click the **Tasks** button to display the Tasks pane.
- Click **Make titles or credits** in the Tasks pane's Edit Movie section. Windows Movie Maker displays the Where Do You Want to Add A Title section of the Make Titles or Credits pane.
- Click **title on the selected clip** to open the Enter Text for Title section.
- Click **Change the title animation** to open the Choose the Title Animation section.
- Click **Moving Titles, Layered** from the Titles, Two Lines list. Windows Movie Maker displays the title animation in the Preview pane over a preset image (see **Figure 42.6**).

When you create anything other than a basic one-line title, you have to select the title animation before entering the title text.

STEP 3: CREATE THE TITLE TEXT

- Click **Edit the title text** to revert to the Enter Text for Title section. Notice that you now have two separate windows in which to enter title text.
- In the top text window, type **St. John**, press **Enter** to create a new line, and then type **Vacation in Paradise**.

- In the bottom text window, type **Filmed by Doug Sahlin**. When you create titles for your own movies, you can take the credit.
- If desired, click **Change the text font and color** to change text attributes as outlined in Technique 41.
- Click **Done add title To movie** to place the title in the movie and close the Make Credits or Titles pane.
- Click the **Play Timeline** button to preview the movie, which should resemble the one shown in **Figure 42.7**.

The layered animated title makes a good intro for the movie. The moving layer of animated text behind the stationary title adds interest to the footage of the beautiful tropical beach. When you're creating a mini-documentary of vacation footage, you can narrate the clips to identify the various places you've visited, or you can add subtitles.

42.6

STEP 4: ADD SUBTITLES

When you want to identify various parts of a movie, you can add a title over the top of a clip. However, the repeated use of title overlays can be distracting. A better choice is the subtitle, which is an unobtrusive text message towards the bottom of the clip.

- Click the blue **Playhead** and drag it to the right. As you drag the Playhead, a tool tip displays the current timecode.
- Release the mouse button when the timecode reads **0:00:05.00**. When you move the Playhead before creating a subtitle, you specify the timecode at which the subtitle will be inserted.
- Click **Make titles or credits** and, in the Where Do You Want to Add the Title section, click **title on the selected clip** to open the Enter Text for Title section.

- Click **Change title animation** to open the Choose the Title Animation section.
- Choose **Subtitle** from Titles, One Line list and then click **Edit the title text**. When the Enter Text for Title section opens, notice that you now have only one window in which to enter text.
- In the text window, type **Cinnamon Bay**. If desired, click **Change text and font color** to choose a different font and text color as outlined in Technique 41.
- Click **Done, add title to movie** to exit the Make Titles or Credits pane. Notice the new entry on the Text Overlay timeline, positioned precisely where you moved the Playhead (see **Figure 42.8**).
- Click the **Play Timeline** button. As the movie plays, notice the innocuous subtitle that appears after the movie has played for 5 seconds. The text is small enough to inform, yet it does not detract from the movie.

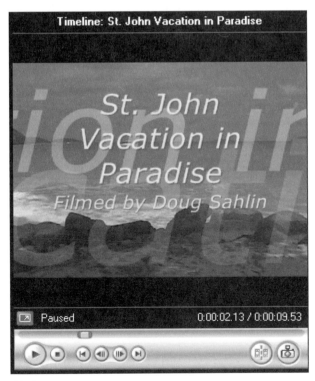

42.7

42.8

CREATING A NARRATIVE TITLE

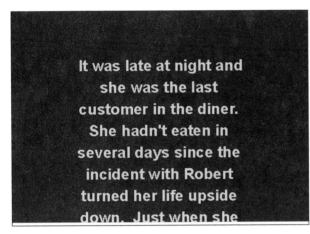

It was late at night and she was the last customer in the diner. She hadn't eaten in several days since the incident with Robert turned her life upside down. Just when she

43.1

43.2

Rolling text is not the exclusive domain of titles and credits. You can also use text as a narrative element to provide background information on the story that is about to unfold.

For long narratives, the amount of information you can display is limited to the height of the frame. By scrolling the text, you can feed more information to the audience over an extended amount of time. Scrolling text dates back to old movies when effects were limited and producers had to rely heavily on narratives to set the stage for the next scene. Narrative text is still effectively used for this purpose. It is an essential element of documentaries and episodic serials.

In this technique, you set up a scrolling text block on a black background that explains the story and then transitions into the first scene.

Figure 43.1 shows the rolling narrative intro text that sets the mood for the beginning of the movie and **Figure 43.2** shows the first clip in the movie that appears after the intro text.

iMOVIE

STEP 1: BEGIN A NEW PROJECT

You first have to import a clip onto the Movie Track before you build the scrolling text block.

- Launch iMovie.
- In the New Project dialog box, type a name for the project in the **Save As** text box and then navigate to the folder in which you want to save the project. Click the **Save** button.
- Choose **File ➤ Import** from the menu. The Import dialog box appears.
- Navigate to the CD-ROM and then select **MacClip050.mov.**
- Click the **Open** button. After the file imports into iMovie, drag the clip from the Shelf to the Movie Track.

STEP 2: CREATE ROLLING TEXT

In this step, you choose a title that works well for a narrative description, the scrolling title. This title enables you to type in a block of text rather than individual lines of text as you would do for titles and credits.

- Click the **Titles** tab. In the Titles pane, check the **Over Black** check box. Doing this ensures that the narrative text overlays a black background as opposed to overlaying the clip. The black background is less distracting than a clip background when there is a lot of text to read.

TIP

If your scrolling text is more than a couple of sentences, try typing it in a word-processing application and then copying and pasting the text into the Scrolling Title pane in iMovie.

- Click the color box and then select a text color from the **Color** palette by clicking and dragging within the color wheel (see **Figure 43.3**). The color you select appears in a swatch to the right of the wheel.
- From the Titles list, select **Scrolling Block.** At the bottom of the pane, select a font from the pop-up font list. (In **Figure 43.4**, Arial Bold is selected.) Drag the **Font Size** slider to the middle, so text will be medium size.
- In the large white text box at the bottom of the pane, type in your narrative text. The formatted text appears in the Preview thumbnail. You can tweak any of the attributes you assigned before you apply the text to the Movie Track.

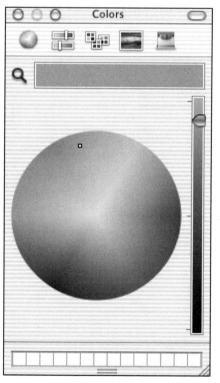

43.3

■ At the top of the Titles pane, drag the **Speed** slider three-quarters of the way toward the right to lengthen the duration of the scrolling title, as shown in **Figure 43.5**. Otherwise, your audience will have to speed read the title as it swiftly scrolls by.

■ Drag the title to the head of the clip in the Movie track. When the title is finished rendering, press the **Home** key and then the **spacebar** to play the title. The text sets the stage for the visuals to come, rather than acting as a title introducing a movie.

■ Save the project by choosing **File** ➢ **Save Project** from the menu.

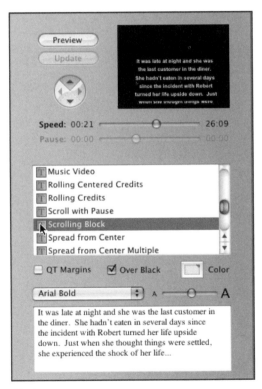

43.4

43.5

OPTIMIZING TEXT QUALITY

Often people are disappointed in the final output quality of their titles, and this issue is not exclusive to iMovie. QuickTime DV compression is known for producing titles that are not very crisp because with QuickTime, the balance of size versus quality is more slanted toward size as opposed to quality. If you are unsatisfied with the output quality, try to stay away from high contrast colors, such as white text on a black background. You can also experiment with various QuickTime compression settings when exporting your movie using Expert Settings. Different settings (Sorenson 3, Cinepak, Motion JPEG A and B) yield different results

TITLE-SAFE MARGINS

Most prosumer and professional video applications offer a title-safe margin feature of some sort. *Title-safe* means that the titles you are creating stay inside a margin within the text field. Older televisions sometimes crop off the portion of the edges of the image. The old cathode ray tubes were curved on the edges, and the consoles overlapped a small portion of the edges, causing titles that came too close to the edges to get clipped off. If your production is full screen and bound for a television monitor, you want to make certain the QT Margins box is not checked (see Figure 43.6). When it is not checked, iMovie will size your text so that it will not crop off part of titles if they fall close to the edges of the frame. You can safely check QT Margins if your final movie is being exported for the Web, CD-ROM, or DVD. Videos played on computer monitors do not require frames with titles within the title-safe area.

43.6

WINDOWS MOVIE MAKER

If you want to tell a back story before rolling your first scene, you can use this technique to display a narrative that slowly scrolls from the bottom of the screen. This is an excellent way to augment your movies and tell viewers what has occurred before the first scene begins. It's also an excellent way to fill a gap when you don't have video, but need to display information pertinent to the scene about to unfold.

STEP 1: CREATE A NEW PROJECT

- Launch Windows Movie Maker and choose **File ➤ New Project**.
- From the CD-ROM that accompanies this book, select **WinClip049.wmv** and then click **Import**. Windows Movie Maker creates a collection for the clip.
- Drag the clip to the storyboard or timeline.

STEP 2: SELECT THE TITLE ANIMATION

The title animation used in this technique is similar to the one used to open classic movies, such as *Star Wars*. When the first words of the title appear, they fill the bottom of the screen and scroll up line by line. The size of the text decreases as it scrolls to the next highest line, creating the illusion of depth as the narrative title plays.

> **NOTE**
>
> When you create a title with a text overlay or subtitle, you can only add it in timeline mode. With all of the other title techniques, you can add and edit the title in either mode.

- Click the **Tasks** button to display the Movie Tasks pane.
- Click **Make credits or titles** to open the Where Do You Want to Add A Title section of the Make Titles or Credits pane.
- Click **title at the beginning** to open the Enter Text for Title section (see **Figure 43.7**).
- Click **Change the title animation** to open the Choose Title Animation section.
- Click **Scroll, Perspective** from the Titles, One Line list and then click **Edit the title text** to revert to the Enter Text for Title section.

After choosing the title animation, all you need to do is type the title text and change the background color.

STEP 3: ADDING THE NARRATION TEXT

When you begin your movie with narrative text, you are telling the back-story of what happened in the past to set the stage for the upcoming events. Rather than take up a paragraph or two of the book with suggested narration text, we suggest that you preview the clip and create your own back-story. Or, if you're

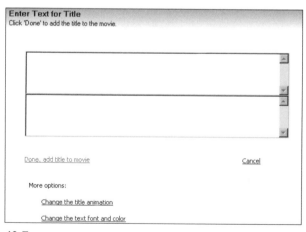

43.7

not feeling especially creative right now, choose the opening lines from your favorite novel, short story, or poem.

- Enter the text for the narrative title (see **Figure 43.8**).
- Click **Change text font and color** to display the Select Title Font and Color section.
- Choose your favorite font and accept the default text size. If you choose a large font size for a narrative title, your title will show only one or two words of text for each line, and the narrative will be hard for your viewers to follow.
- Click the **Background Color** icon, click the **black** color swatch and then click **OK** to exit the Color window.
- Click **Done, add title to movie** to exit the Add Titles or Credits pane.
- Click the **Play Storyboard** or **Play Timeline** button to play the movie in the Preview pane (see **Figure 43.9**).
- Choose **File ➤ Save Project As** to open the Save Project As dialog box.

- Enter **Tech43** in the **File Name** field and then click **Save**.

> **TIP**
>
> If you have word-processing software installed on your computer, use it to create the narrative text. Spell-check the text, press **Ctrl+A** to select all the text, and then press **Ctrl+C** to copy the text to the Clipboard. In Windows Movie Maker, place your cursor in the **Enter Text for Title** section's text window and press **Ctrl+V** to paste the spell-checked text into the window.

43.8

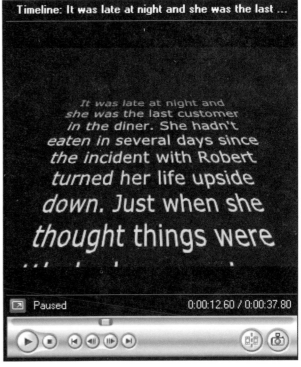

43.9

CREATING TITLES THAT ENGAGE YOUR AUDIENCE

44.1

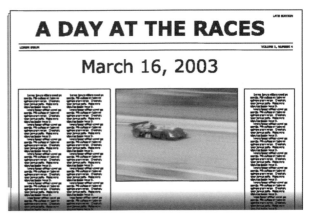

44.2

ABOUT THE VIDEO

The sample video provided for this technique was filmed at the 12 Hours of Sebring automobile race in Sebring, Florida. The footage was filmed with a Sony DCR-TRV27 from a spectator mound and shows the cars queued up for turn 3. The clip was captured with an IEEE 1394 Universal Bus Host Controller FireWire card and trimmed in Windows Movie Maker.

When you've captured exciting footage like a sporting event, you can crank up viewer excitement by creating an exciting title. With this technique, we use the best title effect available in iMovie and Windows Movie Maker to introduce the viewing audience to the excitement of an automobile race. You can use this type of title on any movie when your goal is to catch your viewers' attention before the first scene rolls. By the time you've edited your footage and applied transitions and video effects, you'll have a good idea of a working title for your movie. Plug that into this technique, and if you've done your editing well, you'll have a winning production that will make you the envy of all your moviemaker wannabe friends. The footage shown in **Figure 44.1** is used to create an engaging title, as shown in **Figure 44.2**.

iMOVIE

Sometimes combining titles with dynamic transitions allows you to explore the creative side of titles. In this technique, you combine an animated title with an animated transition. The movie begins with a racing scene and then transitions into the title. The title is a Sweep title, compliments of GeeThree. It "sweeps" the racing clip away to reveal the next clip underneath it, which happens to be the title. For this, you will use a **Gravity Title**. This title drops individual letters that form a word from the top of the screen to the middle screen. The conversion of a clip with a title and a transition makes for an eye-opening experience. Lastly, you add a soundtrack to pull the movie together into a real multimedia event. Before performing this technique, make sure you have downloaded and installed the GeeThree Slick Sampler pack from `www.geethree.com/slicksampler.html`.

STEP 1: BEGIN A NEW PROJECT

- Launch iMovie.
- In the New Project dialog box, type in a name for the project in the **Save As** box. Then, navigate to the folder in which you want to save the project and click the **Save** button.
- Choose **File ➢ Import** from the menu. The Import dialog box appears.
- Navigate to the CD-ROM and select **MacClip082.mov**.
- Click the **Open** button. After the file imports into iMovie, drag the clip from the Shelf to the Movie Track.

STEP 2: CREATE THE TITLE

The racecar clip serves as an introduction to the movie, and the title is gradually revealed after the racecar clip. The following steps show you how to make the title and then place it at the tail of the racecar clip.

- Click the **Titles** tab. Then, navigate to the title named **Gravity** in the Titles list. As the thumbnail preview shows, the letters drop one by one to form the title at mid-screen.
- Click the **Over Black** box to ensure that the clip is displayed over a black background, as opposed to an overlay on the racecar clip.
- Adjust the font, font size, and font color in the Titles pane.
- Highlight the first line of placement text in the Text Input box and type in a title. Then, highlight

44.3

the second line of placement text and input the second line of text (see **Figure 44.3**).

■ Drag the **Gravity** title from the Titles list to the tail of the race clip.

You can adjust the direction of your Gravity title as it enters the screen. In the default direction, the letters fall down from outside the top of the screen. By clicking the Up directional arrow in the top of the Titles pane, you instruct the letters to defy gravity by falling up to the middle screen instead of falling down (see **Figure 44.4**).

STEP 3: ADD A TRANSITION

If you play the movie at this point, the race clip cuts to the title in a mundane manner. You'll add a **sweep** transition to create a lively change from one clip to another. Before you use this transition, make certain that you have installed the transitions from the GeeThree Sampler available at `www.geethree.com/slicksampler.html`.

■ Click the **Trans** tab to transform the Titles pane into the Transitions pane.
■ Click the transition named **Sweep (Gee Three Sampler)** available for download at `www.geethree.com/slicksampler.html`. Note that in the thumbnail preview, the racecar is "swept" into a black title.
■ At the top of the Transitions pane, drag the **Duration** slider to the right, until the timecode

readout on the thumbnail preview reads **02:00**, as shown in **Figure 44.5**. This tells the transition to last for two seconds.

■ Drag the **Sweep** transition from the Transitions list to the Movie Track, in between the two clips on the Movie Track (see **Figure 44.6**).

44.5

44.4

44.6

STEP 4: ADD A SOUNDTRACK

To jazz up this title, you'll add a soundtrack. The soundtrack you are about to import is fast, loud, and upbeat, just like the racecars in the clip.

- Above the Movie Track, click the **Timeline Viewer** icon (clock icon) to display the Movie Track in Timeline mode.
- From the menu, choose **File ➢ Import**. The Import dialog box appears.
- Navigate to the Mac Files folder and select the file **kick.wav**. (This sound file imports directly onto the Audio Track in the Timeline.)
- Click the sound and drag it all the way to the beginning of the Timeline (timecode 00:00).
- Press the **Home** key and then the **spacebar** to play the movie. As you can see, all the components (title, transition, sound) work in concert with one another to create a dynamic movie. This combination of techniques works well for the introduction to a movie. You may want to try mixing and matching a variety of titles, transitions, and sounds together to see what interesting combinations you can invent.
- Choose **File ➢ Save Project** from the menu to save the project.

WINDOWS MOVIE MAKER

When you need to add pizzazz to a production, you can do it right from the start with your opening title. In our humble opinion, the best title Windows Movie Maker has to offer is the Newspaper title. Extra, extra, learn all about it by following the upcoming steps.

STEP 1: CREATE A NEW PROJECT

- Launch Windows Movie Maker and choose **File ➢ New Project**.
- Choose **File ➢ Import Into Collections**. Navigate to the CD-ROM that accompanies this book, select **WinClip017.wmv**, and then click **Import**. Windows Movie Maker creates a collection for the clip.
- Click the **Show Timeline** button if you're currently working in storyboard mode. Remember, you can only use an overlay title animation if you're working in timeline mode.
- Drag the movie clip onto the timeline. Windows Movie Maker snaps the clip to timecode 0:00:00.00.

STEP 2: SELECT THE TITLE ANIMATION

- Click the **Tasks** button to display the Movie Tasks pane.
- Click **Make titles or credits** to display the Where Do Want To Add A Title? section of the Make Titles or Credits pane.
- Click **title on the selected clip** to display the Enter Text for Title section.
- Click **Change the title animation** to display the Choose the Title Animation section.

■ Click **Newspaper** from the Titles, Two Lines section. After selecting the title animation, Windows Movie Maker previews the animation over a pre-set image (see **Figure 44.7**).

After choosing a title animation, your next step is to add the title you've thought up while painstakingly editing your footage. Of course, in this case, you have to use our title, because we painstakingly recorded the clip.

STEP 3: ADD THE TITLE TEXT

■ Click **Edit the title text** to revert to the Enter Text for Title section. Notice that you have two windows in which to enter text.
■ In the top window, type **A DAY AT THE RACES**.
■ In the bottom window, type **March 16, 2003**, which, of course, is the date the event took place.
■ Click **Done**, **add title to movie** to exit the Make Titles or Credits pane.

44.7

CHOOSING TITLE FONTS

When you create titles for your movies, avoid choosing highly stylized fonts with swooping curves. Font families, such as Kaufman and Staccato, may look fine when you preview your work in Windows Movie Maker. However, when you save your work as a movie and choose an option that renders the movie at a small size and compresses it for e-mail delivery or the Web, the text may become distorted or, worse yet, illegible. To guard against this, drop a short clip on the timeline, add your favorite title animation to the piece and experiment with your favorite font types. Save the movie with different options. When you play the rendered movies in Windows Media Player, you'll know which fonts you can safely use for your titles. To learn more about saving movie files for specific destinations, see Chapter 9.

■ Click the **Play Timeline** button to preview the movie. The newspaper spirals and zooms into view, displaying the title text while the clip plays in a small window (see **Figure 44.8**). If that doesn't get your viewers' attention, make sure that they're still breathing.

■ Choose **File ➤ Save Project As** to open the Save Project As dialog box.

■ Type **Tech44** in the **File Name** field and then click **Save**.

TIP

To take this technique over the top, add a music track to the Audio/Music timeline. Trim the audio clip to match the duration of the title clip, and fade the clip out as outlined in Chapter 7. The combination of music and a newspaper title will rev up your audience for the footage that follows.

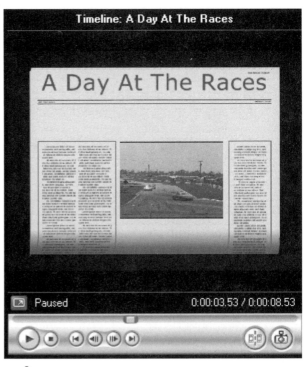

44.8

FINESSING YOUR MOVIE WITH ROLLING CREDITS

Daydream Believer	By Bonnie Blake
Starring	Kelly Blake
Best Boy	Matt Cicitta
Makeup	Dale Kroll
Location	Botanical Gardens

45.1

45.2

ABOUT THE VIDEO

This video was shot on a sunny afternoon in the spring. The DV camcorder used was a Canon GL-2 on automatic settings, using a UV filter and then captured in iMovie. The movie was trimmed in iMovie.

When you take the time and effort to edit your footage, and create an interesting movie to entertain your friends and family, you ought to take some credit for your talent. You could walk around saying, "I made this," after your movie finishes playing. Your audience may think you're a little strange, but if they're friends or relatives, they'll understand. Or you could take the safe route and add credits at the end of your movie. Rolling credits is an excellent way to do this. You can pack as much text into a rolling credit as you think your audience is willing to sit still for. But your best bet is to adhere to the KISS acronym and keep it short and simple.

Figure 45.1 shows the rolling text in action as the movie ends. **Figure 45.2** shows the final scene of the movie beginning to unfold.

iMOVIE

Rolling credits help give your movie a professional touch. They are generally used to give credit to the people who worked on the movie production team. In this technique, you create a simple rolling credit much like you've seen in movies through the years. In the movie you create here, the credits gradually appear at the end of a clip, and they display against a black background. They are very simple to make in iMovie, and, like making other credits, the process basically involves selecting the title, typing it in, and applying it.

STEP 1: BEGIN A NEW PROJECT

- Launch iMovie.
- In the New Project dialog box, type a name for the project in the **Save As** box and then navigate to the folder in which you want to save the project. Click the **Save** button.
- Choose **File ➤ Import** from the menu. The Import dialog box appears.
- Navigate to the CD-ROM and select **MacClip066.mov**.
- Click the **Open** button. After the file imports into iMovie, drag the clip from the Shelf to the Movie Track.

STEP 2: CREATE THE TITLE

- Click the **Titles** tab. Click the title named **Rolling Centered Credits** in the Titles list. As you can see in the thumbnail preview, the credits scroll up from the bottom of the screen. To change the direction to a downward scroll, click the down-ward-pointing arrow button from the cluster of four arrow buttons at the top of the Titles pane.
- Click the **Over Black** box to display the credits over a black background for this technique.

- Adjust the font, font size, and font color in the Titles pane.
- Highlight the first line of placement text in the **Text Input** box and type in a title. Then, highlight the second line of placement text and type the text that you want to appear to the right of the name, as shown in **Figure 45.3**.
- Repeat this process for the third and fourth lines of placement text (title to the left and name to the right).
- Click the **plus** (+) sign to the left of the Text Input box to create another text box. Repeat the process once again of highlighting the placement text and typing in new titles.
- Click again to create a text input box for the name to the right of the title (see **Figure 45.4**).

45.3

- If you need to delete a line of text, click the **minus** (−) sign situated under the Plus sign. You can repeat this process of entering titles in the credit list to accommodate as many credits at the end or the beginning of a movie as you like.
- To finish this movie, add a transition in between the two clips. In the movie sample included on the book's CD-ROM, a Cross Dissolve was added so that the clip of the girl would gradually transition into rolling credits (see **Figure 45.5**).
- Press the **Home** key and then the **spacebar** to play the movie.
- Save the project by choosing **File ➤ Save Project** from the menu.

You can also create a plain rolling credit appropriately named Rolling Credits. This title appears right under Rolling Centered Credits in the Titles list. This credit is similar the centered rolling credit. The difference is that the text is all aligned left, and there are leaders in between name and title (see **Figure 45.6**).

45.5

TIP

To add space in between credits, click the last entry in the text input box, click the **plus** (+) icon, and then leave the space blank. Doing this adds a blank space in between credits if you feel that the line spacing is too tight.

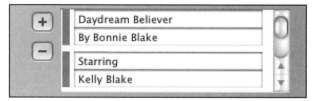

45.4

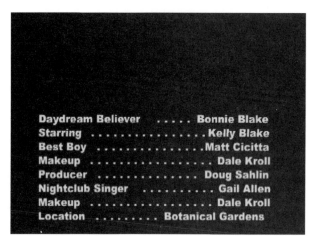

45.6

WINDOWS MOVIE MAKER

When the movie's over, turn on the lights. Of course, your viewers may not know when to quit munching on popcorn and organize a hasty retreat unless you let your viewers know your flick has ended. Follow the upcoming steps and your viewers will know it's: The End.

STEP 1: CREATE A NEW PROJECT

- Launch Windows Movie Maker and choose **File ➤ New Project**.
- Choose **File ➤ Import Into Collections**. Navigate to the CD-ROM that accompanies this book, select **WinClip064.wmv**, and then click **Import**. Windows Movie Maker creates a collection for the clip.
- Click the **Show Storyboard** button. You'll be adding a transition between the movie clip and the rolling credits, a task that is easier to accomplish in storyboard mode.
- Drag the clip into the first slot in the storyboard.

At this point in a project, you'd normally choose a title animation and create the title text. You can create a title if you choose before going to the next step. If you decide to do so, experiment with one of the title animations not covered in this chapter. You can use Windows Movie Maker as a tool to express your creativity through digital video. And like any other tool, you don't master it until you start experimenting with all the bells and whistles. Windows Movie Maker has a lot of bells and whistles when it comes to title animations.

STEP 2: ADD CREDITS TO THE END OF THE MOVIE

The ending credits used in this technique display a single-line title followed by lines of side-by-side credits. When you use rolling credits in your projects, you can use the side-by-side credits to acknowledge actors — or friends, relatives, significant others, and so on — in your movie, yourself as the filmmaker, or to display the location where the movie was filmed.

- Click the **Tasks** button to display the Movie Tasks pane.
- Click **Make titles or credits** to display the Where Do You Want To Add A Title? section.
- Click **credits at end** to display the Enter Text for Title section. Notice that the text area is divided into several windows.
- In the top window, type **Daydream Believer**.
- Click inside the first window in the second row and type **Starring**.
- Click inside the second window in the second row and type **Kelly Blake**.
- Click inside the first window in the third row and type **Filmed by** and then type **Bonnie Blake** inside the third row's second window.
- Click **Done, add title to movie**.
- Click the **Play Storyboard** button to preview the movie (see **Figure 45.7**).

The ending credits finish the movie with a professional touch. However, the transition from ending clip to credits is a bit abrupt. You can add another touch of professionalism if you fade from the final clip to ending credits.

STEP 3: ADD A TRANSITION BETWEEN FINAL SCENE AND CREDITS

You can add additional flare to ending credits through the effective use of a transition. When you decide to add a transition before ending credits, choose a subtle transition that won't detract from the final scene or ending credits.

- Click **View video transitions** to display all video transitions.
- Drag the **Fade** transition into the slot between the first and second clip.

- Click the **Play Storyboard** button to preview the movie (see **Figure 45.8**).
- Choose **File ➢ Save Project As** to open the Save Project As dialog box.
- Type **Tech45** in the **File Name** field and then click **Save**.

As the video plays, notice the subtle transition between the final scene and ending credits. While you still have the clips on the storyboard, experiment with the Reveal, Down, and Wipe, Normal, Down video transitions to explore other ways of segueing from the final scene to rolling credits.

45.7

45.8

ENDING YOUR MOVIE WITH PIZZAZZ

46.1

46.2

The footage for this technique was filmed in an Italian restaurant in historic Ybor City near Tampa, Florida. In 1898, Teddy Roosevelt assembled his Rough Riders in Ybor City prior to the Spanish-American War. This clip was filmed with a Sony DCR-TRV 27, captured to PC, and trimmed in Windows Movie Maker.

I f you start a movie with a bang by using a title that wows your audience, you should give it your best shot during ending credits as well. iMovie and Windows Movie Maker give you several different choices for ending a movie. This technique shows you how to create a lasting impression by using the best ending credit each program offers. You can end your movies on a high note by segueing from the final scene to this technique's ending credits as shown in **Figures 46.1** and **46.2**. iMovie and Windows Movie Maker have different ways of achieving this technique, but produce similar results. When you use this technique, your movie definitely doesn't go out like a lamb as does the month of March.

iMOVIE

iMovie offers many titles that can be used for a fun and light effect. In this technique, you use an Unscramble title. This title starts out with letters scattered randomly in the middle of the screen, reminiscent of the letters in the board game Scrabble. As the motion picks up, the animated letters move into place to form a word. Later, a transition pushes the clip of a man in a restaurant into the title. If you look closely at the accompanying movie for this technique included on the CD-ROM, the man glances to his right, he is pushed off the stage, and then the title gradually scrambles into place. Lastly, an upbeat soundtrack gives the title sequence an airy, lyrical feel, setting the mood of the movie to come.

STEP 1: BEGIN A NEW PROJECT

- Launch iMovie.
- In the New Project dialog box, type a name for the project in the **Save As** box and then navigate to the folder in which you want to save the project. Click the **Save** button.
- Choose **File ➢ Import** from the menu. The Import dialog box appears.
- Navigate to the CD-ROM and select **MacClip045.mov**.
- Click the **Open** button. After the file imports into iMovie, drag the clip from the Shelf to the Movie Track.

STEP 2: CREATE THE TITLE

In this step, the title you make appears after the clip of the man eating in a restaurant.

- Click the **Titles** tab and click **Unscramble Multiple** in the Titles list. An Unscramble title lies directly above the Unscramble Multiple. The titles are identical except Unscramble Multiple enables you to input more than two lines of text.
- Click the **Over Black** box to ensure that the new title will overlay a black background.
- Adjust the font, font size, and font color in the Titles pane.

- Highlight the first line of placement text in the text input box and type in your text. Repeat the process by highlighting the second line of placement text and typing again.
- Repeat this process for the third and fourth lines of placement text (see **Figure 46.3**). If you need more text input boxes, click the **Plus** (+) sign to the left of the text input box to create another text input box.

STEP 3: ADD A TRANSITION

To make the text slide into the clip of the man, you add a Push transition. If you recall from Chapter 12, the Push transition literally pushes one clip out of the way for another, like an animated slide show.

46.3

- Click the **Trans** tab and then click **Push** in the Transitions pane**.**
- At the top of the Transitions pane, drag the **Speed** slider all the way to the right, until the timecode readout on the thumbnail preview reads

TIP

To change the direction of the Push transition, click one of the arrows in the Direction dial at the top of the Transitions pane. You can push the previous clip to the left or right of the frame.

46.4

04:00, as shown in **Figure 46.4.** This tells the transition to last for four seconds.

- Drag the **Push** transition from the Transitions list to the Movie Track, in between the two clips (see **Figure 46.5**).

STEP 4: ADD A SOUNDTRACK

Sound often enhances a movie if you are trying to wow your audience. With this in mind, you can add a soundtrack to give the movie a more finished delivery.

- Above the Movie Track, click the **Timeline Viewer** icon (clock icon) to display the Movie Track in Timeline mode.
- From the menu, choose **File ➢ Import.** Navigate to the Clips folder, select the file **ambient noise.aif,** and click **Open.** Note that this sound file imports directly onto the first Audio Track in the timeline.
- Click the sound and center it underneath the clips on the Movie Track.
- From the menu, choose **File ➢ Import** again. Navigate to the Mac Files folder, select the file **Cool.wav**, and then click **Open.** This sound file

46.5

imports onto the second Audio Track in the Timeline. Drag this clip all the way to the left in the track it resides on, as shown in **Figure 46.6**.

■ Press the **Home** key and then the **spacebar** to play the movie. The combination of the upbeat music, the scrambled title, and the clip creates an engaging movie introduction.

■ Save the project, by choosing **File ➢ Save Project** from the menu.

TIP

If you want to adjust the volume on selected sound clips, click the **Edit Volume** box and drag the **Volume** slider left to lower the volume or to the right to increase it. Alternatively, you can click the **Edit Sound** button under the Timeline to display volume lines on the sound clip. See Chapter 7 to learn more about editing sound on clips.

WINDOWS MOVIE MAKER

When you've created your ultimate masterpiece, you can stand up, bow, and take credit for the production as soon as the final scene airs, which is OK when you're with friends and family. However, you can really impress your viewing audience when you use what we consider to be Windows Movie Maker's best ending credits option.

STEP 1: CREATE A NEW PROJECT

■ Launch Windows Movie Maker and choose **File ➢ New Project**.

■ Choose **File ➢ Import Into Collections**. Navigate to the CD-ROM that accompanies this book, select **WinClip044.wmv**, and then click **Import**. Windows Movie Maker creates a collection for the clip.

■ Click the **Show Timeline** button if you're currently working in storyboard mode.

■ Drag the clip onto the timeline. Windows Movie Maker snaps the clip to timecode position 0:00:00.00.

TIP

Select any clip on the timeline and then press **Page Down** once or twice to zoom in on the timeline. Doing this makes it easier to for you to precisely align clips on the different timeline tracks.

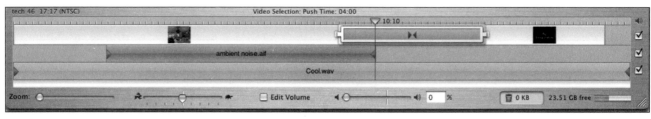

46.6

STEP 2: ADD THE ENDING CREDITS

For this technique, you specify a title over the clip, but you choosing an ending credit for the animation. The actual credit scrunches the video to the left, displays the title of the movie in a marquee banner near the top of the screen, and rolls the credits to the right of the video.

- Click the **Tasks** button to display the Movie Tasks pane and then click **Make titles or credits.** The Where Do You Want To Add The Title? section of the Make Titles or Credits pane appears.
- Click **title on the selected clip** to display the Enter Text for Title section.
- Click **Change the title animation** to open the Choose A Title Animation section.
- Click **Credits: Video Left** from the Credits list and then click **Edit the title text** to return to the Enter Text for Title section.
- Click inside the appropriate text box and enter the title and credits for the movie, as shown in **Figure 46.7**.

When you use this technique on the final scene of a movie, you can display multiple lines of credits. However, you need a long clip when you are displaying multiple credits using this credit animation. To display a movie title and two lines of credits, you'll need a clip that's at least 15 seconds in duration.

STEP 3: ADDING THE FINISHING TOUCHES

When you create an ending credit overlay, Windows Movie Maker snaps it to the beginning of the clip you select. If your clip is longer than the ending credits, as is the case in this example, you can reposition the clip to suit the movie you are creating. In this step, you synch the ending credits with the end of the video clip.

- Click **Done, add title to movie** to exit the Add Titles or Credits pane. Windows Movie Maker adds the ending credits to the Title Overlay

46.7

timeline. Notice that the credits clip is aligned with the beginning of the clip.

■ Drag the ending credit clip so that it is aligned with the end of the movie (see **Figure 46.8**).

■ Click the **Play Timeline** button to preview the technique (see **Figure 46.9**).

■ Choose **File ➢ Save Project As** to open the Save Project As dialog box.

■ Type **Tech46** in the **File Name** field and then click **Save**.

When you use this ending credit on your movies, you can edit the font attributes by clicking **Change the text font and color** after typing the title and credits. While you're in this section, you can also change the background color for the title marquee by clicking the color swatch and choosing a color that suits your movie.

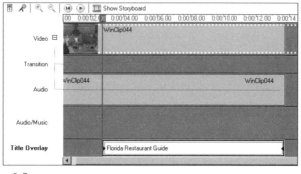

46.8

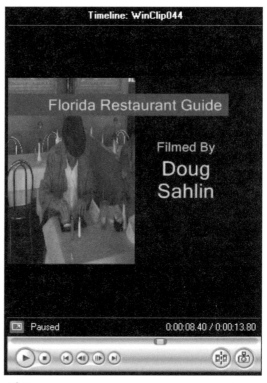

46.9

CHAPTER **9**

EXPORTING YOUR MOVIE

After you master the iMovie or Windows Movie Maker techniques in this book, you'll want to share your video creations with your friends and relatives, and maybe the world if you have a Web site. But you may have a hard time doing this until you learn how to save your projects as standalone movie files. When you save a project as a movie file, iMovie or Windows Movie Maker renders the project. With many video-editing applications, you have to be a genius to create a movie file for a specific destination. Fortunately, the process is pretty straightforward with iMovie and Windows Movie Maker. Each program has a series of easy-to-understand dialog boxes that gives you the option of choosing a setting for a specific destination, such as an Internet Web site, e-mail, a DVD, and so on. In this chapter, you learn how to save movies for specific uses. The last techniques in this chapter show you how to use software to create your own VCDs (video CD-ROMs) or DVDs (digital video discs).

EXPORTING CLIPS FOR THE INTERNET

47.1

47.2

The Internet is a wonderful tool. You can communicate with friends, relatives, and even people you've never met via e-mail. When you create movies in iMovie or Windows Movie Maker, you can share them with your friends and relatives via the Internet. Instead of attaching a scanned snapshot of your new baby, car, or other prized possession to an e-mail, now you can attach a movie. The possibilities are only limited by your imagination. You can greet friends or relatives with a small introduction video of yourself and then use one of the transition techniques to segue to footage of your child, pet, or whatever the subject of your e-mail video happens to be. When you create a video e-greeting, keep it fairly short. Not everyone has the luxury of fast cable modems, so download time is still a factor.

Figure 47.1 shows a frame from a movie that has been rendered in high resolution. **Figure 47.2** shows the result of exporting this movie to the Internet. The image in **Figure 47.1** shows a frame exported from a

QuickTime movie created in iMovie. **Figure 47.2** shows a frame from a Web-friendly version of the same movie as exported from Windows Movie Maker playing in the Windows Media Player.

iMOVIE

If you intend to share your movies with friends and family online, iMovie offers three different export options for Internet delivery. Each option addresses a specific need including e-mail, the Web, and a custom configuration that allows you to configure your own settings. For e-mail and the Web, the iMovie Export interface works in a simple, straightforward manner, essentially making all the technical decisions for you after you indicate your output goal. On the other end of the spectrum, the Expert Settings allow you to adjust the size and frame rate, add filters, and specify compression format. In this technique, we explore iMovie's quick and simple way of generating movies for e-mail and the Web.

STEP 1: OPEN AN iMOVIE FILE

■ Open the iMovie project file you saved from Technique 43. You use this file in the proceeding steps to learn the Export to e-mail and Web features of iMovie.

STEP 2: EXPORT FOR E-MAIL AND WEB

When you export a clip for e-mail, iMovie creates a movie with a size of 160 x 120 pixels and a rate of 10 frames per second. Although the movie is obviously small in size and dimension, low quality, and slow, sending a video via e-mail rather than just a mundane text message is still a miraculous event. This step walks through the process of exporting a movie for e-mail.

■ Choose **File ➤ Export** in the menu.

■ In the iMovie: Export dialog box, for Export, choose **To QuickTime** from the pop-up list. For Formats, select **Email,** as shown in **Figure 47.3.**

■ Click the **Export** button. In the **Save As** dialog box, type a name for the file. Make certain that after the name you include the **.mov** extension (see **Figure 47.4**). This identifies the type of compressor used for this movie, which in this case is QuickTime. This way, the file can be viewed on multiple platforms.

■ Navigate to the folder where you want the movie to save. Then click the **Save** button, and the movie begins to export, and while doing so, displays a progress bar (see **Figure 47.5**).

■ To test the movie before you e-mail it, navigate to the folder where you saved it and double-click the QuickTime file icon. The movie opens in your QuickTime Player. The QuickTime Player serves as a container for the movie. Users can control the playback of the movie in the Player with the Stop, Play, Rewind, Fast Forward, and Volume Control

47·3

buttons, all on the bottom of the console, as shown in **Figure 47.6**.

■ To e-mail the movie, simply attach it to an e-mail correspondence.

■ To export the movie for the Web (dimensions are 240 x 180), repeat the above process, except in the iMovie: Export dialog box, choose **web** instead of **Email**.

If you want more control over the quality and size of your e-mail or Web movie, in the iMovie: Export dialog box, for Formats, from the pop-up menu, choose **Expert Settings** ➢ **Export**. The export process is similar to that of the prefab choices. The difference is the **Export Options** button in the **Save exported file as....** dialog box. If you click this, you can access

47.4

Exporting Movie

Stop

47.5

> **TIP**
>
> The recipient of your e-mail must have the QuickTime Player installed on their system to see the movie you attach. Most new computers ship with the QuickTime Player, so it may not be a problem. Recipients who do **not** have QuickTime can download the QuickTime Player for free at `www.apple.com/quicktime/products/qt/`.

47.6

the Movie Settings dialog box where you are presented with a plethora of choices buried in additional dialog boxes (see **Figure 47.7**). Here you can tweak

iMovie: Export

Export: To QuickTime

Email
✓ Web
Web Streaming
CD–ROM
Full Quality DV

Expert Settings...

Cancel   Export

47.7

COMPRESSION

Before delivering files over the Internet, you must compress them. *Compression* refers to the science of making files smaller so that they are more portable. Compression works by eliminating redundant information in each file to reduce the file size. In iMovie, the compressor is QuickTime, and the compression formats (codecs) are as varied as are flavors of ice cream. Two of the most popular QuickTime codecs are Cinepak and Sorenson 3. Cinepak is an old standard, which offers ho-hum quality. In general, Sorenson 3 offers a much better image quality: file size ratio. When you export using the e-mail and Web prefab settings, the encoding used is H.263, which is targeted toward smaller file size rather than superior quality. You can also individually adjust codecs in most cases, to reduce frame rate and image quality. By doing this, you can scale down file sizes even more. Custom Compression formats are only available if you export with Expert Settings.

your export in a multitude of ways. In fact, if you are serious about making movies in iMovie, you want to experiment with different settings to judge which combination best suits your output goals.

WINDOWS MOVIE MAKER

If you want to surprise a friend or relative, attach a video to an e-mail. You can easily do this by selecting the proper settings when you save the file as a movie, as outlined in the upcoming steps.

STEP 1: OPEN A PROJECT

When you decide to surprise a friend or relative by attaching a movie to an e-mail, you can e-mail the movie on which you are currently working or send a movie from a previously saved project file. Skip this step when you want to send a movie from the project you currently have open.

■ Launch Windows Movie Maker.
■ Choose **File ➤ Open.** Then navigate to your desktop or the folder in which you store your movie files and select **tech43.MWMSM,** which you saved from the last chapter. When you click **Open,** Windows Movie Maker assembles the clips and transitions on the timeline.

STEP 2: SEND THE MOVIE VIA E-MAIL

When you send a movie via e-mail, you initiate a wizard that saves the movie in a format acceptable for e-mail. Keep in mind that file size is still a factor even in this day of broadband Internet access. When you send a movie via e-mail, it should be 20 seconds in duration or less; otherwise, you run the risk of creating a movie with a large file size that will take considerable time to download.

- Click the **Tasks** button to display the Movie Tasks pane.
- Click **Send in E Mail** in the Finish Movie section. Windows Movie Maker begins rendering the movie and, when finished, displays the Ready To Send By Email section of the Save Movie Wizard (see **Figure 47.8**).
- Click **Play the Movie** to preview the finished movie in Windows Media Player. If you choose this option, close Windows Media Player after previewing the movie.
- Click **Save a copy of my movie on my computer** if you want to save a copy of the movie. Choosing this option opens the Save Movie dialog box, where you can accept the default project name or enter a different name in the File Name field. After choosing a name, click **Save** and Windows Movie Maker saves a copy of the file in the My Videos folder, which is a subfolder of the My Documents folder.
- Click **Next** to advance to open your default e-mail application. The rendered movie file is already attached to a blank e-mail message.

- Enter the e-mail address of the person to whom you want to send the movie and, if desired, type a message (see **Figure 47.9**). You can send the movie to more than one person by entering multiple e-mail addresses. Separate each e-mail address with a comma.
- Click **Send**. Your default e-mail application sends the rendered movie to your desired recipients.

When you choose the E-mail option from the Save Movie Wizard, Windows Movie Maker renders the file the same size as the clips you have on the timeline. This is fine if you have imported clips with small dimensions. However, if you are using video clips as captured from your digital camcorder, the file size may be huge. If this is the case, you're better off using the alternate method listed next.

STEP 2: (ALTERNATE) SAVE MOVIE AND THEN E-MAIL

When you capture video clips from your digital camcorder, the movie dimension is 720 x 480 pixels. When you choose the My Computer option from the Save Movie Wizard, you can modify the dimensions of the movie and data rate at which the movie is played back.

47.8

47.9

■ Choose **File ➤ Save Movie File** to open the Save Movie Wizard (see **Figure 47.10**).

■ Click **My Computer** and then click **Next** to open the Save Movie File section of the Wizard.

■ Enter a name for the movie in **field 1**. When you save a file for use on the Internet, do not leave any spaces in the filename. Spaces may cause errors with some e-mail applications and Web browsers.

47.10

UNDERSTANDING DATA RATE

The *data rate* for media is the amount of data (measured in kilobytes) that is transmitted per second. When you save movies with high data rates, the movie looks and sounds better but is considerably larger in file size and takes longer to download from the Internet. When you watch movies on the Internet, most movie file formats stream the content into your browser, which means you don't have to wait for the entire movie to download. As soon as enough data has downloaded to play the first few frames, the movie begins playing. However, if the data rate of any given frame exceeds the amount of data you can receive at a given connection speed, the movie halts until sufficient data has downloaded to display the next few frames. For example, if you access the Web with a dial-up modem, the movie halts if data rate exceeds 56 Kbps. Keep this in mind when saving movies for viewing at a Web site. If your viewers access the Internet with a dialup modem, their maximum connection speed is 56 Kbps, so use the Video For Dialup Access (38 Kbps) setting when saving a movie for your Web site. To learn more about viewing multimedia content over the Web, read *Teach Yourself VISUALLY Computers*, 3rd Edition (Wiley Publishing, 2000).

- Accept the default directory (My Videos sub-folder of My Documents) or click **Browse** to navigate to a different directory, which will be displayed in **field 2**.
- Click the **Other Settings** radio button and then click the triangle to the right of the field to display the list of available settings (see **Figure 47.11**).
- Choose the applicable setting. For example, if the person to whom you are e-mailing the message accesses the Internet via dial-up modem, choose **Video for Dialup Access (38kbps)**, or if your recipient has a cable modem connection, choose one of the **Video for broadband** settings.
- Click **Next,** and Windows Movie Maker renders the file.
- After the movie is rendered, exit Windows Movie Maker, launch your e-mail application, and send the movie as an attachment.

Save Movie Wizard ⊠

Movie Setting
Select the setting you want to use to save your movie. The setting you select determines the quality and file size of your saved movie.

- ○ Best quality for playback on my computer (recommended)
- ○ Best fit to file size: 675 KB
- ⦿ Other settings: Video for local playback (2.1 Mbps)

Show fewer choices.

| Video for Pocket PC (218 Kbps) |
| Video for Pocket PC (143 Kbps) |
| Video for Pocket PC (Full screen 218 Kbps) |
| High quality video (large) |
| High quality video (small) |
| Video for local playback (2.1 Mbps) |
| Video for local playback (1.5 Mbps) |
| Video for LAN (1.0 Mbps) |
| Video for LAN (768 Kbps) |
| Video for broadband (512 Kbps) |
| Video for broadband (340 Kbps) |
| Video for broadband (150 Kbps) |
| Video for ISDN (48 Kbps) |
| Video for dial-up access (38 Kbps) |
| DV-AVI (NTSC) |
| High quality video (NTSC) |
| Video for local playback (2.1 Mbps NTSC) |
| Video for local playback (1.5 Mbps NTSC) |

Setting details
File type: Windows
Bit rate: 2.1 Mbps
Display size: 640 x
Aspect ratio: 4:3
Frames per second: 30

Estimated disk space available on drive C:
19.24 GB

< Back   Next >   Cancel

47.11

PRINTING TO TAPE

48.1

48.2

After you create a really cool digital video in iMovie or Windows Movie Maker, the first thing you want to do is show it to your friends. Of course, unless you have a very big computer room and a very big monitor, you can only show it to a few friends at a time. That is, of course, unless you get the movie files out of your computer and onto media that users can view with a home entertainment center. If you own a DVD burner, the logical choice is to burn a DVD with your movies as outlined in Technique 50. But if you don't own a DVD burner, and you want to show your videos on a VHS machine, your only choice is to output the movies to tape. By following this technique, you can record your home movies back to your camcorder and then record them to VHS tape.

iMOVIE

iMovie has made the process of printing your final production to tape very easy. Just like the capture setup, you connect the DV camcorder via the FireWire on your Mac. When it's hooked up, you select the print to tape settings in the menu. In this technique, you review the process of printing to DV tape and then recording the DV tape to VHS tape.

STEP 1: OPEN AN iMOVIE FILE

Open the iMovie project file you saved from Technique 44. You can use this movie to practice the technique reviewed in this chapter.

STEP 2: CONNECT THE DV CAMCORDER

Before printing to tape, you must connect the DV camcorder to your computer via FireWire and plug the camcorder into the wall outlet as opposed to running off of battery power.

- Connect your DV camcorder to your computer with your FireWire connector.
- Turn on your DV camcorder and put it in VCR/VTR mode.
- In iMovie, choose **File ➢ Export**. In the iMovie Export dialog box, to Export, select **To Camera**.
- You can change the default number of seconds for Wait 5 seconds for camcorder to get ready. However, it is best to leave this setting at the default of 5 seconds. Doing this gives the DV camcorder enough time to get up to normal speed (see **Figure 48.3**).
- Add 2 seconds of black before/after a movie inserts black footage so your movie doesn't automatically begin; rather, you see a moment of block footage beforehand. It's a good idea to put at least 1 to 2 seconds of black footage both before and after the movie.
- Click the Export button. The export processing bar crawls along as it indicates the status of the import (see **Figure 48.4**).

- When the export is done, disconnect the DV camcorder from your computer. Rewind the DV tape in your DV camcorder and play it. You see a full-screen version of your movie, and the resulting quality is surprisingly crisp and clean. To print

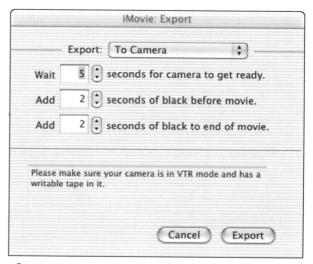

48.3

48.4

your DV tape to VHS, see Step 4 in the Windows Movie Maker section.

CONNECTING A DV CAMCORDER TO A TV

To get your iMovie production from DV camcorder to VHS tape, you first need to connect the DV camcorder to a VCR. The DV camcorder comes equipped with its own mini VCR (sometimes named "VTR" on the DV camcorder), so essentially you copy from one tape (DV tape) to another (VHS tape). To connect, you need an S-video cable. This cable was most likely included with your DV camcorder when you purchased it. Connect both the camcorder and VCR via the S-Video, as shown in Figure 48.6 in the Windows Movie Maker section of this technique. To record to tape, you must set the VCR to Line or Auxiliary, and the DV camcorder to VCR/VTR mode. Make sure that you cue the DV tape and VHS tape where you want to start recording. Press the Record button on the VCR and the Play button on the DV camcorder to copy from your camcorder to VHS tape.

WINDOWS MOVIE MAKER

STEP 1: OPEN A PROJECT

When you create your own movies in Windows Movie Maker, you'll be tempted to immediately record them to tape and dupe them to VHS as soon as you finish them. However, like a fine wine improves with age, so will your talent as a moviemaker, which of course will be reflected in your movies. When you have several movies you want to transfer to tape, pop a tape into your camcorder and follow these steps.

- Launch Windows Movie Maker.
- Choose **File ➤ Open**, navigate to your desktop or the folder in which you store your movie files, select **tech44.MWMSM** that you saved in the last

chapter, and click **Open**. Windows Movie Maker assembles the clips and transitions on the timeline.

STEP 2: CONNECT YOUR CAMCORDER TO YOUR FIREWIRE CARD

This step shows basically the same setup that you use when you capture video. The only exception is now your camcorder captures video from, instead of transmitting video to, your PC. So, in a sense, you can say the process has come full circle.

- Connect your digital camcorder to the FireWire cable attached to your computer. Refer to your camcorder's operating manual for detailed instructions.
- Switch your camcorder to VCR or VTR mode. When you switch to this mode, you can record directly from PC to tape. As soon as you switch your camcorder to VTR or VCR mode, Windows XP plays a sound alerting you that the camcorder has successfully been connected to your computer.

STEP 3: RECORD THE MOVIE

- Click the **Tasks** button to display the Movie Tasks pane.
- Click **Send to DV Camera** in the Finish Movie section. The Save Movie Wizard opens. Your digital camcorder and any other capture devices are listed in the Save Movie Wizard dialog box (see **Figure 48.5**). Make sure that the proper device is selected before proceeding to the next instruction. In **Figure 48.5**, the digital camcorder is selected and not the Pinnacle video capture card.
- Click **Next**. Windows Movie Maker displays a dialog box prompting you to cue the tape to the position where you want the recording to begin. If you want to record to a new tape, disregard this dialog box. If necessary, cue your tape to the place where you want to begin recording.

48.5

■ Click **Next**. Windows Movie Maker displays a warning telling you that it will overwrite any content on the tape. If you're sure you've properly cued your tape, click **Yes**. Windows Movie Maker takes control of your digital camcorder and records the movie tape. Windows Movie Maker stops your camcorder from recording as soon as it detects the end of the clip.

After recording a movie to DV tape, you can open additional projects and click **Send To DV Tape**, to add more movies to the tape. Before adding additional movies to the tape, you may want to advance the tape a few seconds, so you have a blank screen before the next movie begins.

STEP 4: TRANSFER YOUR MOVIES TO VHS TAPE

Most digital videotapes record an hour of footage. After sending the desired movies to DV tape, you have three options: you can watch them on your digital camcorder, which is limited due to the small screen size, and which prematurely wears out the mechanical devices inside the camcorder; you can connect the digital camcorder to your TV and then watch the movies; or you can transfer the movies to VHS tape, which is the desired method.

■ Switch off your camcorder and disconnect it from your PC. When you have turned off the camcorder, Windows plays a sound alerting you that it is safe to remove the device from your PC.

■ Connect the camcorder to your VHS recorder. Most digital camcorders have a cable that you use to connect from the camcorder to a VHS recorder or television set. Refer to your camcorder owner's manual for detailed instructions on connecting your camcorder to a VHS recorder. **Figure 48.6** shows a Sony DCR-TRV27 connected to a VHS recorder.

■ Switch on your camcorder and choose VCR or VTR mode.

■ Rewind the tape to the beginning, or the point at which you began recording the movies you captured from Windows Movie Maker.

■ Insert a tape in your VHS recorder. If you insert a tape with previously recorded material, make sure that you cue the tape properly so as not to erase any previously recorded material you want to save.

■ Select your VHS recorder's option to **record from Line Input**. The actual nomenclature varies from model to model. Consult your VHS manual if you're not sure how to record from line input.

■ Press the **Pause** button on your digital camcorder and VHS recorder.

■ Simultaneously press the **Play** button on your digital camcorder and the **Record** button on your VHS recorder. Your digital camcorder plays your Windows Movie Maker productions while the VHS machine records them.

> **TIP**
>
> You can prolong the life of your digital camcorder if you invest in a cassette rewinder. These devices are available for popular digital video cassette formats and are relatively inexpensive. Maxell makes a MiniDV tape rewinder (model MDV/RW-1) that sells for less than $50.00.

> **TIP**
>
> After recording your movies to VHS tape, you can prevent the tape from being accidentally erased by removing the write protect tab at the rear of the tape.

48.6

EXPORTING TO CD-ROM

49.1

49.2

The videos for the projects you will render for this technique were filmed with a Sony DCR-TRV 27 and a Canon GL-1. The clips were filmed at various locations in Florida and New Jersey and were captured and trimmed in iMovie and Windows Movie Maker.

VHS tape has a limited life span and is easily broken or jammed if your VHS player runs amuck. DVD discs are the ultimate format for displaying your digital video movies; however, DVD burners are still quite expensive. If you own a CD-ROM burner, you can archive your movies on disc using the VCD (Video Compact Disc) format. When you create a VCD disc, you have video that is near VHS quality. Video files are large and by comparison, CD-ROM discs are relatively small, holding 650 or 700MB of data. Therefore, VCD-authoring applications accept video files that are 320 x 240 pixels and expand them to full screen when you view them with a DVD player.

iMOVIE

There are two different ways to get your production on a CD. In iMovie, you can export the movie for CD-ROM. If you have a CD drive on your computer, you are probably familiar with the process of burning a disk. When the user plays the file, he or she must click the icon and play the file. The user must also have the QuickTime Player installed on their computer to play the movie. The good news is the QuickTime Player is available on the Mac and PC for free, and you can download it at `www.apple.com/quicktime`.

The second way to get your movie onto CD-ROM is to create a video CD, also known as a VCD. Video CDs are similar to DVDs, but the resolution of the movie is more similar to VHS tape quality. The downside of creating a VCD is that iMovie does not offer any direct way of doing so. To do so, you need to use a third-party application like Toast Titanium (`www.roxio.com`).

If you use the default settings in iMovie to create a file for a CD as we discuss in this technique, iMovie compresses the file in a QuickTime format, at a frame size of 240 x 180, and at 15 frames per second. The resulting movie is small and compact, which will work well on computers with slower CD drives. If the QuickTime file you are exporting is very large in size, when played on slower CD players, the movie can skip and pause because the speed of the CD drive can't keep up with the frames playing on the computer. If you are inexperienced in the art of expert export settings for CDs, choosing the default settings to export a file for CDs is the foolproof way to go.

STEP 1: OPEN AN EXISTING MOVIE

For this technique, you use the movie you previously constructed in Technique 45.

- Launch iMovie and choose **File ➢ Open**. Navigate to the Technique 45 movie.

STEP 2: EXPORT TO CD-ROM

- Insert a blank CD into your computer's CD-burning drive.
- From the menu, choose **File ➢ Export**. In the Export field of the iMovie Export dialog box, select QuickTime. For Formats, select CD-ROM (see **Figure 49.3**). Then, click the **Export** button. The Save As dialog box appears.
- In the **Save As** dialog box, assign the file a name. For "where," navigate to the folder where you want to save the file. Click the **Save** button.
- After the movie exports, drag the file to the CD icon on your hard drive to copy it. The resulting movie has a frame size of 240 x 180, is compressed in an H263 format, and plays at 15 frames per second. **Figure 49.4** displays information about a QuickTime file exported for CD in iMovie.

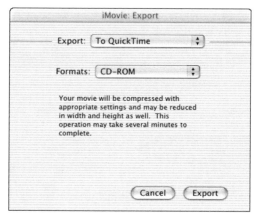

49.3

49.4

- Drag the disk to the **Trash** icon to burn it. If you decide not to burn it, select **Eject** from the desktop.
- You can play the resulting CD-ROM by clicking the QuickTime icon for your named file on the CD. The file opens in a QuickTime Player frame complete with control console on the bottom. You can play it on a Mac and a PC assuming the user's computer has the QuickTime Player installed.

WINDOWS MOVIE MAKER

Although Windows XP gives you the necessary tools to burn a CD-ROM, it has no VCD authoring programs as part of the operating system. However, Sonic has a program called MyDVD Plus 4, that supports the Windows Movie Maker *.wmv format and enables you to author and burn VCD discs and DVD discs. The Sonic MyDVD application ships with many DVD burners. If you do not own MyDVD, you can purchase MyDVD Plus 4 at Sonic's Web site, www.mydvd.com/default.asp. As of this writing, the software sells for $79.99. You can use this application to author VCDs and DVDs from movies saved with Windows Movie Maker's native *.wmv format and several other video formats.

STEP 1: SAVE PROJECTS AS MOVIE FILES

You have a lot of different settings available when saving movie files. With Windows Movie Maker, you don't need a degree in the fine art of compressing videos, all you need to do is select the proper setting and Windows Movie Maker takes care of the rest. When you save movie files for a VCD disk, you use the High Quality Video (small) setting.

- Launch Windows Movie Maker and choose **File ➢ Open Project**.

- Navigate to the folder where you saved the projects from the last chapter, select **tech43.MSMWM**, and then click **Open**. Windows Movie Maker assembles the project on the timeline.
- Click **Save To My Computer** in the Finish Movie section of the Movie Tasks pane. Windows Movie Maker opens the Save Movie Wizard.
- Enter a filename for the movie and then click **Next** to display the Movie Setting section.
- Click the **Other Settings** radio button and from the drop-down menu choose **High Quality Video (small)**.
- Click **Next** to render the movie.

After the movie renders, repeat this step to render the following project files that you saved while performing the techniques in the last chapter: **tech44.MSMWM**, **tech45.MSMWM**, and **tech46.MSMWM**.

STEP 2: AUTHOR THE VCD

You use Sonic MyDVD Plus 4 to author the VCD. The program is well documented and easy to use. When you create a VCD disc, you can choose the menu background color, outlines for the menu buttons, and more.

> **NOTE**
>
> VCD menu buttons look exactly like menu buttons on a DVD disc, however, do not function in the same manner. VCD menu buttons are merely thumbnail images of the poster frame for each movie on the disc. When you play the VCD on your DVD player, you use the DVD controller to select individual movies, advance to other movies, etc. Refer to your DVD manual for additional information.

■ Launch Sonic **MyDVD Plus 4**.

■ Choose **File ➢ New ➢ VCD Project**.

■ Click the **Get Movie Files** icon to open the Add Movies To Menu dialog box.

■ Select the movies you rendered in Step 2 and click **Open** to add the movies to the project. MyDVD Plus 4 creates a menu button for each movie (see **Figure 49.5**).

■ Click any movie title to select the title text. Accept the default title text (the movie filename without the extension) or enter new text.

■ Click **Change here to change text** to select the default project title text. After selecting the text, you can enter a new title for the VCD.

■ Click the **Edit Style** icon to open the Edit Style dialog box (see **Figure 49.6**). You can choose different styles, change font type, text size, and more. Refer to the Sonic MyDVD Plus 4 help menu for additional information.

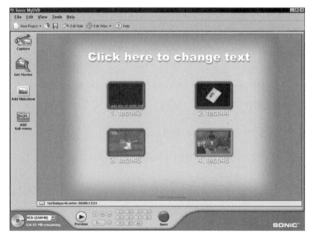

49.5

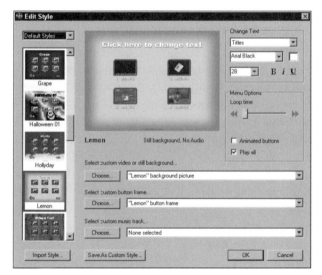

49.6

- Place a blank CD-R disc in your CD-ROM drive. Note that you must use a CD-R or CD-RW disc to create a VCD Disc. Most recent DVD players play 700MB discs, while older machines can only read 650MB discs. Refer to your DVD Player owner's manual to see which media your player supports.
- Click the triangle to the right of the field at the lower-left corner of the interface and select **VCD (650 MB)** or **VCD (700 MB)**. Select the option that matches the size of the CD-ROM media you are using.
- Click **Burn**. MyDVD Plus 4 prompts you to save the project. After saving the project, MyDVD Plus 4 creates the VCD disc.

TIP

You can recycle failed CD-ROM burns, outdated program discs, and free ISP trial offer discs. They make wonderful coasters. You can also create colorful mobiles for your porch or den by using dowels, fishing line, paper clips, and unwanted CD-ROM discs.

This process may take some time, especially when you add several minutes of movies to the project. MyDVD Plus 4 creates the necessary files to play the VCD in your DVD player, and then transcodes an audio and video file for each movie. Unless you're particularly fond of staring at a progress bar scrolling slowly across the screen, we suggest you do something more stimulating, like bathing your cat. Unless you have a very powerful computer, do not use the computer for other tasks while you create the VCDs; otherwise, you may crash your computer. MyDVD Plus 4 ejects the disc and sounds a warning when the file is done. When you begin experimenting with creating your own VCD discs, you're bound to make a few mistakes. That's the beauty of this format; CD-R discs are cheap, especially if you buy them in bulk.

AUTHORING A DVD

50.1

50.2

The videos for the projects you will be rendering for this technique were filmed with a Sony DCR-TRV 27 and a Canon GL-1. The clips were filmed in Florida and New Jersey and were trimmed and edited in iMovie and Windows Movie Maker.

I f you've been keeping up with the Joneses, you know that DVDs (Digital Video Discs) are the hottest thing since VHS tapes. No wonder. They're small, easy to care for, and offer excellent audio and video quality. If you have a DVD burner hooked up to your computer, you can easily create stunning DVDs of your home movies. Mac OS X has all the tools you need to burn your own DVD discs with movies you create with iMovie. If you're a PC user and have a DVD burner hooked up to your computer, your DVD burner probably shipped with proprietary software you can use to author your own DVD discs. When you create a DVD disc, the authoring software doesn't have to compress the video as severely as when it creates a VCD disc. After all, a DVD disc gives you 4.7GB worth of storage space.

iMOVIE

If you have a DVD burner or a SuperDrive, you can author DVDs directly from iMovie. Apple computers with SuperDrives ship with iDVD, a utility that allows you to make custom quality DVDs complete with menus and interactive buttons. If you do have a third-party DVD burner, chances are it shipped with a utility application that allows you to burn DVDs. If you prefer to use iDVD, you can download it from the Apple site. You can access iDVD from within iMovie if you have the proper hardware setup and are ready to go.

STEP 1: OPEN AN EXISTING MOVIE

For this technique you use the movie you previously constructed in Technique 46.

- Launch iMovie.
- Choose **File ➢ Open**. Navigate to the **Technique 46 movie**.

STEP 2: CREATE CHAPTER MARKERS

In iMovie, you can create **chapter markers**. Chapter markers flag parts of the Movie Track, so you can later go back and create interactive buttons so the audience can navigate to specific sequences in the movie. Chapter markers provide an easy way for users to navigate around your movie in a non-linear fashion without having to watch the movie from start to finish.

- Click the **iDVD** tab to display the iDVD Chapter Markers pane.
- Under the monitor, drag the **Playhead** to a point in the movie right before the title appears (see **Figure 50.3**).
- In the iDVD pane, highlight the default title in the Chapter Title column and type a name for the title. In **Figure 50.4**, the title reads "end."

- Repeat this process for more chapter titles. You can have as many titles as you want. If you change your mind and want to delete a title, click **Remove Chapter** at the bottom of the iDVD pane.
- When you finish making your markers, click the **Create iDVD Project** button at the bottom of the iDVD pane. This launches iDVD and allows you to do one-stop processing of your file. DVDs are encoded in the mpeg-2 format. iDVD does background encoding before burning to DVD, thus eliminating many steps in the DVD authoring process.

If you do not have a DVD burner connected to your computer, iDVD installed on your computer, or you have a version of iDVD installed that is incompatible with your version of iMovie, a warning message appears alerting you to the fact that you need to update your configuration.

50.3

50.4

WINDOWS MOVIE MAKER

Most video editing applications give you the option of saving a file using the MPEG2 format, which is widely used as the basis for DVD videos. Windows Movie Maker does not support the MPEG2 format, but you can create stunning DVDs by saving movies using the DV-AVI (NTSC) setting, and high quality DVDs using the High Quality Video (NTSC) setting. The latter setting saves the movie using the Windows Movie Maker *.wmv format. NTSC stands for National Television System Committee.

STEP 1: SAVE PROJECTS AS MOVIE FILES

When you decide to create a DVD disc, your first step is to save your projects in the proper format.

- Launch Windows Movie Maker and choose **File ➢ Open Project**.
- Navigate to the folder where you saved the projects from the last chapter, select **tech43.MSMWM**, and then click **Open**.
- Click **Save To My Computer** in the Finish Movie section of the Movie Tasks pane. Windows Movie Maker opens the Save Movie Wizard.
- Enter a **filename** for the movie and then click **Next** to display the Movie Setting section.
- Click the **Other Settings** radio button and from the drop-down menu choose **DV-AVI (NTSC)**.
- Click **Next** to render the movie.

After the movie renders, repeat this step to render the project files **tech44.MSMWM**, **tech45.MSMWM**, and **tech46.MSMWM**.

STEP 2: AUTHOR THE DVD

This technique shows steps to use Sonic MyDVD Plus 4 to author a DVD disc. A version of Sonic MyDVD ships as proprietary software with many DVD burners. If you're using different authoring software, refer to your operating manual for specific instructions. This step is for MyDVD Plus 4 users only. MyDVD Plus 4 gives you plenty of options when authoring a DVD. You can choose different backgrounds, menu buttons, styles, and so on. For additional information, refer to the MyDVD Plus 4 Help menu.

- Launch MyDVD Plus 4.
- Choose **File ➣ New ➣ DVD Project**.

CAUTION

Rendering a movie may take a while depending on the length of your production. Rendering is also a processor-intensive process. Avoid multitasking while Windows Movie Maker is rendering video. Otherwise, you run the risk of taxing your system's resources, which may cause your computer to crash.

- Click the **Get Movie Files** icon to open the Add Movies To Menu dialog box.
- Select the movies you rendered in Step 1 and click **Open** to add the movies to the project. MyDVD Plus 4 creates a menu button for each movie.
- Click any movie title to select the title text. Accept the default title text (the movie filename without the extension) or type new text.
- Drag a **menu button** to change its position on the menu. When you release the mouse button, MyDVD Plus 4 realigns all menu buttons, which ensures you of a neatly organized DVD menu.
- Click **Click here to change text** to select the default DVD title text. After selecting the text, you can enter a new title for your DVD (see **Figure 50.5**).
- Click the **Edit Style** icon to open the Edit Styles dialog box. From this dialog box, you can choose different styles, change font type and text size, and

---

TIP

If your DVD burner accepts DVD-R media and DVD+R media, and you're creating a DVD disc to send to a friend or relative, consider choosing DVD-R. Most DVD players support DVD-R, but many popular DVD players do not support DVD+R.

---

more. Refer to the Sonic MyDVD Plus 4 help menu for additional information.

■ Place a blank DVD disc in your DVD/CD ROM drive. DVD discs are available in the following formats: DVD-R, DVD-RW, DVD+, and DVD+RW. Choose the media that is right for your DVD burner. If your burner supports multiple media types, choose the media type that matches the device on which the completed disc will be played.

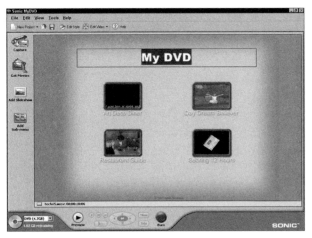

50.5

■ Click **Burn**. MyDVD Plus 4 prompts you to save the project. After you save the project, MyDVD Plus 4 creates the DVD disc.

The actual creation of the DVD disc takes a great deal of time. A DVD authoring application, such as MyDVD Plus 4, creates the menus and associated files before transcoding the video and audio for the movie files you created in Windows Movie Maker. Burning a DVD disc also takes considerably longer, because the current generation of DVD burners cannot record at the high speeds of CD-ROM burners.

TIP

DVD is still fairly expensive media. Before committing a project to a disc, do a test burn on a rewritable disc (DVD-RW or DVD+RW). Rewritable discs are good for about 1,000 burns. If the disc plays successfully, you can burn the disc image to one-time recordable DVD media and avoid wasting discs.

APPENDIX A
WHAT'S ON THE CD-ROM

This appendix provides you with information on the contents of the CD-ROM that accompanies this book. For the latest and greatest information, please refer to the ReadMe file located at the root of the CD-ROM. Here is what you will find:

- System Requirements
- CD-ROM Installation Instructions
- What's on the CD-ROM?
- Troubleshooting

SYSTEM REQUIREMENTS

Make sure that your computer meets the minimum system requirements listed in this section. If your computer doesn't match up to most of these requirements, you may have a problem using the contents of the CD-ROM.

FOR WINDOWS XP:

- PC with 300 megahertz (MHz)or higher processor clock speed recommended; 233 MHz minimum required (single or dual processor system); Intel Pentium/Celeron family, or AMD K6/Athlon/Duron family, or compatible processor recommended
- 128 megabytes (MB) of RAM or higher recommended (64MB minimum supported; may limit performance and some features)
- 1.5 gigabytes (GB) of available hard disk space
- Super VGA (800 × 600) or higher-resolution video adapter and monitor
- CD-ROM or DVD drive
- Keyboard and Microsoft Mouse or compatible pointing device

FOR MACINTOSH:

- Mac OS X v10.1.5 or later
- 400 MHz PowerPC G3 or faster required (700 MHz recommended)
- 256MB RAM recommended; 2GB of free hard disk space; Macintosh with built-in FireWire ports
- 1,024 x 768 screen resolution or higher; QuickTime 6.1 required (download via Software Update)

WINDOWS SOFTWARE INSTALLATION INSTRUCTIONS

To install a particular piece of software, open its folder with My Computer or Internet Explorer. What you do next depends on what you find in the software's folder:

1. First, look for a ReadMe.txt file or a .doc or .htm document. If this is present, it should contain installation instructions and other useful information.

2. If the folder contains an executable (.exe) file, this is usually an installation program. Often it will be called Setup.exe or Install.exe, but in some cases the filename reflects an abbreviated version of the software's name and version number. Run the .exe file to start the installation process.

MACINTOSH SOFTWARE INSTALLATION INSTRUCTIONS

To install a particular piece of software, double-click the icon of its folder. What you do next depends on what you find in the software's folder:

1. First, look for a ReadMe.txt file or a .doc or .htm document. If this is present, it should contain installation instructions and other useful information.

2. To open a program that comes with an installer, double-click the Install or Installer icon.

WHAT'S ON THE CD-ROM

The following sections provide a summary of the software and other materials you'll find on the CD-ROM.

SOURCE CLIPS FOR 50 TECHNIQUES

The audio, video, and image clips for the techniques are located on the CD-ROM in a folder called Clips. The clips are 640 x 480, 30 frames per second. For the Windows side, the clips are saved in Movie Maker's native *.wmv format. For the Macintosh side, the clips are saved in the QuickTime *.mov format. These clips yield good results as you work your way through the techniques. You get even better results when you capture video from your digital camcorders.

FLASH VIDEO RESULTS CLIPS FOR ALL 50 TECHNIQUES

Over 50 results clips are included on the CD-ROM in Flash SWF format to illustrate the desired final result of each technique. The clips can be played using the interface that is accessed through the CD-ROM 50 Fast interface. Occasionally, a technique may differ between platforms. When this is the case, we provide two clips for the technique and a parenthetical reference to which operating platform was used to create the clip. Furthermore, when there is a difference, we list the platform with the title of each video clip.

APPLICATIONS AND GOODIES

The following applications are on the CD-ROM:

Macintosh-Related Goodies

Bias Peak Demo

Bias' Peak 4 is a masterful professional audio- and sound-editing software application for the Macintosh. It includes the capability of Redbook CD burning from directly within the application, and many new DSP tools and enhancements.

GraphicConverter v4.5.4

This shareware utility allows users to import still pictures, crop them, and save them in various formats for both multimedia and print delivery.

Still Life Demo

Still Life by Granted Software, made exclusively for Mac OS X, arms users with the ability to take multiple pan and zoom shots of still photographs to produce videos for incorporation into iMovie, iDVD, and other projects of a multimedia genre.

Stupendous Software Plug-in Demo Pack

This demo pack for iMovie includes title effects ranging from crops and zooms, color manipulation, applying artistic and abstract effects, glows and blurs, to various Photoshop-style image abstracts. The demos included on the disc are Ascii & Art, Big & Bold, Color Effects, Crops & Zooms, Glows & Blurs, Labels & Overlays, Levels & Balances, Makes & Compositing, Scratch & Dirt, Smoke & Glass, Split Screen & PiP, Time Effects and Time Effects 2.

Virtix Sample Pack

This samples pack includes many cool special effects, such as Flame effect, Extreme Black and White, and a Letterbox, which allows you to simulate a widescreen movie.

Windows XP Applications and Goodies

Video Factory

You can use this powerful nonlinear video-editing application to augment your work in Movie Maker.

Cool Edit 2000 v1.1 (Shareware)

With Cool Edit 2000, you can record, mix, and edit sounds as well as export to .mp3 format. You can use this software to create sound effects and add soundtracks to your projects.

ACID® Music (Demo)

With Acid Music, you can create soundtracks for your projects by mixing and matching sound samples. Sonic Foundry has a plethora of sound samples from popular instruments, such as drum, piano, guitar, violin, and so on. The music genres run the gamut from classical to hip-hop.

Sound Forge 6.0 (Demo)

With Sound Forge, you can record, edit, and mix sounds. This powerful application makes it possible for you to create sound effects for your movies. Hook a microphone to your computer, launch Sound Forge, record some sounds, and then use the various menu commands, tools, and effects to modify the sound.

SpiceFX Packs for Movie Maker 2 (Demo)

SpiceFX Packs are video transitions and effects that pick up where Movie Maker leaves off. You can use these effects to add picture-in-picture transitions, and apply effects, such as color correction, to your clips.

1,001 Free Sound Effects

We've included 30 sound effects files from this Sonic Foundry compilation. These .wav files are ready for you to add them to your Movie Maker productions.

TROUBLESHOOTING

If you have difficulty installing or using any of the materials on the companion CD-ROM, try the following solutions:

- **Turn off any antivirus software that you may have running.** Installers sometimes mimic virus activity and can make your computer incorrectly believe that a virus is infecting it. (Be sure to turn the antivirus software back on later.)
- **Close all running programs.** The more programs you're running, the less memory is available to other programs. Installers also typically update files and programs; if you keep other programs running, installation may not work properly.
- **Reference the ReadMe.** Please refer to the ReadMe file located at the root of the CD-ROM for the latest product information at the time of publication.

  If you still have trouble with the CD-ROM, please call the Wiley Product Technical Support phone number: (800) 762-2974. Outside the United States, call 1 (317) 572-3994. You can also contact Wiley Customer Care from our Web site at `www.wiley.com/techsupport`. Wiley will provide technical support only for installation and other general quality control items; for technical support on the applications themselves, consult the program's vendor or author.

APPENDIX B
RESOURCES

Thousands of resources are available on the Internet for digital video, iMovie, and Windows Movie Maker. The following list is just a small portion of what the Internet has to offer. The Internet is in a constant state of flux. The URLs for these resources have all been verified at the time of this writing. However, we cannot guarantee the accuracy of these URLs when you read this. You can find your own resources for digital video by entering a keyword in your favorite search engine for the subject on which you need more information.

ASSOCIATIONS, PUBLICATIONS, AND FORUMS

www.dmnforums.com/htm/homeset.htm: Here you can find excellent forums on all sorts of topics related to digital video, including editing, post production, audio, compression, effects, and also information on iMovie and Windows Movie Maker.

www.dvcreators.net: This Web site offers a CD entitled *Make Awesome iMovies* for $39.95.

www.dvpa.com: The Digital Video Professionals Association is a group of new media professionals. Their site also offers tutorials, a job bank, and a gallery of members' works. You do need to register first.

www.filmmakermagazine.com: This is a magazine for independent filmmakers. It includes resources, a film festival calendar, and film site links.

AUDIO, AUDIO-EDITING, AND FILE-CONVERSION LINKS

GENERAL SITES

www.cyberfilmschool.com: This is a very strong site, which, among other things, offers information about film formats.

www.pblmm.k12.ca.us: This site offers sound information on using audio in moviemaking.

www.shockwave-sound.com: Need royalty-free music and sound effects? Well, here you can purchase full tracks or mini-loops. This site includes recommended resources with clips for sound tutorials, such as turning several music loops into a "whole song."

www.sounddogs.com: Downloadable sounds, effects, vocals, and royalty-free music.

iMOVIE SPECIFIC AUDIO LINKS

www.apple.com/itunes: iTunes 3 comes with iMovie 3 and is available as a separate download. A digital music player, iTunes boasts the fabulous iTunes Music Store stocked with hundreds of thousands of songs you can preview and own with just one click.

www.danslagle.com: This site shows you how to organize and edit sounds for iMovie 3.

MAC-SPECIFIC RESOURCES

www.macinstein.com: This site offers a wealth of Mac information with tools, events, downloads, press releases, and a lot of information on Mac users groups.

www.macreviewzone.com: This site offers plenty of information and great links to digital video information inclusive of that which relates to iMovie.

www.macrumors.com: This site allows you to stay abreast of the latest Macintosh rumors including Mac Forums, all located under Discussion Forums.

www.macworld.com: This magazine site offers a rather thorough, insightful, and current review of iMovie 3 as well as other relevant and helpful information.

iMOVIE RESOURCES

www.ali.apple.com: This is the Apple Learning Interchange Resource Guide site and contains all types of information regarding iMovie usage in education. You'll find a tutorial called Digital Video Made Easy, which is very useful and helpful.

www.apple.com/imovie: This is Apple's Web site offering a plethora of information on iMovie and all of its incarnations.

www.d23.org/Macarthur/Teacher%20pages/imovie/imovie.htm: This is an outstanding link on how to use iMovie.

www.atomiclearning.com: This site offers iMovie 2 and 3 tutorials that are free and cover such topics as basic camera shots, importing QuickTime movies, plugging clips into the timeline, the clip viewer versus timeline viewer, copying and pasting clips, and so on. For a fee, you can obtain more elaborate libraries of tutorials.

www.danslagle.com: This invaluable site provides an iMovie FAQ with information gleaned off the various Mac forums. It includes tips and techniques for using iMovie 3.

www.etc.sccoe.k12.ca.us: SCCOE Internet Institute offers a very good, basic tutorial in the use of iMovie.

www.inkvision.com: This site offers iMovie tutorials as well as downloads and examples.

www.macdevcenter.com: This is the O'Reilly Mac Development Center with information about iMovie.

www.rubistar.4teachers.org: At this site you can learn to create a rubric for your iMovie project. A *rubric* is a scoring tool that lists the criteria for a piece of work or "what counts" to help define quality. With rubrics templates for video, digital storytelling, multimedia, creating documentaries, and so on, this site is very helpful for the beginner movie maker.

www.springfield.k12.il.us: This site offers a free online course for iMovie. It also serves as a solid resource for free audio and video content through Copyright Friendly Images for Education, Newsfilm Library, and Webshot Photos.

www.umanitoba.ca: This is the University of Manitoba Web site, which contains iMovie workshops and many excellent tips and techniques for using iMovie.

PLUG-INS AND DOWNLOADS FOR iMOVIE

www.csb-digital.com/iplugins/about/index.php: This site offers several stunning plug-ins in the Special Effects Pack 1 and the Video Effects Pack 2, both of which start at $29.00 and include several different effects. In some techniques in this book, you need to download the CSB free iPlug-in pack and install it on your Mac. The free plug-ins offered as a sampler include Spy Scope, Solarization, and Movie Mosaic.

www.geethree.com: This is a site that offers a slick sampler of transitions and effects (9 free plug-ins) and four volumes for purchase with everything from split screens to cookie cutter. Plug-ins range in price from $29.95 to $49.95.

www.macosxhints.com: A very helpful site that offers help with OSX as it relates to working with iMovie 3 plug-ins.

www.mindspring.com: This site offers iMovie 3 solutions and a four-sample iMovie plug-in, which consists of a disk image file. There's also a helpful FAQ.

www.stupendous-software.com: Interested in 54 different plug-ins with three for free with downloadable demos available? Here's the place. Stupendous offers a nice selection of different effects for iMovie. If you are looking for a particular effect and can't find it elsewhere, try this link.

www.virtix.com: This site offers effects including iBubble, Bravo, and Echo (with 38 effects for iMovie). There is a 16 x 9 converter, which converts footage to 4 x 3, a Virtix Cinematic (with 29 transitions to achieve the look of classic films), Spectra (this has 24 color effects), and Zoom & Pan, all priced from $24.99 to $34.99.

WINDOWS MOVIE MAKER RESOURCES

www.microsoft.com/windowsxp/moviemaker/default.asp: This is the home page for Windows Movie Maker at Microsoft's Web site. Here you'll find the latest information about the software, as well as informative tutorials. Occasionally, Microsoft will post free plug-ins and accessories for Windows Movie Maker.

www.pixelan.com/mm/intro.htm: At this Web site you'll find plug-ins for Windows Movie Maker. The Spice FX Packs plug-ins augment the software by providing you with additional transitions and effects. Pixelan has graciously provided us with a demo version of the Spice FX Packs, which you'll find on the CD-ROM that accompanies this book.

TRAINING, TUTORIAL, AND TECHNICAL SITES

DV TRAINING AND EQUIPMENT

www.apple.com/quicktime: Here you can download the QuickTime Player plug-in for free. You can also upgrade QuickTime to QuickTime Pro, an inexpensive little application that allows you to perform some sophisticated functions with QuickTime movie files, like layering and alpha masks.

www.cyberfilmschool.com: One of the best sites around for learning about DVD, this site offers outstanding articles on moviemaking education, links, and tips in filmmaking. There's an entire section on digital video moviemaking that covers topics such as using your digital video movie on the big screen, adventures in real time, video storage, writing your digital video script, working with slow motion, making a digital video feature, video for the Internet, film formats, and so much more.

www.dv.com: Although you have to register to log on, it's well worth it for outstanding information on digital video.

www.michaelmino.com: This site offers many links for project-based techniques in moviemaking and general information on digital video.

www.mwp.com: Michael Wiese Productions has great articles and information on digital moviemaking from word to image. Here you can find book reviews on film and digital editing, movie reviews, and sample chapters on the many books this organization has authored.

www.pblmm.k12.ca.us: This site offers project-based learning with multimedia. It's an outstanding site. Check out the Video Guide in the lower-left menu — it offers great information, such as a glossary of helpful terms and concepts from basic video editing to lighting to tripod use. It includes information on production, post-production, editing, and audio.

www.shortcourses.com: This site offers courses in digital video as well as digital photography. You can purchase the courses in book form, or in some cases, they offer courses online.

www.uemedia.com: Digital Filmmaker's Resource Site. This site contains everything you can imagine about digital filmmaking and videography.

www.vcdhelp.com: This site offers all sorts of helpful tips on how to prepare files to import to video CD. It also tells you what kind of software you need and where to purchase it.

www.videoguys.com: Videoguys sells all sorts of DV-related equipment, software, DV camcorders, and so on. The company also offers compatibility charts to help you determine the best configuration for your system. There are also tutorials.

FILMMAKING TIPS AND TECHNIQUES

www.creativecow.com: An array of very helpful tips, tutorials, discussion groups, and articles related to digital video.

www.desktopvideo.about.com: This site is unbelievably vast and phenomenal! It offers all types of articles and tutorials, product reviews, and digital filmmaking interviews. When you do a search for iMovie, it brings you to 62 sections of information including iMovie tutorials, iMovie help, and iMovie plug-ins. There are even iMovie lesson plans and how to apply iMovie in real-life applications. There's a section on DV filmmaking with interviews of "great people" in filmmaking that are quite inspiring, especially for beginners.

www.filmmaking.com: For those who really want to stay "in the know," this site contains everything from FAQs to tutorials to magazines and dailies to firsthand directions to criticisms to short film works for review. There are tutorials on basic filmmaking, preparing for the shoot, equipment and how to use it, and transferring tape to film.

www.macosxhints.com: A very helpful site because it includes Mac OSX hints and offers all kinds of Mac stuff as it relates to working with iMovie 3 plug-ins.

www.movieworkshops.com: To keep your skills polished and honed, this site offers online courses in screenwriting, cinematography, sound, editing, and production for moviemakers.

www.pbs.org: Interested in filmmaking on the Web? This site offers tons of resources and links for alternative filmmaking.

www.digitalfilmmaker.net: Home of The Digital Filmmaker, this site is dedicated to the art of visual storytelling, uniting the worlds of the photojournalist, the videojournalist, and the independent digital filmmaker. Some outstanding filmmaking tips are offered here.

www.wrigleyvideo.com: This site provides obscure information, tutorials, and tips you can't find elsewhere.

INSPIRATIONAL DV AND STOCK FOOTAGE

www.artbeats.com: Here you find a collection of royalty-free stock film footage. The site also offers five free samples of their footage. Their video collection ships on CD-ROM and includes a low-resolution thumbnail video of each clip as well as a high-resolution, full-screen version.

www.atomiclearning.com: This site offers video samplers and links to 16 free video examples.

TRADE SHOWS AND CONFERENCES FOR DIGITAL VIDEO

www.dvexpo.com: Lists events and conferences coming up for digital video.

COLOPHON

This book was produced electronically in Indianapolis, Indiana. Microsoft Word 2000 was used for word processing; design and layout were produced using QuarkXPress 4.11. The typeface families used are: Chicago Laser, Minion, Myriad, Myriad Multiple Master, Prestige Elite, Symbol, Trajan, and Zapf Dingbats.

Acquisitions Editor: **Mike Roney**

Project Editor: **Tim Borek**

Technical Editor: **Dennis Short**

Copy Editor: **Beth Taylor**

Permissions Editor: **Laura Moss**

Production Coordinator: **Nancee Reeves**

Production: **Elizabeth Brooks, Lauren Goddard, Joyce Haughey, LeAndra Hosier, Kristin McMullan, Lynsey Osborn**

Proofreading and Indexing: **Christine Pingleton; Infodex Indexing Services Inc.**

ABOUT THE AUTHORS

Bonnie Blake is an award-winning designer specializing in video for the Web and multimedia design. She is a faculty member at a college in New Jersey where she teaches new media design and video editing. She is the author of *The Premiere Virtual Classroom, How to Do Everything with Macromedia Flash 5*, co-author of *Flash DeCONSTRUCT,* and author of *How to Do Everything with Macromedia Flash MX.*

Doug Sahlin is a graphic designer and Web site designer living in Lakeland, Florida. He is the author of ten books on graphic and Web design including *Fireworks 4 For Dummies, Flash ActionScript For Dummies,* and other titles. Doug has also written an online Flash course for DigitalThink and created two video training CDs for Virtual Training Company.

INDEX

Continued

Continued

WILEY PUBLISHING, INC. END-USER LICENSE AGREEMENT

READ THIS. You should carefully read these terms and conditions before opening the software packet(s) included with this book "Book". This is a license agreement "Agreement" between you and Wiley Publishing, Inc. "WPI". By opening the accompanying software packet(s), you acknowledge that you have read and accept the following terms and conditions. If you do not agree and do not want to be bound by such terms and conditions, promptly return the Book and the unopened software packet(s) to the place you obtained them for a full refund.

1. **License Grant.** WPI grants to you (either an individual or entity) a nonexclusive license to use one copy of the enclosed software program(s) (collectively, the "Software" solely for your own personal or business purposes on a single computer (whether a standard computer or a workstation component of a multi-user network). The Software is in use on a computer when it is loaded into temporary memory (RAM) or installed into permanent memory (hard disk, CD-ROM, or other storage device). WPI reserves all rights not expressly granted herein.

2. **Ownership.** WPI is the owner of all right, title, and interest, including copyright, in and to the compilation of the Software recorded on the disk(s) or CD-ROM "Software Media". Copyright to the individual programs recorded on the Software Media is owned by the author or other authorized copyright owner of each program. Ownership of the Software and all proprietary rights relating thereto remain with WPI and its licensers.

3. **Restrictions on Use and Transfer.**

    (a) You may only (i) make one copy of the Software for backup or archival purposes, or (ii) transfer the Software to a single hard disk, provided that you keep the original for backup or archival purposes. You may not (i) rent or lease the Software, (ii) copy or reproduce the Software through a LAN or other network system or through any computer subscriber system or bulletin- board system, or (iii) modify, adapt, or create derivative works based on the Software.

    (b) You may not reverse engineer, decompile, or disassemble the Software. You may transfer the Software and user documentation on a permanent basis, provided that the transferee agrees to accept the terms and conditions of this Agreement and you retain no copies. If the Software is an update or has been updated, any transfer must include the most recent update and all prior versions.

4. **Restrictions on Use of Individual Programs.** You must follow the individual requirements and restrictions detailed for each individual program in the About the CD-ROM appendix of this Book. These limitations are also contained in the individual license agreements recorded on the Software Media. These limitations may include a requirement that after using the program for a specified period of time, the user must pay a registration fee or discontinue use. By opening the Software packet(s), you will be agreeing to abide by the licenses and restrictions for these individual programs that are detailed in the About the CD-ROM appendix and on the Software Media. None of the material on this Software Media or listed in this Book may ever be redistributed, in original or modified form, for commercial purposes.